AN ALTERNATIVE MACROECONOMIC THEORY: THE KALECKIAN MODEL AND POST-KEYNESIAN ECONOMICS

RECENT ECONOMIC THOUGHT SERIES

Editors:

Warren J. Samuels
Michigan State University
East Lansing, Michigan, USA

William Darity, Jr.
University of North Carolina
Chapel Hill, North Carolina, USA

Other books in the series:

Tool, Marc R.: INSTITUTIONAL ECONOMICS:
 THEORY, METHOD, POLICY
Babe, Robert E.: INFORMATION AND COMMUNICATION IN
 ECONOMICS
Magnusson, Lars: MERCANTILIST ECONOMICS
Garston, Neil: BUREAUCRACY: THREE PARADIGMS
Friedman, James W.: PROBLEMS OF COORDINATION IN
 ECONOMIC ACTIVITY
Magnusson, Lars: EVOLUTIONARY AND NEO-SCHUMPETERIAN
 APPROACHES TO ECONOMICS
Reisman, D.: ECONOMIC THOUGHT AND POLITICAL THEORY
Burley, P. and Foster, J.: ECONOMICS AND THERMODYNAMICS:
 NEW PERSPECTIVES ON ECONOMIC ANALYSIS
Brennan, H.G. and Waterman, A.C.: ECONOMICS AND RELIGION:
 ARE THEY DISTINCT?
Klein, Philip A.: THE ROLE OF ECONOMIC THEORY
Semmler, Willi.: BUSINESS CYCLES: THEORY AND EMPIRICS
Little, Daniel: ON THE RELIABILITY OF ECOONOMIC MODELS:
 ESSAYS IN THE PHILOSOPHY OF ECONOMICS
Weimer, David L.:
 INSTITUTIONAL DESIGN
Davis, John B.:
 THE STATE OF THE INTERPRETATION OF KEYNES
Wells, Paul:
 POST-KEYNESIAN ECONOMIC THEORY
Hoover, Kevin D.:
 MACROECONOMETRICS: Developments, Tensions
 and Prospects
Kendrick, John W.:
 THE NEW SYSTEMS OF NATURAL ACCOUNTS
Groenewegen, John:
 TRANSACTION COST ECONOMICS AND BEYOND

AN ALTERNATIVE MACROECONOMIC THEORY: THE KALECKIAN MODEL AND POST-KEYNESIAN ECONOMICS

edited by

J.E. King

of

La Trobe University
Australia

Kluwer Academic Publishers
Boston/Dordrecht/London

Distributors for North America:
Kluwer Academic Publishers
101 Philip Drive
Assinippi Park
Norwell, Massachusetts 02061 USA

Distributors for all other countries:
Kluwer Academic Publishers Group
Distribution Centre
Post Office Box 322
3300 AH Dordrecht, THE NETHERLANDS

Library of Congress Cataloging-in-Publication Data

A C.I.P. Catalogue record for this book is available from
the Library of Congress.

Contents

INTRODUCTION

J.E. King

Michael Kalecki (1899-1970) was one of the most important, and also one of the most underrated, economists of the twentieth century. In the 1930s he made a series of fundamental contributions to macroeconomic theory which anticipated, complemented and in some ways surpassed those of Keynes. Almost entirely self-educated in economics, and influenced as much by Marxism as by mainstream theory, Kalecki very largely escaped the fatal embrace of pre-Keynesian orthodoxy, which blunted the thrust of the *General Theory*. Many Post Keynesians, in particular, have found in his work the elements of a convincing alternative to what Joan Robinson - Kalecki's greatest advocate in the English-speaking world - was scathingly to describe as 'bastard Keynesianism'.

But Kalecki was never interested in theory for its own sake. He approached economics from a practical perspective, wrote extensively on applied and policy questions, and in the final decades of his life turned his attention increasingly to problems of economic development and the management of state socialist economies. If there were indeed 'three worlds' in the quarter-century after 1945, Kalecki was at home in each of them.

He was born into a middle-class Jewish family in Lodz in 1899, and initially trained as an engineer. His formal education curtailed by his father's financial difficulties, the young Kalecki earned his living as a commercial journalist, and his earliest theoretical work was published in trade papers and the socialist press; many important articles have only recently been translated. In the mid-1930s Kalecki moved first to Sweden and then to England. He spent the war years at the Institute of Statistics in Oxford and ten years in North America, working first for the International Labour Organisation and then for the United Nations. In 1955 Kalecki returned to Poland, where he served as an adviser and critic to successive Communist governments, sometimes enjoying official favour, sometimes not. He died in 1970, in the middle of a particularly unpleasant episode of anti-Semitism, an unhappy and frustrated man.

During his lifetime a few of Kalecki's contemporaries recognised the significance of his work, and said so. For the most part he was simply overwhelmed, in terms of influence and prestige, by the success of the Keynesian Revolution. Kalecki had none of Keynes's social assets, in upbringing, family background, reputation or personal charm. He wrote sparingly, and without any pretensions to literary elegance : articles rather than books, in the utilitarian style one might expect from an engineer. No-one reads Kalecki for pleasure. Nor did his politics help, except perhaps in Cambridge. In the United States Kalecki was a dangerous radical; in Poland he was a bourgeois individualist. Not bad credentials, in fact, for an economic heretic.

Since his death a substantial secondary literature has grown up around him, including the book-length appraisals of his work by Feiwel (1975) and Sawyer (1985) and an important symposium in the *Oxford Bulletin of Economics and Statistics* (Dell 1977; Eshag 1977; Robinson 1977; Worswick 1977). Only in the 1990s, however, with the publication in English of Kalecki's *Collected Works*,[1] has a full appreciation of his significance become possible. The nine papers in this book survey the principal components of Kalecki's theoretical system and promote his claim to recognition as a dominant influence on modern non-neoclassical economic thought.

In the first chapter Philip Arestis summarises Kalecki's analysis of advanced capitalist economies, emphasising the role of effective demand (and in particular investment) in his theoretical system. Arestis's survey serves as a valuable introduction to several subsequent chapters, in which aspects of Kalecki's ideas are investigated in greater detail. He begins by setting out Kalecki's pricing theory, and assesses subsequent extensions to it by Asimakopulos, Cowling, Eichner and Wood. Arestis demonstrates the close connection between price theory and the analysis of income distribution, establishing the role of the degree of monopoly and the relative price of raw materials in determining the income shares of wages and profits. He compares Kalecki's model of distribution with that of Nicholas Kaldor, who (unlike Kalecki) assumes the maintenance of full employment.

Arestis then discusses Kalecki's treatment of class conflict, where the Marxian aspects of his thinking are most obvious. For Kalecki, class struggle generates wage and price inflation via wage-earners' efforts to obtain a target real wage and the subsequent validation of wage and price increases by the monetary and credit system. This leads Arestis to a consideration of Kalecki's theory of endogenous money, which was adopted by later Post Keynesian writers such as Kaldor and Basil Moore, and can be extended to analyse liquidity preference on the part of the banks and also to the context of an open economy. Arestis outlines Kalecki's theory of investment, which stresses the influence of the rate of profit and the rate of interest. His 'principle of increasing risk' identifies a major constraint on the growth of the firm, and explains the corporation's preference for internal financing. This aspect of Kalecki's thinking, as Arestis shows, was taken over and extended by his colleague and disciple, the Austrian economist Josef Steindl (Steindl 1952, 1990).

Kalecki's war-time work on international monetary arrangements, neglected but now again highly topical, is the next issue raised by Arestis. Kalecki argued that surplus countries should be required to bear the main burden of adjustment to balance of payments disequilibria, a proposal which is not without its attraction for US economists in the mid-1990s. Arestis concludes by outlining Kalecki's views on economic policy in developed capitalist countries, which emphasised the inevitable limits to private investment expenditure and the political and social (rather than narrowly economic) constraints on full employment. He points to Kalecki as an early proponent of Gunnar Myrdal's notion of 'circular and cumulative causation', with the implication that regional policies (within and between nation-states) are inescapable.

Simon Chapple's chapter has a much narrower focus than Arestis's but the same starting-point: Kalecki's theory of effective demand. Chapple deliberately refrains from a detailed comparison of Kaleckian and Keynesian macroeconomics, which would raise broader questions explored in the chapters by Sawyer, Dymski and King. Instead he focuses on the question of priority. Did Kalecki get there first? Did he anticipate the essentials of the *General Theory*? Chapple describes Kalecki's own claims to priority, which were confidently and continuously, if not at all stridently, advanced. He notes that early recognition of the similarities between Kalecki and Keynes came from such authorities as Ragnar Frisch and Oskar Lange and, most insistently, from Joan Robinson.

Kalecki's claims have been opposed by Robert Solow, Paul Samuelson and Don Patinkin, whose objections are summarised by Chapple. He rejects Patinkin's view that an author's central message should never be inferred from non-professional publications, like the journalistic pieces in which Kalecki first set out his ideas (in Polish) in the early 1930s. As Chapple observes, Kalecki was not a doctoral product of the modern North American academic assembly line, and should not be judged by criteria relevant only to such. Having established the credentials of Kalecki's early writings, Chapple highlights two important articles, published in full in English only very recently. The 'Essay on the Business Cycle Theory' (Kalecki 1933) and the paper, 'Three Systems' (Kalecki 1934) demonstrate for Chapple that Kalecki had by this early date developed a theory of effective demand as comprehensive and as convincing as that of the *General Theory*.

It should be noted here that Chapple's interpretation of Kalecki's analysis is a controversial one. Some commentators - including at least two contributors to this book - reject his contention that Kalecki made use in these papers of a concept of macroeconomic equilibrium, and vigorously deny his suggestion that an IS-LM model is implicit in Kalecki's analysis. The reader should turn to 'Three Systems' and make up his or her own mind on this issue. My own view is that there are significant neoclassical elements in Kalecki's early work, which become more prominent after his move to England but fade rapidly from the mid-1940s and disappear entirely (it is scarcely necessary to add) after his return to Poland. This must have been partly tactical : his review of the *General Theory*, for example (Kalecki 1936), with its U-shaped marginal cost curve, was clearly intended to promote the principle of effective demand among a predominantly neoclassical readership. And there is also a substantial Marxian component, rarely explicit but always present, even in his earlier writings. Kalecki was never a neoclassical, nor in any simple way a Marxist. He was an original thinker of genius, and an opponent of all dogmatism, whether bourgeois or socialist.

In the third chapter Peter Kriesler identifies a clear line of demarcation dividing Kalecki from all varieties of orthodox economics, including both 'bastard' and New Keynesians, where questions of methodology are concerned. Kriesler describes the ways in which the relationship between microeconomics and macroeconomics is dealt with in the work of classical, neoclassical, Marxian and Post Keynesian economists. He argues that Kalecki broke both with the methodological individualist reductionism of the mainstream, which regards macroeconomics as a pure aggregate of microeconomic elements, and with what might be termed the structuralism of the Marxians, and many Post Keynesians, for whom the analytical priorities are reversed.

Concentrating on Kalecki's three books of essays on the dynamics of advanced capitalist economies (Kalecki 1939, 1943, 1954), Kriesler explains the connection between Kalecki's method and his treatment of the macro-micro relationship. He lucidly outlines Kalecki's macroeconomic theory of profits, in which capitalist incomes are determined, in aggregate, by their expenditures. This is Kalecki's greatest analytical achievement, hinted at by Keynes in the *Treatise on Money* but entirely absent from the *General Theory*. Kriesler argues, however, that for Kalecki the microanalysis is also required, to establish the levels of real wages, output and employment which correspond to the volume of profits that is determined by the macroanalysis. Thus, for Kalecki, the macro and the micro have equal theoretical status, even if the macro is more important in explaining the aggregate operation of actual capitalist economies.

Concentrating on Kalecki's microanalysis, but with repeated references to its significance for the macroanalysis, Peter Reynolds begins his chapter by discussing Kalecki's important and influential distinction between cost-determined and demand-determined prices. Reynolds identifies a strong marginalist strand in Kalecki's early work on pricing, which was all but eliminated in his later writings. He considers Kalecki's definition and analysis of the 'degree of monopoly' in a non-marginalist framework, where the extent of concentration, the ratio of advertising to sales revenue, and the factors affecting the propensity to collude, all play an important role. Reynolds surveys the recent literature on the degree of monopoly, discussing the relationship between the profit margin and the rate of return on capital in the context of post-Kaleckian work by Riach, Asimakopulos and Cowling.

Next Reynolds shows how the Kalecki mark-up pricing equation provides a theory of income distribution, and integrates this microeconomic theory of the profit share with Kalecki's macroeconomic analysis of the *level* of profits. (As is suggested in my own chapter, Kalecki had reservations about this dichotomy when applied to conditions of full employment). Reynolds identifies one very important conclusion that may be drawn from Kalecki's analysis. Although the money wage is determined in the labour market, perhaps by wage bargaining with trade unions, the real wage depends on the degree to which firms mark up their variable (wage plus raw material) costs, and is therefore determined by product market phenomena. The inflation rate in turn depends on the rate of growth of money wages, and many Post Keynesians have inferred from this the need for a tax-based incomes policy or some form of inflation tax; Kalecki himself may well have demurred.

With the next two chapters the focus returns to Kalecki's macroanalysis. In his discussion of Kalecki's work on the trade cycle and economic growth, Malcolm Sawyer points to several significant features of the Kaleckian analysis of capitalism. He stresses demand constraints upon output; believes unemployed resources and surplus capacity to be the rule; rejects equilibrium analysis in favour of a model of cyclical instability; and regards investment, not consumption, as the driving force in aggregate demand. Sawyer touches briefly on certain technical issues before outlining the three main versions of Kalecki's business cycle model. The first, dating from the mid-1930s, specifies investment as a function of current profitability, interpreted as a proxy for (expected) future profits. His second formulation, published in 1943, emphasises current profits as a source of internal finance, and derives cycles from the effect on investment of changes in profitability. In his third model, which appeared in 1968, Kalecki broke with his previous assumption of a stationary economy and allowed explicitly for technical change, thereby generating a growth cycle.

Kalecki's analysis of economic growth is quite distinctive. Sawyer cites Kalecki's 'laconic statement' that the long period is simply `a slowly changing component of a chain of short-period situations; it has no independent entity' (Kalecki 1971,165). He interprets this as an attack on the equilibrium approach to macroanalysis typified by both neoclassical growth theory and the Sraffian treatment of long-period positions as centres of gravity for market prices. Sawyer's exposition of Kalecki's own theory of growth hinges on its demand-side emphasis, and his related refusal to view full employment outcomes as in any sense normal or natural. Sawyer briefly discusses the application of Kalecki's growth theory to a socialist economy (this question is elaborated on in the later chapter by Jan Toporowski). He concludes by suggesting that Kalecki's analysis might be broadened to include the effects of class struggles over relative income shares, and a role for money and finance.

While Kalecki is not generally regarded as a monetary economist, it can be argued that he paid more attention to financial factors than he is usually (so to speak) given credit for. In chapter 6 Gary Dymski shows that a coherent and original monetary theory can legitimately be constructed out of Kalecki's admittedly rather brief and fragmentary writings in this area. Dymski begins by setting out Kalecki's macro model, in its mature form in *Theory of Economic Dynamics* (Kalecki 1954). As Dymski observes, this includes a monetary theory of both the short-period and long-period rates of interest, and an important role for interest rates as a determinant of investment expenditure. At one point Kalecki identifies a tendency for the ownership of capital to pass from capitalists to rentiers. In conjunction with the principle of increasing risk, this implies a slowdown in investment demand because of the corporations' growing reliance on external finance.

Dymski compares Kalecki's vision with that of the Sraffian and Davidsonian approaches to macroeconomic modelling. He points to some of the problems with Kalecki's analysis, especially owing to its shallow treatment of uncertainty. Dymski suggests that Kalecki's structural model of investment cycles can, nevertheless, be linked with the monetary or Davidsonian version, strengthening both models by allowing a deeper appreciation of financial constraints and credit rationing. His own schematic presentation of the relations between investment, finance and uncertainty distinguishes five stages, from the planning of investment through the placing of orders and the delivery of capital equipment to its use and eventual full depreciation. Comparing this Kaleckian model with recent developments in New Keynesian economics, Dymski notes certain similarities. He concludes, however, that Kalecki's cycle is dynamic and monetary in character, embodying the institutional context of the real-world capitalist economy in a way that New Keynesians have been unable to achieve.

If Kalecki's model needs to be extended in this manner to incorporate the monetary aspects of economic fluctuations, Hyman Minsky's financial instability hypothesis can be criticised for paying insufficient attention to real variables. Dymski argues that Kalecki's analysis complements that of Minsky, integrating into it an account of production and the extraction of an economic surplus. He concludes by discussing Kalecki's treatment of the link between micro and macro analyses, again contrasting Kalecki with the New Keynesians, and commenting on his views on the tension between industrial capitalists and rentiers as rival claimants to a share of the surplus product.

In chapter 7 I deal with one of the questions considered by Dymski : Kalecki's relations with American economists, and especially with Post Keynesians in the United States. Kalecki spent a full decade in North America and yet, as Joan Robinson wrote, his influence was always much greater in Cambridge (England). I provide a brief account of Kalecki's writings from this period, including those under the imprint of the United Nations for which he had primary responsibility. While he was an international civil servant Kalecki formulated a model of the relationship between investment and the profit share which anticipated Nicholas Kaldor's famous article (Kaldor 1956) and the contemporary writings of Robinson herself (Robinson 1956), to explain the operation of capitalist economies in an era of excess (rather than deficient) effective demand. He later developed both an interest in the problems of economic development and a conviction that an essentially Marxian framework was required to understand them. (Kalecki's approach to development economics is discussed at length in Bruce McFarlane's chapter below).

The second, much longer part of my own chapter deals with Kalecki's influence, or lack of influence, on Post Keynesian economics in the United States. I concentrate on the writings of Sidney Weintraub, Paul Davidson, Hyman Minsky and Alfred Eichner, supplementing the evidence (in Eichner's case) with his extensive unpublished correspondence with Joan Robinson. Weintraub's intellectual odyssey, from expositor of the neoclassical synthesis to one of its most vocal critics, was a long and tortuous one, in which he slowly overcame an initial and quite powerful antipathy to Kalecki's ideas. His pupil, Paul Davidson, rejected Kalecki's theory of distribution from the start and never regarded Kalecki as a serious rival to Keynes. Minsky's evolution resembled Weintraub's, leading him eventually to incorporate Kalecki's theory of aggregate profits as an essential support for his own analysis of financial instability.   As for Eichner, the correspondence with Robinson reveals a young, impressionable theorist bludgeoned into accepting Kaleckian macroeconomics by a most insistent (and persistent) mentor. I conclude by suggesting some intellectual and political reasons why Kalecki's influence in America was so limited, and so hard-won.

In Eastern Europe he encountered quite different obstacles, as Jan Toporowski explains in chapter 8. Kalecki began his economics of socialism with a critique of capitalism, and of the Keynesian demand management policies that were believed by many in the West to be capable of overcoming its inherent instability. Kalecki advocated socialism primarily because of his conviction that it was an improvement over the irrationalities of capitalism. Unlike Hayek and Kornai, he thought that socialist planners would possess better information than was available to agents in a free market. Central planning, he claimed, was (at least in principle) more efficient than capitalism. As Toporowski argues, Kalecki was also aware of the limitations of the central planners, an awareness that was sharpened by the experience of their appalling policy errors in the 1960s and which made him increasingly unpopular in official circles.

Toporowski discusses Kalecki's contributions to the theory and practice of planning, which included his articulation of a 15-year perspective plan as a check on the feasibility of shorter, medium-term plans. He outlines Kalecki's theory of socialist growth, which he used to criticise the contemporary Polish strategy of adopting ever more capital-intensive techniques of production. Kalecki recognised the barriers to faster growth that were presented by current consumption needs and by foreign exchange constraints, and repeatedly attacked the planners for underestimating them. His analysis, Toporowski concludes, was more realistic than that of the apologists for Stalinism and of the Austrian eulogists of capitalism.

The book concludes with Bruce McFarlane's account of Kalecki's political economy of development. McFarlane is the only contributor who knew the Polish economist personally, having worked with him as a young economist at the Indian Planning Commission. He begins his chapter by summarising Kalecki's thinking on development issues during his period at the United Nations, and the impact on his ideas of later visits to India and Cuba. As McFarlane shows, Kalecki became a strong critic of the orthodox approach to development, attacking its neglect of distributional questions and its reliance on the static theory of comparative advantage. Kalecki used an essentially Marxian framework to analyse the financing of economic development, but took issue - as Toporowski shows in the context of Eastern Europe - with the Stalinist supporters of highly capital-intensive methods of production.

On practical policy issues Kalecki advocated land reform to improve the plight of the rural poor, and redistributive taxation both to raise revenue for development and to relieve the balance of payments difficulties caused by the high marginal propensity to import of the rich. McFarlane emphasises the political aspects of Kalecki's development economics, praising the perceptiveness of his analysis of 'intermediate regimes', which was again primarily Marxian in its inspiration. Kalecki's influence has been considerable, not least in the spread of 'structuralist' ideas in Latin America. His formal analysis can be extended to allow for the growth of manufacturing output in the newly-industrialising countries of East and South-East Asia, as is shown by the three-sector model of Joseph Lim, which McFarlane describes towards the end of his chapter, and in Joseph Halevi's application of Pasinetti's vertical integration analysis to a Kaleckian model of development. McFarlane himself concludes that it is Kalecki's underlying vision, together with his concern for the plight of the poor and his awareness of the bottlenecks to development, which are the principal strengths of his political economy of development.

Note

1 By 1994 five volumes, out of a projected seven, had appeared, containing all of Kalecki's theoretical writings; the two remaining volumes will include his applied economic studies, a bibliography, and miscellaneous items. No attempt has been made to provide a complete list of Kalecki's writings, as a full bibliography will be contained in the seventh and final volume of his *Collected Works*, due for publication in 1996. A very substantial list, including many items from non-English language sources, can be found in Feiwel (1975, 527-54).

References

Dell, S. 1977. 'Kalecki at the United Nations, 1946-54'. *Oxford Bulletin of Economics and Statistics* 39(1), February: 31-45.

Eshag, E. 1977. 'Kalecki's Political Economy : a Comparison with Keynes'. *Oxford Bulletin of Economics and Statistics.* 39(1), February : 79-85.

Feiwel, G. R. 1975. *The intellectual Capital of Michal Kalecki : a Study in Economic*

Theory and Policy. Knoxville : University of Tennessee Press.

Kaldor, N. 1956. 'Alternative Theories of Distribution.' *Review of Economic Studies*. 23(2): 83-100.

Kalecki, M. 1933. 'Essay on the Business Cycle Theory' (in Polish). English translation in Kalecki (1990): 65-108.

Kalecki, M. 1934. 'Three Systems' (in Polish). English translation in Kalecki (1990): 201-19.

Kalecki, M. 1936. 'Some Remarks on Keynes's Theory' (in Polish). English translation in Kalecki (1990): 223-32.

Kalecki, M. 1939. *Essays in the Theory of Economic Fluctuations*. London: Allen and Unwin.

Kalecki, M. 1943. *Studies in Economic Dynamics*. London: Allen and Unwin.

Kalecki, M. 1954. *Theory of Economic Dynamics* London: Allen and Unwin.

Kalecki, M. 1971. *Selected Essays on the* Dynamics of the Capitalist Economy, 1933-1970. Cambridge: Cambridge University Press.

Kalecki, M. 1990. *Collected Works of Michal Kalecki. Volume I. Capitalism, Business Cycles and Full Employment*. Ed. J. Osiatynski. Oxford: Clarendon Press.

Robinson, J. 1956. *The Accumulation of Capital*. London: Macmillan.

Robinson, J. 1977. 'Michal Kalecki on the Economics of Capitalism.' *Oxford bulletin of Economics and Statistics* 39(1), February: 7-17.

Sawyer, M. C. 1985. *The Economics of Michal Kalecki*. London: Macmillan.

Steindl, J. 1952. *Maturity and Stagnation in American Capitalism*. Oxford: Blackwell.

Steindl, J. 1990. *Economic Papers 1941-88*. London: Macmillan.

Worswick, G. D. N. 1977. 'Kalecki at Oxford 1940-44.' *Oxford Bulletin of Economics and Statistics*. 39(1), February: 19-29.

1 KALECKI'S ROLE IN POST KEYNESIAN ECONOMICS: AN OVERVIEW

Philip Arestis

Introduction

There is very little doubt that Kalecki's role in post-Keynesian economics is both extensive and paramount. This may very well explain the recent resurgent of interest amongst post-Keynesians in Kalecki's work. So much so that there are writers who acknowledge the existence of a coherent Kaleckian paradigm which sits very comfortably within the post-Keynesian ethos and tradition (Hamouda and Harcourt 1988; Sawyer 1982, 1985). It is the purpose of this chapter to show that Kalecki's economics possesses a central role in the development of post-Keynesian economics. This proposition is very much consistent with the thesis developed elsewhere, that Kalecki's economics is one of a number of approaches within post-Keynesian economics (Arestis 1992; Arestis and Sawyer 1993; Hamouda and Harcourt 1988).

I am extremely grateful to Geoff Harcourt, John King and Malcolm Sawyer for extremely useful comments and helpful suggestions. In no way should they be held responsible for any remaining errors or omissions.

The *principle of effective demand* is the backbone of Kalecki's analysis as it was in Keynes's *General Theory* (1936). Effective demand in Kalecki and post-Keynesian analyses implies that it is scarcity of demand rather than scarcity of resources that is to be confronted in modern economies, so that output is ordinarily limited by effective demand and not by (physical) supply. Kalecki argued that scarcity of demand rather than scarcity of resources tends to characterise capitalist and not socialist economies. The latter experienced the opposite tendency, a scarcity of resources rather than of demand. There is now accumulated evidence which suggests that actually Kalecki had formulated the principle of 'effective demand' before Keynes (Robinson 1977; Targetti and Kinda-Hass 1982; Asimakopulos 1989; Harcourt 1991). Not everybody agrees, however, that Kalecki and Keynes discovered 'effective demand' independently. Davidson (1992), for example, holds the view that they did not, and has argued that Kalecki is closer to the new-Keynesians' non-market clearing models than to Keynes's non-neutral money and uncertainty analysis. Davidson's proposition, however, cannot be upheld in the light of Kalecki's view of the *General Theory* (Harcourt 1991). A further example is Patinkin (1982, 1989) who argues that since Keynes's central message is the theory of effective demand with its novel feature that it is changes in output that act as the equilibrating force, a very different message from Kalecki's, the claim that he had discovered 'effective demand' before Keynes does not have any basis. A closer study of the similarities and differences between the two approaches (Sawyer 1985) clearly indicates that these claims are not valid.

Kalecki's economics concerns itself with the capitalist mode of production. Social relationships are recognised to be of paramount importance in production, so that social classes are explicitly accounted for within the analysis. As such, Kalecki's economics sets out to demonstrate that markets distribute income according to relative power. This is so since the output produced by one class of society (the wage earners) is planned, directed and managed by another class of society that does not participate physically in production (the recipients of residual income or profit). In this power relationship capital's objectives are in conflict with labour's objectives, so that 'class conflict' is at the heart of analysis. This analysis justifies the claim that 'the institutional framework of a social system is a basic element of its economic dynamics' (Kalecki 1970, 311), and that Kalecki 'always incorporated the institutional framework into his models' (Kriesler 1987, 3). There are further aspects in Kalecki's work which have been influential in the development of post-Keynesian economics. The non-equilibrium character of his analysis which integrates microeconomics and macroeconomics, based on the cyclical aspects of an economy with strong elements of historical time and hysteresis, are a few examples. Of equal significance is Kalecki's notion that the long-run trend is dependent on a chain of short-period situations, and as such it does not have an independent existence. The long-run simply does not exist, and therefore it cannot be a unique centre of gravity.

Effective demand, and investment in particular, as the prime mover of the capitalist system, is the most important theoretical element underpinning Kalecki's model. In addition, pricing, distribution and conflict, business cycles and money, international monetary arrangements, as well as economic policy, comprise a comprehensive coverage of the essential theoretical elements of post-Keynesian economics where Kalecki has a significant role to play. In what follows we discuss them at length, beginning with pricing.

Kalecki's Pricing Theory and Extensions

It should be stated at the outset that a lot of post-Keynesian pricing theory is related to Kalecki (1954), as for example, Eichner (1973, 1976), Wood (1975), Harcourt and Kenyon (1976), amongst others. These contributions recognise that not all markets are perfectly competitive and that there is a distinction between sectors where price changes are 'cost-determined' and those where they are 'demand-determined'. They also postulate that prices of finished goods are determined by a mark-up on some measure of unit costs. We discuss first Kalecki's own pricing theory, followed by developments initiated by post-Keynesians but firmly embedded in Kalecki.

Kalecki's Pricing Theory

In this section we concentrate on the essence of Kalecki's pricing theory, which is the *degree of monopoly*. Average variable costs are thought to remain constant until full capacity is reached, an assumption supported by empirical evidence. Excess capacity exists, so that prices are determined by a mark-up on average costs. Once full capacity is reached, demand may very well have a role to play. However, this is considered to be highly exceptional. Firms are further assumed to pay attention to the prices of other firms producing similar products (Kalecki 1954). We may express these observations in (1.1) as:

$$p = mh + n\eta \tag{1.1}$$

which is the firm's pricing equation, where p = firm's price, h = average variable costs, η = the weighted average price of all the other firms in the industry producing similar products, and m and n are parameters which reflect the firm's *degree of monopoly*. These parameters are determined by factors such as the degree of industrial concentration, trade union influence, and the importance of fixed costs in relation to variable costs, although the influence of the latter factor is rather unclear in that 'The degree of monopoly may but need not necessarily increase as a result of a rise in overheads in relation to prime costs' (Kalecki 1954, 18).

Moving from the individual firm to the industry as a whole, we may consider the general case where m and n differ between firms. Kalecki (1954) employs the notion of the representative firm, which enables him to write:

$$p = mh/(1 - n) \qquad (1.2)$$

where p and h are average price and average variable costs for the industry as a whole, and m and n are weighted averages of individual firms' pricing parameters. Prices are thus determined by a mark-up on variable costs, with the mark-up determined by the degree of monopoly which summarises the set of environmental and institutional factors as described above.

Recent debate on Kalecki's pricing theory has concentrated on its historical roots. Basile and Salvadori (1984-85; but see Casson 1994) have argued that there is continuity in Kalecki's pricing theory, whilst Kriesler 'suggests that a discontinuity existed in Kalecki's formulation of price decisions. However, a common element runs through the discontinuous stages: 'the degree of monopoly (or some parameter reflecting non-competitive influences) and the ratio of the cost of raw materials to wage costs' (*op. cit.*, 100).

Extensions of Kalecki's Pricing Theory

A number of extensions of Kalecki's pricing model have taken place. One is Asimakopulos's (1975), which assumed complete vertical integration in industry so that labour costs (W) are the only variable cost, such that:

$$p = (1 + n)(W/a) \qquad (1.3)$$

where n is the mark-up and a is the average output per unit of labour. There is a price leader who sets the price. The mark-up over unit variable costs, which reflects the degree of monopoly, is designed to cover both fixed costs and an expected rate of return, or profit, on investment. A relationship is established between pricing and investment and thus between pricing and the rate of growth of the economy.

Another extension is the contribution by Cowling (1982) and Cowling and Waterson (1976). In this pricing model the industry consists of a number of firms each pursuing independent *profit maximisation*, but the expected reactions of each firm's rivals are taken into account.[1] The model predicts a relationship between mark-ups and the industry price elasticity of demand, industrial concentration as measured by the Herfindahl index, and expected responses by firms to output changes by rivals. However, short-run fluctuations in price are expected to be affected by cost changes, so that this model is consistent with Kalecki's view that short-run price changes in the manufacturing are essentially due to cost factors rather than to variables emanating from demand. An interesting feature of Cowling's model is that profit maximisation is re-introduced into the analysis. Another feature is that investment in excess capacity is viewed as an effective barrier to entry.

The extension initiated by Eichner (1976) emphasises the 'corporate revolution' which produced the notion of the oligopolistic sector where the typical firm is the 'megacorp'. The emergence of the oligopolistic sector has meant that the 'megacorp' has replaced the neoclassical type of firm and has become the dominant form of enterprise in modern advanced industrial societies. The pricing behaviour of the megacorps is simply to add a certain percentage mark-up to their unit cost of production. The mark-up is determined by the needs of the megacorps to finance their investment plans (see also Ball 1964), so that *pricing theory* is inevitably and inextricably linked to the theory of *investment*. It has been argued (Reynolds 1989) that Eichner's model provides microeconomic underpinnings to Kalecki's analysis which are closer to the spirit of Kalecki's own work than those provided by the Cowling model considered above. On the other hand, the Cowling model more than the Eichner model can be said to highlight the importance of market structure, thus providing more rigorous underpinnings to the notion of 'the degree of monopoly'.

Kalecki (1954, 7) argued that an important cause of change in the degree of monopoly was 'the significance of the power of trade unions' as it provides the channel whereby labour may affect its share of output. Kalecki (1971) demonstrated that changes in money wages would be reflected wholly as changes in the mark-up, so that class struggle finds expression not in the process of wage setting but in mark-up determination. Such an effect does not appear in Eichner's model but, as Reynolds (1989) has correctly noted, such an effect can easily be incorporated in it. This would take the form of an additional cost associated with increases in the mark-up, so that as the mark-up is raised beyond a certain level, it could very well trigger militant action by trade unions. Unions may feel that since the firm is achieving high profit rates they, too, deserve a higher share. In this way an explicit role for class struggle is introduced in Eichner's model, just as it exists in Kalecki (1971) - see, also, Harcourt (1965) where a model is postulated which contains these features and is very 'Kaleckian'.

Wood (1975) attempts to build a model which takes explicit account of the financial side. The broad objective of this model is the same as Eichner's, in that it aims to establish the size of the target mark-up. It is the firm's investment requirements which determine target profits and thus the mark-up. In this sense Wood casts his model as an explanation of target profits at normal long-run capacity and utilisation levels. Another important ingredient of

Wood's contribution is the explicit modelling of the financial constraints on the firm in a way that is consistent with Kalecki's (1954) 'principle of increasing risk' (see below). There is an important similarity between this theory, Eichner's, and Kalecki's 'degree of monopoly'. This is that prices are determined, at least in a significant proportion of the economy, by a process of mark-up on costs. In determining the price, firms take unit costs as given, even though this level of unit costs is influenced by firms through their investment activities. The price will remain constant in the medium to longer term in the face of demand variations, so that realised profit may differ from planned profit. Furthermore, both Eichner's and Wood's contributions are *golden age*, logical time, models, unlike the analysis of Harcourt and Kenyon (1976) which is conducted in historical time. In this sense the Harcourt and Kenyon (1976) model is much more within the spirit of post-Keynesian analysis in general, and pricing in particular.

Distribution Theory

One important aspect of Kalecki's pricing theory is that it is linked to distribution. This aspect is highlighted by referring to Kalecki's well-known formulae:[2]

$$(W/Y) = 1/[\beta + (\beta - 1)j] \tag{1.4}$$

$$(\Pi/Y) = 1 - 1/[\beta + (\beta - 1)j] \tag{1.5}$$

which are the share of wages (W) to income (Y) and the share of profits (Π) to income, respectively. The rest of the symbols in (1.4) and (1.5) are as follows: $\beta = m/(1-n)$, where m and n are as defined above, and j is the ratio of total spending on materials to the wage bill. It follows that distribution is related crucially to j and the mark-up, and thus to the degree of monopoly.

We may further define Π as:

$$\Pi = I + C_c + BD + XS - S_w \tag{1.6}$$

where I is investment, C_c is capitalist's consumption, BD is the budget deficit, XS is the export surplus and S_w is workers' savings. Combining (1.5) and (1.6) we may arrive at:

$$Y = [I + C_c + BD + XS - S_w]/[1 - 1/[\beta + (\beta - 1)j] \tag{1.7}$$

which shows that, from the relationship of the share of profits and that of the volume of profits, the level of income is determined, and depends on aggregate expenditure and the degree of monopoly as well as on j. An increase in aggregate expenditure affects profits on a one-to-one basis, and also income, which depends on the degree of monopoly and the j-ratio. A higher degree of monopoly leads to a lower level of income and to an unchanged volume of profits. Any attempt, therefore, to increase profits via a higher degree of monopoly would have no impact on the level of profits in the absence of changes in aggregate expenditure.

Post-Keynesian distribution theory has been influenced by the approach of Kaldor (1955-6), although Kalecki's influence on writers such as Baran (1957), Cowling (1982) and Steindl (1952) is both obvious and substantial. Kaldor's model of distribution has some similarities with, and differences from, Kalecki's model. Whilst Kaldor refers to his model as Keynesian - it is actually from the *Treatise on Money* (Keynes 1980a) - Pasinetti (1974) suggests that it should be labelled as Kaleckian. It is, therefore, important that we bring out the differences between the two models. We may begin our exploration into the Kaldorian model with (1.8):

$$Y = W + \Pi \tag{1.8}$$

which states that national income is divided into wage income (W) and profit income (Π). We can also write Y as:

$$Y = C_w + C_c + I \tag{1.9}$$

where the variables are as above, with the exception of C_w which stands for consumption by workers. We may also adopt the following simplifying assumptions:

$$C_w = c_w W \tag{1.10}$$

$$C_c = c_c \Pi \tag{1.11}$$

that is to say, workers' consumption is proportional to wages and capitalists' consumption is proportional to profits. Investment can be treated as fully exogenous for the purposes of this analysis.

Expressions (1.8) to (1.11) can be combined and manipulated to arrive at:

$$(\Pi/Y) = - [(1 - c_w) / (c_w - c_c)] + [1/(c_w - c_c)] (I/Y) \tag{1.12}$$

If we assume that $c_w = 1$ we derive the result:

$$(\Pi/Y) = [1/(1 - c_c)](I/Y) \hspace{6cm} (1.13)$$

which suggests that, in a steady-state, the greater the rate of economic expansion as a result of a higher share of investment to income, and the higher the marginal propensity to consume out of profits, the greater the share of profits and the lower the share going to workers. This is the essence of Kaldor's distribution model.

The most obvious difference between the two models is that, contrary to Kalecki, Kaldor conducted his analysis within a full employment, steady-state theoretical framework. In Kalecki constant marginal propensities to consume out of wages and profits were not assumed. The share of profits to income is determined by aggregate expenditure and workers' savings as well as by the degree of monopoly and j, with the level of income adjusting to satisfy this requirement. In Kaldor it is essentially the share of investment to income and the marginal propensity to consume out of profits that determine the profit share. For Kalecki, whilst investment is central to growth, it alone is inadequate for the maintenance of full employment. Steindl (1952) emphasises the growth in monopoly power to justify this proposition. The argument is that monopolistic conditions are associated with high profit margins and thus lower levels of aggregate demand, and also with higher planned rates of capacity utilisation which reduce investment incentives. Further models in this tradition which are firmly based on Kaleckian principles are, amongst others, those of Dutt (1992), Bhaduri and Marglin (1990), Harcourt (1963, 1965), Robinson (1977) and Rowthorn (1981).

Class Conflict: Wage and Price Inflation

Concern with distributional matters, in the way we have just described them, implies a 'conflict' of interests between workers and capitalists. This is particularly relevant in the case of wage and price inflation theory, where collective bargaining in the labour market is the kernel of this analysis. Kalecki (1971,7) was clear on the importance of this type of analysis when he argued that 'The existence of high mark-ups will encourage strong trade unions to bargain for higher wages, since they know that firms can 'afford' to pay them. If their demands are granted ..... prices will also increase'. This suggests that unions have some notion of an acceptable profit margin which they compare with the actual profit margin, and demand higher wages when the actual is higher than the acceptable (Sawyer 1985, 114-15). The acceptable profit margin can be seen as corresponding to a target real wage which is compared to the actual real wage. The latter is adjusted whenever there is a mismatch. This is the backbone of the post-Keynesian analysis of wage determination (see, for example, Arestis 1986), and it is clearly based on notions propounded by Kalecki.

Inflationary processes are embedded in the structure of mature capitalist economies and are the consequence of a struggle over shares in national income. The rate of wage inflation relative to productivity, along with prices of imports and raw materials, are taken to be the most vital determinants of price inflation. Consequently the theory of inflation belongs squarely to the 'conflict theory' framework, reflecting the struggle of labour for its income share. It is a conflict theory of wage and price inflation. The conflict is expressed in the wage setting process and the price setting process, the former being used by labour, the latter by corporations, to influence the share of wage and profit income respectively. There are three essential and interlinked factors in this explanation of the inflationary process: collective bargaining, real wage determination, and validation of wage and price levels by the monetary authorities and the credit system. Any attempt to isolate any one of the three factors as *the cause* of inflation is misdirected. Certainly money wage increases lead to price increases, but to say that the former *cause* the latter is to ignore the structural features of mature capitalism that allow corporations to determine these prices. Equally, price rises lead to money wage increases as workers seek to re-establish real wage levels. The process is akin to Marshall's famous analogy, used in a different context, of a pair of scissors. To argue about which blade does the cutting is absurd. The power of labour to influence money wages and the power of corporations to pass on wage rises in the form of higher prices are the two blades and *jointly* cause inflation. At the risk of stretching the analogy, the accommodation of the monetary system may be seen as the pivot, the factor which allows the blades to move at all. Monetary expansion is not the *cause* of inflation. It merely allows the expression of the conflict inherent in mature capitalism. We proceed next to discuss these three conditions in turn, beginning with collective bargaining.

Collective Bargaining

Labour uses collective bargaining to seek a target real wage, the exact outcome of the process depending on factors beyond its control, as agreements are only established in terms of a *money* wage. Workers have drives and aspirations, as well as economic and political power, which are expressed in terms of *a target relative real wage*. Deviations of actual real wages from the target level affect the level of money wage demands, thereby causing upward pressure on money wages if the desired level is greater than the actual. Similarly, there would be downward pressure on money wages when the real wage falls short of the target relative real wage. Another pertinent variable which should be seriously considered is the ability of firms to grant wage demands. This is proxied by profitability, which can be measured by the profit rate on sales in relation to a minimum acceptable rate of profit for the firms. There are two further objectives which should be considered: the maintenance of the current real wage, and restoration of differentials. Expectations of price inflation over the contract period, and the rate of change of unemployment seen as a proxy of the speed of expansion or contraction of 'the reserve army of unemployed', are variables which unions take into account in ensuring the maintenance of current real wage levels. The workers' position in the income distribution relative to certain reference groups is a variable which can be utilised to capture the attempt to restore wage differentials by workers.

It may be helpful to summarise the analysis in this section as follows (see also Marglin 1984):

$$W_t = w_0 + w_1[(W/P)^d - (W/P)_{t-1}] + w_2(\Pi_{t-1}) + w_3(P_t^e/P_{t-1}/\Pi_{min})$$
$$+ w_4(W_{ct-1}/W_{t-1}) + w_5 u_t \qquad (1.14)$$

where $(W/P)^d$ is the target real wage, $(W/P)_{t-1}$ is the current (at the time of negotiation) real wage, Π_{t-1} is the profit rate (at the time of bargaining), Π_{min} is the minimum acceptable rate of profit, P^e is the expected price level at time t, P_{t-1} is the known price level at the time of negotiation, W_{ct-1} is the average wage in industries regarded by unions as compatible with their own, and u is the rate of change in unemployment.

Real Wage Determination

Given the money wage, the degree of monopoly determines the pricing policy of firms. The level of the *real* wage is thus beyond the control of the worker. Increases in money wages can usually be passed on through the mark-up process as firms attempt to preserve real profit levels in the face of money wage rises. Real wages are thus not determined in the labour market, whilst money wages are determined in the labour market as explained above. Trade union activity is an important feature of the determination of money wages. Their impact on the real wage is only through the degree of monopoly, since the real wage is mainly determined by the degree of monopoly, a variable which is the outcome of events which take place in the product market (Kalecki 1966).[3] We may demonstrate this result as follows. From (1.2) above we may write:

$$p = kh \qquad (1.2')$$

where $k = m/(1 - n)$, so that k is related to the degree of monopoly. Furthermore, since

$$h = [WL + p_m Q_m]/Q \qquad (1.15)$$

where the symbols are as above, with the exception of p_m and Q_m which stand for the price and quantity of imported raw materials respectively, and Q is output. Combining (1.2') and (1.15), and using P rather than p, we arrive at (1.16):

$$P = k[WL + p_m Q_m]/Q \qquad\qquad (1.16)$$

which may be re-written as:

$$(W/P) = (Q/kL) - [p_m Q_m/PL] \qquad\qquad (1.17)$$

thus confirming the proposition put forward above that the real wage is determined in the product market and is little influenced by conditions in the labour market. The degree of monopoly as embedded in k, the techniques of production and the intensity of labour as they are reflected in (Q/L) and (Q_m/L), the relationship between p_m and domestic output prices, and the speed of adjustment of prices to costs, are the factors which determine (1.17), none of which has much to do with the labour market.

Validation of Wage and Price Claims

The role of the monetary and credit system is essentially passive, in that it is geared towards satisfying the 'needs of the trade'. Post-Keynesians have long argued that the supply of money is endogenous, responding to changes in the demand for credit and thus allowing the cycle of money wage rise and price rise to take place. In the section that follows I wish to argue that this proposition is based on, and directly descends from, Kalecki's theory of money and credit.

Kalecki's Theory of Money and Credit

Post-Keynesian economics views money as essentially endogenous in a credit money economy. Money is completely integrated within production, and exchange, so that any attempt to curtail the required flow of money will produce severe cutbacks in production. The aim of monetary authorities is to create financial stability to discourage the use of funds for speculation rather than for productive activity. However, when speculation causes liquidity to increase excessively, direct credit controls should be used to curb it. This analysis is actually based on Kalecki (1944a, 1954) as I now wish to demonstrate.[4]

There are three financial assets in Kalecki: money, short-term bills and long-term loans. Money has a zero rate of interest, so that there are two interest rates: short-term and long-term. Their determination is a monetary phenomenon, for they are determined by the forces of demand and supply of money. Money is created as a result of meeting the 'needs of trade'. When firms wish to invest they call upon the banks to borrow the required funds, and in the process money is created. Money is endogenously determined. There is a downward-sloping demand curve for bank lending which is related to a downward-sloping demand for money relationship that depends crucially on the short-term rate of interest. Kalecki is clear on the nature of the latter relationship when he argues that 'it seems fairly obvious that the velocity of circulation in fact depends on the short-term rate of interest. Indeed, the higher the short-term rate the greater is the inducement to invest money for short periods rather than to keep it as cash reserve' (Kalecki 1954, 73). The supply curve of money is upward-sloping: as more funds are supplied essentially for investment, then, given the 'principle of increasing risk', there has to be a higher rate of interest paid on those loans, precisely because, given the firms' assets, their liabilities increase and consequently there is a higher risk, and so there should be a higher short-term rate of interest forthcoming. The interaction of the demand for money and the supply of money determine the short-term rate of interest. The long-term rate of interest is related to the short-term rate, but Kalecki (1971, 1954) believed that the long-term rate was expected to change relatively little over the business cycle.

Three types of post-Keynesian development have taken place which are heavily based on these Kaleckian general principles. There was first the Kaldor (1980) approach, which is essentially based on the same premise, that is to say, money comes into the economy from the production side. The difference, however, with Kalecki is that Kaldor was assuming not an upward-sloping supply curve of money but a horizontal one, which also coincides with the demand for money. That is to say, the central bank administers the discount rate, and at that rate money is supplied as the needs of the trade dictate. We, therefore, arrive at what Moore (1988) labels the 'horizontalist' position. Moore has taken the argument a step further by looking carefully into the institutional detail and all the monetary developments, especially 'financial innovations'. In Moore's framework monetary authorities control the discount rate, changes in which influence changes in the market interest rates directly via a mark-up. It is, therefore, apparent that Kalecki's (1971) theory of mark-up pricing as applied to interest rate determination is alluded to in this regard. Consequently, it is the rate of interest that is viewed as being the control variable in this approach.

The second development argues that the Kaldor-Moore analysis should be extended to embrace liquidity preference on the part of the banks (see, for example, Arestis and Howells, 1994). Even when the central bank administers the rate of interest, liquidity preference may be such that commercial banks may curtail the amount of borrowing that they would otherwise have allowed the private sector to undertake. And in that case an upward-sloping supply function of money is more appropriate than a horizontal one. In these developments the 'principle of increasing risk' is very much at the heart of the analysis, where the distinction between 'borrower's risk' and 'lender's risk' is paramount. On a priori grounds, 'borrower's risk' inhibits firms from borrowing to finance investment, whilst 'lender's risk' prohibits the supply of funds to expand in tandem with demand.

The third development refers to the open economy case, where domestic interest rates affect the exchange rate (Arestis and Eichner 1988). This aspect is incorporated into the analysis through the current and capital accounts of the balance of payments. The exchange rate influences and is influenced by the state of both accounts, in addition to the interest rate effect just referred to. A novel feature of the imports element of the current account is the hypothesis embedded in it that suggests that the marginal propensities to import out of workers' wages and out of capitalists' profits differ (Arestis and Driver 1987). This is, of course, an extension of the Kaleckian idea in terms of distinguishing income classes in consumption. A novel implication of this analysis is that, unlike the orthodox approach which distinguishes sharply between a fixed exchange rate system and a flexible exchange rate system,[5] this approach implies that, once the money supply is credit-driven and demand-determined, 'the exchange rate regime is of absolutely no consequence in the determination of money and credit' (Arestis and Eichner 1988, 1015).

Kalecki's Investment Theory

In Kalecki's writings, investment depends on the level of profits relative to capital, as well as on the rate of interest. Profits affect investment in two different ways. First, profits are seen as a source of funds which enable investment to be undertaken. Obviously, then, retained profits, along with funds set aside for depreciation purposes, assume a very significant role in the investment decision process. The larger retained profits and depreciation allowances are, the greater the ability of firms to proceed with the capital expenditure programmes. External sources of funds are also important, but because of the 'principle of increasing risk' the level of investment is still constrained by available internal funds. The 'principle of increasing risk' suggests that firms do not realise their full investment potential because 'risk increases with the amount invested' (Kalecki 1971, 106). The greater the volume of investment the greater the loss a firm is liable to sustain in the case of unsuccessful investment ventures. This, according to Robinson (1966), provides an answer to the case where investment may not be undertaken, even when it could return more than the rate of interest; this is a possibility left unexplored by Keynes.

There is a further related argument here which emphasises the importance of the stock of capital in enabling firms to secure outside finance. Since 'firms below a certain size have no access whatever to the capital market' (*op. cit.*, 106) two propositions follow: first, the size of a firm's capital stock becomes important in securing external finance and, second, the expansion of firms relies heavily on their ability to accumulate capital out of retained profits. These propositions highlight the importance Kalecki puts on the role of the capital stock in investment theory. Accumulation of capital 'will enable the firm to undertake new investment without encountering the obstacles of the limited capital market or "increasing risk". Not only can savings out of current profits be directly invested in the business, but this increase in the firm's capital will make it possible to contract new loans' (Kalecki, 107). This analysis clearly indicates the enormous influence of Kalecki on post-Keynesian thinking. We may refer to Eichner's (1973) pricing theory - as well as to Ball (1964), Harcourt and Kenyon (1976), Wood (1975) and others - to pinpoint the importance of internal funds, a thesis which emanates from Kalecki.

The second way in which profits affect investment is through firms' expectations about the future, in that they indicate the extent to which these are likely to materialise. Rising profits signal healthy economic conditions, which are likely to make firms adopt a more optimistic stance and thus proceed with their investment plans. Falling profits indicate to firms deteriorating economic conditions. Firms become pessimistic and are more reluctant to go ahead with planned investment. The relevant variable in this regard is the change in the level of profits rather than the absolute level.

In addition to profits, the degree of utilisation of the existing capital stock is thought to be a contributory factor in explaining investment. Underutilised capacity encourages firms to cut back on their capital expenditure, and a period of cumulative decline is expected to ensue. Similarly, when demand increases relative to capacity it puts pressure on the existing capital stock, which encourages firms to be more adventurous in their investment decisions. A period of cumulative expansion is now predicted to follow.

Kalecki also considers the possibility that the investment relationship is interest-elastic. His argument is that, whilst the rate of interest can be relevant to long-term investment decisions, a number of reasons suggest that the link may not be strong. To begin with, Kalecki felt that interest rates should not be expected to change by much to affect investment significantly. In any case the effects of changes in interest rates are incorporated in profit rate movements. A more important consideration is the role played by internal financing out of profits, which he sees as more prevalent than external financing, so that interest rate changes assume less significance than otherwise. It should be noted, though, that when Kalecki wrote nominal and real interest rates were not as high as they have been recently.

The impact of the determinants of investment within this theoretical framework is subject to a certain time-lag. Actual investment materialises well after the decision to undertake the investment has been taken. This lagged effect is responsible for introducing a dynamic element in investment behaviour. A further dynamic element is introduced in Kalecki's model in the case of inventory investment, where the 'acceleration principle' is invoked. The rate of change in output or the volume of sales influences inventory investment positively, where Kalecki is very much concerned with the lags involved between cause and effect, justified on the premise that firms would wait to ascertain whether the change in output is permanent or not before they proceed to make the necessary adjustments.

Steindl (1952, 1979) has expanded Kalecki's theory of investment to account for increases in concentration. This leads to higher mark-ups and, with profits determined by past investment decisions, a slow-down in capacity utilisation ensues which increases excess capacity and adversely affects investment decisions. The economy, therefore, tends to stagnate. This is Steindl's 'maturity thesis'. Furthermore, utilising the distinction between internally and externally financed investment, Steindl argues that the 'gearing ratio' affects investment. If insufficient internal funds were forthcoming to maintain the desired level of the 'gearing ratio', total investment would decline. *Mutatis mutandis*, investment would be boosted if internal funds were in abundance. Steindl (1982) also argued that, as 'outside' savings increase relative to 'inside' savings, they would not encourage investment in that the constraint of the 'gearing ratio' does not allow full utilisation of outside savings.

Investment in the post-Keynesian tradition is very much influenced by Kalecki's contributions. For example, in Robinson (1962, 48 in particular) where the famous 'banana' diagram is to be found, this influence is conspicuous.[6] It is thus argued that investment is determined by expected profitability. But it is recognised that whilst it is *expected* profitability that induces capital accumulation, *realised* investment creates the profitability which makes investment possible, partly through internally generated funds. Emphasis on expectations implies that uncertainty must be considered explicitly. The analysis here is based to some considerable extent on the 'principle of increasing risk' which implies that the higher the uncertainty the lower the level of investment. The possibility of uncertainty being a major influence on investment has been further explored recently by Driver and Moreton (1992), who strongly support Kalecki's basic premise and also provide empirical evidence for their case (see also Aiginger 1987). Henley and Tsakalotos (1991) demonstrate that in countries of corporatist inclination, taken to be cases where there is lower uncertainty, investment is less sensitive to fluctuations in income than in non-corporatist countries, where uncertainty is higher.

A further influence on post-Keynesian economics is the proposition that investment is the dominant variable in business cycle theory. Business cycles are depicted as endogenous phenomena, caused by the normal functioning of the capitalist economic system (Kalecki 1971, chapter 11). Exogenous shocks, like technological innovations, oil price changes etc., can set off cyclical fluctuations, but they simply accentuate an underlying endogenously embedded instability. This instability arises from the motive of producers and financial investors alike to accumulate wealth for its sake. It is, therefore, not surprising to find that investment is at the heart of this business cycles theory.

International Monetary Arrangements

This aspect of Kalecki's (1946; see also Kalecki and Schumacher, 1943) work is the least explored and it has only recently been recognised by post-Keynesians (see, for example, Arestis 1993).[7] One reason for this neglect may be the fact that Kalecki's proposals were not fully developed, although he was advocating the creation of financial institutions similar to the ones embedded in Keynes's clearing union plan (see Keynes 1980b). This suggests that another reason for the neglect of this aspect of Kalecki's work is the similarity of the institutions proposed by the two authors. Furthermore, Keynes's views were afforded a lot more exposure than Kalecki's proposals at the time, in view of Keynes's prominence at the Bretton Woods proceedings. Kalecki's proposals were not as comprehensive as Keynes's and, given that both were propounded at the same period, it was inevitable that Keynes's views had more of an impact. The recent interest in a 'New World Order' and in the shape of a future European Monetary System has forced post-Keynesians to revisit not just Keynes but also Kalecki.

Kalecki's views on international monetary arrangements were formulated in the 1940s when discussions of Keynes's clearing union were at their peak. Like Keynes he proposed the creation of an international clearing union to operate as an institution which would periodically settle outstanding balances between central banks. Kalecki's clearing union would be a 'double-entry bookkeeping clearing institution', providing overdraft facilities so that unused credit balances could be mobilised effectively. Kalecki also proposed the establishment of an international investment office, the aim of which would be to provide enough short-term and long-term lending facilities to help overcome foreign exchange difficulties (Kalecki and Schumacher 1943; Kalecki 1946; see also Schumacher 1943).

Kalecki (1946) was mindful of the disadvantages of making the burden of adjustment fall on deficit countries, especially on those with small or weak economies. He argued that eventually this would have deflationary consequences, not just for the weak but also for the stronger countries, thus imparting a serious deflationary bias to the system. Kalecki insisted that 'no country will experience difficulties in balancing its foreign trade if all countries maintain their expenditure on goods and services at a level adequate to secure full employment with no export surplus in existence' (Kalecki 1946, 323). This could be arrived at, if each country maintained full employment, based on domestic expenditure and on net foreign expenditure financed by international long-term lending' (*ibid.*, 327). He insisted that any international monetary arrangement which precluded full employment as priority would simply fail. Surplus countries should stimulate their imports and hence the exports of the deficit countries. The latter should improve their export performance and discourage their imports at the same time, so that their balance-of-payments problems would be alleviated.

Kalecki, therefore, recognised the importance of devising a mechanism that requires surplus countries to bear the main burden of adjustment of balance of payments disequilibria, without at the same time removing all responsibilities from the deficit members. This would be helped by the adoption of a combination of fixed but adjustable rate system to reduce the possibility of massive currency misalignments. However, Kalecki recognised that mere transfer of excess credit balances to the debtor nations could not be relied upon to produce a satisfactory permanent solution, unless an international agency were set up to satisfy long-term financial needs - thus the proposal to create the international investment office.

Economic Policies

Post-Keynesian analysis on economic policy follows closely Kalecki (1943) to suggest that, although governments are able to influence economic magnitudes, this prerogative will not be utilised to its full potential, essentially because there are severe obstacles to reaching the goals of economic policy. This is entirely due to the 'power of vested interests' which Kalecki emphasised so much. Kaldor (1983) has also argued that the changes in the power structure of society, as a result of post-World War II Keynesian economic policies, are responsible for the hostility towards these ideas.

In Kalecki (1944b) three ways of achieving and maintaining full employment are considered: (i) government spending on public investment and subsidies to consumption, financed by borrowing; (ii) stimulating private investment; and (iii) income redistribution from higher to lower income classes.[8] But he was fully aware of the difficulties of reaching, let alone maintaining, full employment. These constraints were viewed by Kalecki (1943) as being rooted in the objections to full employment by the 'industrial leaders'. They emanate from a dislike of government interference in the private sector and are based on the following. There is, to begin with, the objection to government interference in the area of full employment. Such intervention is thought to threaten the replacement of capitalism by socialism. It is also seen by capitalists as a threat to the health of profitability and investment, since government intervention would crowd out the 'efficient' and 'wealth-creating' private sector by the 'inefficient' public sector. There is also an objection to government spending on public investment projects and subsidies on consumption. This is based on arguments like 'not spending more than one's means', 'the need for sound finance', 'the need to balance the budget' etc., which are justified by the 'moral principle' that Kalecki describes ironically as follows: 'The fundamentals of capitalist ethics require that "you shall earn your bread in sweat" - unless you happen to have private means' (Kalecki 1971, 140).

Another objection relates to the social and political changes caused by the achievement and maintenance of full employment. There is the possibility here of workers 'getting out of hand', a situation which the 'captains of industry' would not be prepared to tolerate. Rentiers, too, would not tolerate this situation since they would be disadvantaged by the inflationary pressures which are inevitable at full employment. Kalecki suggests that under these circumstances there could very well develop 'a powerful bloc.....between big business and the rentiers' interests, and they would probably find more than one economist to declare that the situation was manifestly unsound. The pressure of all these forces, and in particular of big business, would most probably induce the Government to return to the orthodox policy of cutting down the budget deficit' (Kalecki 1971, 144).

There is another significant element in Kalecki's (1943) analysis. The elimination of budget deficits near full employment, as a result of insistence by powerful industrial and financial interests, not only precludes the achievement and maintenance of full employment but also leads to unemployment. As the next election approaches, however, pressures to relieve unemployment result in expansionary economic policies, so that a period of expansion ensues until the economy reaches a near full employment stage, where again pressures for contraction reappear. Here the 'business cycle' is replaced by a 'political cycle'.

There are, of course, other economic obstacles to lasting full employment beyond the ones discussed above. Poor research and development, inadequate excess capacity, lack of trained and skilled labour force, lack of high educational standards and consequently lack of skill and talent amongst all economic agents, and thus absence of innovation which is so vital to boost investment, are some of the more important examples. In the case of open economies, there is a further awkward problem in that the balance of payments can be a severe constraint in terms of allowing the economy to move to full employment. Expansion of demand meets severe balance-of-payments deficits and undesirable movements in the country's exchange rate, so that the expansionary policy would have to be reversed. This difficulty could very well arise from a weak supply-side sector, due to inability of the economy to respond to the increased demand, well before full employment is reached. The balance-of-payments constraint is of particular significance here. Kalecki (1946) clearly suggested that international trade is likely to be a binding constraint to attempts by governments to achieve full employment. This argument was further developed and has become an integral part of the post-Keynesian open-economy theoretical framework, in the form of 'Thirlwall's Law' (Thirlwall 1979).

These views are reinforced by the important contributions of Myrdal (1939, 1957), known as the theory of 'circular and cumulative causation', which is essentially based on the dynamic interplay between investment and productivity growth which reinforces *inequalities* and *regional disparities*. Regions which are already developed enjoy competitive advantages so that the growth that takes place generates dynamic economies of scale, by attracting more skilled labour (especially young) and capital. Higher productivity and higher rate of profit in the faster-growing regions ensue, with the slower regions finding it progressively harder to compete.[9] This inflow of capital and skilled labour allows still further expansion of production and the reaping of further economies of scale, higher productivity and rate of profit. There may be certain advantages accruing to the slower regions, such as transfer of new technology, expanded markets etc., which, however, can never be strong enough to outweigh the negative effects emanating from 'cumulative causation'. Even if by chance these effects were in balance, this would not be a stable equilibrium, for any change in the balance of the two forces would be followed by cumulative movements.

The policy implications of this analysis are that not only intervention at the national level is necessary, but also at the regional level, where regions can be countries, as for example in the case of the European Union. The effectiveness of such policy prescriptions are recognised to be limited for the achievement and maintenance of full employment, in view of Kalecki's analysis as expounded above. Institutional changes are required which would remove the constraints Kalecki was so much concerned about then, and post-Keynesians are now. At the top of the agenda for these changes must surely be co-ordination of economic policies at the international level and more 'corporatist' institutions at the national level.

Summary and Conclusions

We have argued in this chapter that Kalecki's role in post-Keynesian economics is both extensive and significant. Furthermore, our analysis supports strongly Geoff Harcourt's belief that 'Kalecki's analysis of the political economy of capitalism is the most profound of the twentieth century, as relevant today as when he originally developed it' (Foreword to Kriesler 1987, xi-xii). Effective demand, and investment in particular, has been emphasised. We have also argued that there are other aspects which are of equal importance. The capitalist system, which is Kalecki's focus, is thought to be marred with inequalities which market forces cannot eradicate. By contrast, market forces tend to exacerbate the disparities that are evident in such a system. The capitalist system based on free market principles is inherently cyclical and unstable. Left to itself it would not achieve, let alone maintain, either full use of existing resources or their equitable distribution.

These features of the capitalist system are due mainly to the behaviour of private investment. Full employment requires a radical change in income distribution and in the organisation of production. Kalecki (1943) realised that long-run full employment would be unsustainable for a number of reasons: it reduces the threat of dismissal for there is the strong possibility that workers 'get out of hand'; the dislike of big business of full employment; the unfounded argument of crowding-out; and the need to balance the budget. Substantial institutional changes to remove the obstacles to full employment at both the national and the international levels are vital. Whatever these institutional changes may be, the priority of any economic policy should be the achievement and maintenance of full employment.

Notes

1 It might be argued that Cowling's model may not be within the spirit of Kalecki's analysis in view of its assumptions. This would be too hasty a conclusion given the predictions of the model and the arguments advanced by a number of writers to suggest that it is actually very much Kaleckian (see, for example, Sawyer 1990).

2 The interested reader can find the derivation of the formulae that appear in the text in Arestis (1992, chapters 5 and 6).

3 There is an interesting and important contrast here with orthodox economics, where the real wage is determined in the labour market.

4   Our analysis of Kalecki's theory of money and finance refers to advanced western industrialised economies. FitzGerald (1993) considers the case of semi-industrialised economies.

5 In the orthodox approach, the supply of money is exogenous under a flexible exchange rate with the exchange rate itself changes to clear the market. By contrast, the money supply is endogenous under a fixed exchange rate regime where the exchange rate is exogenously determined.

6 This is merely one example of Kalecki's influence on Robinson. Geoff Harcourt suggested that Robinson's post-war contributions were increasingly expositions of Kalecki's views. Space constraints do not allow full exposition of this thesis, which needs a fully-fledged paper, if not a book, to do it justice.

7 Although Davidson's (1992-93) recent proposals are based on Keynes's 'clearing union', they are nonetheless very consistent with Kalecki's proposals. Arestis (1993) discusses both Kalecki's and Keynes's proposals, and in this analysis it is clear that they are very consistent with each other.

8 An interesting development, in terms of the distributional aspects of economic policy, is the work undertaken recently on the impact of different taxes on economic activity and distribution of income. Damania and Mair provide a critical review of the literature which leads them to 'doubt that neo-classical analytical techniques are sufficiently robust' (1992, 141) to investigate questions of tax incidence. They develop, instead, a Kaleckian model which enables them to offer 'a fuller appreciation of the macroeconomic effects of tax reforms' (ibid., 141).

9 There is further the idea that 'cumulative causation' in economic terms generates inequalities in non-economic terms, such as political power, cultural domination etc. (Cowling 1985). Relatively rich regions are expected to dominate, not just in the sense of economic power, but also in terms of their ability to exert political superiority. They are in a position to impose their policies and culture over the less powerful regions, so that democratic institutions are under threat.

References

Aiginger, K. 1987. *Production and Decision Theory Under Uncertainty*. Oxford: Blackwell.
Arestis, P. 1986. 'Wages and Prices in the UK: the Post Keynesian View'. *Journal of Post Keynesian Economics* 8 (3), Spring: 339-358.
Arestis, P. 1992. *The Post-Keynesian Approach to Economics: An Alternative Analysis to Economic Theory and Policy*. Aldershot: Elgar.
Arestis, P. 1993. 'An Independent European Central Bank: A Post-Keynesian Perspective'. Paper delivered at the Eleventh Keynes Seminar, *Keynes and the Post-Keynesians*, at the University of Kent, November. To be published in V. Chick (ed.), *Keynes and the Post-Keynesians*. London: Macmillan.
Arestis, P. and Chick, V. (eds) 1992. *Recent Developments in Post-Keynesian Economics*. Aldershot: Elgar.
Arestis, P. and Driver, C. 1980. 'Consumption Out of Different Types of Income in the UK'. *Bulletin of Economic Research* 32 (4), November: 85-96.
Arestis, P. and Driver, C. 1987. 'The Effects of Income Distribution on Consumer Imports'. *Journal of Macroeconomics* 9(1), Winter: 83-94.
Arestis, P. and Eichner, A.S. 1988. 'The Post-Keynesian and Institutionalist Theory of Money and Credit'. *Journal of Economic Issues* 22(4), December: 1003-1033.
Arestis, P. and Howells, P.G.A. 1994. 'Theoretical Reflections on Endogenous Money: The Problem with 'Convenience Lending''. *Mimeo*.
Arestis, P. and Kitromilides. Y. (eds) 1990. *Theory and Policy in Political Economy: Essays in Pricing, Distribution and Growth*. Aldershot: Elgar.
Arestis, P. and Sawyer, M.C. 1993. 'Political Economy: An Editorial Manifesto'. *International Papers in Political Economy* 1(1): 1-38.
Asimakopulos, A. 1975. 'A Kaleckian Theory of Income Distribution'. *Canadian Journal of Economics* 8(3), August: 313-333.
Asimakopulos, A. 1989. 'Kalecki and Robinson'. In Sebastiani 1989: 10-24.
Ball, R.J. 1964. *Inflation and the Theory of Money*. London: Allen and Unwin.
Baran, P. 1957. *The Political Economy of Growth*. New York: Monthly Review.
Basile, L. and Salvadori, N. 1984-85. 'Kalecki's Pricing Theory'. *Journal of Post Keynesian Economics* 7 (2): 249-262.
Bhaduri, A. and Marglin, S. 1990. 'Unemployment and the Real Wage: The Economic Basis for Contesting Political Ideologies'. *Cambridge Journal of Economics* 14(4), December: 375-393.
Carson, J. 1994. 'Existence and Uniqueness of Solutions to Kalecki's Pricing Equations'. *Journal of Post Keynesian Economics* 16 (3), Spring: 411-434.
Cowling, K. 1982. *Monopoly Capitalism*. London: Macmillan.
Cowling, K. 1985. 'Economic Obstacles to Democracy'. In R.C.O. Matthews (ed.). *Economy and Democracy*. London: Macmillan.

Cowling, K. and Waterson, M. 1976. 'Price-cost Margins and Market Structure'. *Economica* 43(171), August: 267-274.

Damania, R. and Mair, D. 1992. 'A Post-Keynesian Approach to the Incidence of Taxation'. In Arestis and Chick (1992).

Davidson, P. 1992. 'The Asimakopulos View of Keynes's General Theory'. Paper read at the a conference on *Employment, Distribution and Markets*. Levy Institute, Bard College, New York, September 24-26.

Davidson, P. 1992-93. 'Reforming the World's Money'. *Journal of Post Keynesian Economics* 15 (2), Winter: 153-179.

Driver, C. and Moreton, D. 1992. *Investment, Expectations and Uncertainty*. Oxford: Blackwell.

Dutt, A.K. 1992. 'Rentiers in Post-Keynesian Models'. In Arestis and Chick (1992): 95-122.

Eichner, A.S. 1973. 'A Theory of the Determination of the Mark-up Under Oligopoly'. *Economic Journal* 83(332), December: 1184-2000.

Eichner, A.S. 1976. *The Megacorp and Oligopoly: Micro Foundations of Macro Dynamics*. Cambridge: Cambridge University Press.

FitzGerald, E.V.K. 1993. *The Macroeconomics of Development Finance: A Kaleckian Analysis of the Semi-Industrialised Economy*. London: Macmillan.

Hamouda, O.F. and Harcourt, G.C. 1988. 'Post Keynesianism: From Criticism to Coherence'. *Bulletin of Economic Research* 40 (1), January: 1-33.

Harcourt, G.C. 1963. 'A Critique of Mr Kaldor's Model of Income Distribution and Economic Growth'. *Australian Economic Papers* 2, June: 20-36.

Harcourt, G.C. 1965. 'A Two-sector Model of the Distribution of Income and the Level of Employment in the Short Run'. *Economic Record* 41(93), March: 103-117.

Harcourt, G.C. 1991. Review of *Collected Works of Michal Kalecki, Volume I: Capitalism, Business Cycles and Full Employment*. Edited by Jerzy Osiatynski. *Economic Journal* 101(409), November: 1608-1610.

Harcourt, G.C. and Kenyon, P. 1976. 'Pricing and the Investment Decision'. *Kyklos* 29 (3): 449-72.

Henley, A. and Tsakalotos, E. 1991. 'Corporatism, Profit Sqeeze and Investment'. *Cambridge Journal of Economics* 15 (4), December: 425-50.

Kaldor, N. 1955-6. 'Alternative Theories of Distribution'. *Review of Economic Studies*. 23 8(2): 83-100.

Kaldor, N. 1982. *The Scourge of Monetarism*. Oxford: Oxford University Press.

Kaldor, N. 1983. 'Keynesian Economics After Fifty Years'. In D. Worswick and J. Trevithick (eds), *Keynes and the Modern World*. Cambridge: Cambridge University Press: 11-28.

Kalecki, M. 1943. 'Political Aspects of Full Employment'. *Political Quarterly*. 14 (4), October/December: 322-31.

Kalecki, M. 1944a. 'Professor Pigou on "The Classical Stationary State": A Comment'. *Economic Journal* 54 (1), March: 131-2.

Kalecki, M. 1944b. 'Three Ways to Full Employment'. In *The Economics of Full Employment: Six Studies in Applied Economics Prepared at the Oxford University Institute of Statistics*. Oxford: Blackwell: 39-58.

Kalecki, M. 1946. 'Multilateralism and Full Employment'. *Canadian Journal of Economics and Political Science* 12(3), August: 322-327.

Kalecki, M. 1954. *Theory of Economic Dynamics: An Essay on Cyclical and Long-run Changes in Capitalist Economy*. London: Allen and Unwin.

Kalecki, M. 1966. 'Money and Real Wages'. In M. Kalecki, *Studies in the Theory of Business Cycles*. Oxford, Blackwell: 40-71.

Kalecki, M. 1970. 'Theories of Growth in Different Social Systems'. *Scientia* 105: 311-16.

Kalecki, M. 1971. 'Class Struggle and Distribution of National Income'. *Kyklos* 24 (1): 1-9.

Kalecki, M. and Schumacher, E.F. 1943. 'International Clearing and Long-Term Lending'. *Bulletin of the Oxford Institute of Statistics* 5, Supplement, August: 29-33.

Keynes, J.M. 1936. *The General Theory of Employment, Interest and Money*. London: Macmillan.

Keynes, J.M. 1980a. *The Collected Writings of John Maynard Keynes*. In A. Robinson and D. Moggridge (eds), *Treatise on Money*. London: Macmillan.

Keynes, J.M. 1980b. *The Collected Writings of John Maynard Keynes*. In A. Robinson and D. Moggridge (eds), *Activities 1940-4, Shaping the Post-War World: The Clearing Union*. London: Macmillan.

Kriesler, P. 1987. *Kalecki's Microanalysis: The Development of Kalecki's Analysis of Pricing and Distribution*. Cambridge: Cambridge University Press.

Marglin, S.A. 1984. 'Growth, Distribution and Inflation: A Centennial Synthesis'. *Cambridge Journal of Economics* 8(2), June: 115-144.

Moore, B.J. 1988. *Horizontalists and Verticalists: The Macroeconomics of Credit Money*. Cambridge: Cambridge University Press.

Myrdal, G. 1939. *Monetary Equilibrium*. London: Hodge.

Myrdal, G. 1957. *Economic Theory and the Underdeveloped Regions*. London: Duckworth.

Pasinetti, L.L. 1974. *Growth and Income Distribution: Essays in Economic Theory*. Cambridge: Cambridge University Press.

Patinkin, D. 1982. *Anticipations of the General Theory? And Other Essays on Keynes*. Chicago: University of Chicago Press.

Patinkin, D. 1989. 'Michal Kalecki and the General Theory'. In Sebastiani 1989: 25-44.

Reynolds, P.J. 1989. 'Kaleckian and Post-Keynesian Theories of Pricing: Some Extensions and Implications'. In Arestis and Kitromilides 1990: 229-69.

Robinson, J. 1962. *Essays in the Theory of Economic Growth*. London: Macmillan.

Robinson, J. 1966. 'Kalecki and Keynes'. In *Problems of Economic Dynamics and Planning: Essays in Honour of Michal Kalecki*. Oxford: Pergamon: 335-41.

Robinson, J. 1977. 'Michal Kalecki on the Economics of Capitalism'. *Oxford Bulletin of Economics and Statistics* 39(1), February: 7-18.

Rowthom, R. 1981. 'Demand, Real Wages, and Economic Growth'. *Thames Papers in Political Economy* Autumn: 1-39.

Sardoni, C. (ed). 1992. *On Political Economists and Modern Political Economy: Selected Essays of G.C. Harcourt.* London Routledge.

Sawyer, M.C. 1982. *Macroeconomics in Question: The Keynesian-Monetarist Orthodoxies and the Kaleckian Alternative.* Brighton: Wheatsheaf.

Sawyer, M.C. 1985. *The Economics of Michal Kalecki.* London: Macmillan.

Sawyer, M.C. 1990. 'On the Post-Keynesian Tradition and Industrial Economics'. *Review of Political Economy* 2 (1), March: 43-68.

Schumacher, E.F. 1943. 'Multilateral Clearing'. *Economica* n.s. 10, May: 150-165.

Sebastiani, M. (ed.) 1989. *Kalecki's Relevance Today.* London: Macmillan.

Steindl, J. 1952. *Maturity and Stagnation in American Capitalism.* Oxford: Oxford University Press.

Steindl, J. 1979. 'Stagnation Theory and Stagnation Policy'. *Cambridge Journal of Economics* 3 (1), March: 1-14.

Targetti, F. and Kinda-Hass, B. 1982. 'Kalecki's Review of Keynes's General Theory'. *Australian Economic Papers* 21(39), December: 244-260.

Thirlwall, A.P. 1979. 'The Balance of Payments Constraint as an Explanation of International Growth Rate Differences'. *Banca Nazionale del Lavoro Quarterly Review* 32(128), March: 45-53.

Wood, A. 1975. *A Theory of Profits.* Cambridge: Cambridge University Press.

2 KALECKI AND KEYNES

Simon Chapple

Introduction

Two approaches have been taken by economists writing on Kalecki and Keynes. The first picture is broad, comparing and contrasting the two as political economists.[1] The narrower approach is a consideration of whether Kalecki anticipated important elements of Keynes's *General Theory*. This chapter pursues the latter issue, critically discussing the literature on Kalecki and Keynes in an attempt to answer the question of whether Kalecki anticipated the essentials of the Keynesian model.[2]

Why is the question of Kalecki's possible multiple discovery of the *General Theory* important? A number of commentators have suggested that the question is uninteresting, unimportant or glosses over difference between ideas of the two.[3] There are a number of reasons for pursuing questions of multiple discovery. Indeed the fact that so many prominent economists of the mid-twentieth century have touched on the issue - amongst them names such as Dobb, Frisch, Klein, Lange, Patinkin, Robinson, Samuelson, Shackle and Solow - shows a revealed preference that it is a question of importance within the economics community. And there can be little doubt that priority was important to Kalecki, demonstrated by the following account of Robinson (1977, 186):

[Kalecki] told me that he had taken a year's leave from the institute where he was working in Warsaw to write the *General Theory*. In Stockholm someone gave him Keynes' book. He began to read it - it was the book that he intended to write. He thought that perhaps further on there would be something different. No, all the way it was his book. He said : 'I confess, I was ill, three days I lay in bed. Then I thought - Keynes is more known than I am. These ideas will get across much quicker with him and then we can get on to the interesting question which is their application. Then I got up.'[4]

Later evidence of the importance of multiple discovery to Kalecki is reported by Feiwel, who recalls Maurice Dobb informing him that before one of Kalecki's post-war lectures at Cambridge, he was introduced as the anticipator of the main ideas of the *General Theory* 'so that it could have been called the Kaleckian revolution. Kalecki, although inclined to be expressionless on such occasions, looked as if this pleased him distinctly' (Feiwel 1975, 458 n4).

Why might so many, including Kalecki himself, be concerned with questions of multiple discovery? Sociologist of science Robert Merton has examined multiple discovery in science in detail, pointing out that the norms of science place advancement of knowledge and the act of originality as central institutional goals. Material and honorific rewards are given to those who make scientific progress. Within science the only intellectual property right is that of recognition of originality. Therefore issues of who gets the credit are of importance.

Moreover, if Kalecki and Keynes (and possibly others) did (or did not) discover some of the same ideas around the same time, as a particular case study it casts light more generally on the nature of scientific discovery and the role of individuals in scientific progress. Therefore whether Kalecki independently discovered central elements of the *General Theory* is an important question both to the community of economists and more generally. The issue is not whether there is a 100 per cent overlap in the work of the two on all substantive questions, Indeed, no commentator has argued along these lines. Nor is it the purpose of this chapter to suggest that the only correct way to assess the importance of contributions to macroeconomics before 1936 is via the extent to which they anticipate elements of the *General Theory*. The issue here is the more modest one of ascertaining which parts of Keynes's work Kalecki had arrived at before Keynes and to what extent these add up to the Keynesian revolution.

Kalecki's Claims

Kalecki himself made a number of claims for anticipating elements of the *General Theory*. The first appears in Polish in his 1936 *Ekonomista* review of the *General Theory*, in three footnotes. The first footnote suggests that '[t]he proposition that investment decides the global volume of production has been proved in a similar way to Keynes's in my *Essay on the Business Cycle Theory* [1933a]' (Kalecki 1936a, 228 n4). Kalecki (1936a, 228) goes on to stress that for Keynes 'saving does not determine investment but, on the contrary it is precisely investment which creates savings' and that capital market equilibrium exists 'whatever the rate of interest, because investment always forces savings of the same amount'. Kalecki then adds the second footnote, claiming that '[a]n analogous idea about the demand for and supply of capital has been put forward in my *Essay on the Business Cycle Theory*' (Kalecki 1936a, 228 n5). The third footnote comes after his discussion of money wage cuts in the *General Theory* and claims that 'I have also shown the independence of production from changes in money wages in my *Essay on the Business Cycle Theory*' (Kalecki 1936a, 229 n6). Kalecki's review essay also draws a connection between his work and Keynes's use of 'a given productive apparatus', which he states 'we have previously used' (Kalecki 1936a, 223), presumably a reference to his 1934 *Ekonomista* article 'Three Systems' which makes this assumption.

Kalecki's first English claims are discreetly implied hints. In chapter 3, 'Money and Real Wages', of his 1939 book *Essays in the Theory of Economic Fluctuations* Kalecki discusses at some length what he calls 'the Keynesian theory of wages' (Kalecki 1939, 274) and, after showing that a money wage cut only causes an equivalent reduction in prices with no change in employment, he notes that 'I have already treated the problem of wages in this way in my article "Essai d'une Theorie du Mouvement Cyclique des Affaires," *Revue d'Economie Politique* March-April 1935, 201-2' (Kalecki 1939, 79 n1). In chapter 6 Kalecki (1939, 116 n1) alerts readers to the fact that earlier versions of his business cycle theory had been published in both English (Kalecki 1935a) and French (Kalecki 1935b) prior to 1936, leaving it up to the reader to make a connection between his work and that of Keynes. A stronger claim comes in a 1942 *Economic Journal* article where Kalecki indicates that the 'theory of profits presented here is closely allied to Mr. Keynes' theory of savings and investment. It has been, however, developed independently from Mr Keynes' (Kalecki 1942, 260 n1) and this same footnote is repeated in *Studies in Economic Dynamics* (Kalecki 1943, 50). At the beginning of chapter 3 of his book *Theory of Economic Dynamics*, entitled 'The Determinants of Profits', Kalecki (1954, 45) includes a footnote making the point that his theory of profits was developed in two 1935 articles (Kalecki 1993a, 1935b). Finally, Kalecki's most forthright claim comes in the posthumously published *Selected Essays on the Dynamics of the Capitalist Economy*, where he indicates in the introduction that the 'first part includes three papers published in 1933, 1934 [sic][5] and 1935 in Polish before Keynes' *General Theory* and containing, I believe, its essentials' (Kalecki 1971, vii).

Claims by Others

Kalecki was not a lone voice in the wilderness. He found support from others. An early indication of similarities between Kalecki and Keynes is made by Ragnar Frisch who (at the 1936 Oxford Meeting of the Econometric Society) 'pointed out that the possibility of permanent unemployment even when there was no restriction of the supply of labour, to which Mr. Keynes had called attention in his recent work' had been previously brought out in macrodynamic studies by Kalecki, amongst others (Phelps Brown 1937, 363).

Another early claim on behalf of Kalecki is made by Oscar Lange in a 1939 article written for a Polish encyclopedia (Lange 1939; Patinkin 1982, 60). Lange suggests that 'M. Kalecki entirely independently created a theory of employment similar to the one developed in Cambridge and on its basis constructed a theory of the business cycle' (editorial note, Kalecki 1990, 464). And in his 1939 book *Business Cycles*, Schumpeter hints that Kalecki's theory of the business cycle (to which he devotes four pages of discussion) may have anticipated Keynes, pointing out that Kalecki's theory was published in Polish and in English prior to 1936 and noting that in the 1937 *Review of Economic Studies* version, 'the theory is compared to that of Mr. Keynes. Into the ramifications of that subject we cannot enter here' (Schumpeter 1939, 185 n2).

A further early English language suggestion of a link between Keynes and Kalecki was made by Zweig (1944, 167), who, in an appendix on Polish economic thought between the world wars indicates Kalecki (1933a) 'came very near to the Keynesian General Theory of Employment.'[6] In his 1947 memoir of Keynes, Austin Robinson, while writing that 'Michal Kalecki was independently approaching the same goal' (Robinson 1947, 42) as Keynes, does not suggest that Kalecki discovered the essentials of the *General Theory*. On the other hand, in a review essay of Roy Harrod's biography of Keynes, Lawrence Klein (1951) claims that Kalecki's business cycle theory 'created a system that contains everything of importance in the Keynesian system... he has a theory of employment that is equal to Keynes' (Klein 1951, 447; see also Klein 1964, 1966, 1975).

Along with Klein, Joan Robinson has been a vigorous promoter of Kalecki's claims, setting out as she puts it 'to blow his trumpet for him' (Robinson 1977, 186). 'Mr. Kalecki's discovery of the *General Theory* independently of Keynes', Robinson states, 'was a classic example of the coincidence of science' and she goes on to suggest that '[b]ased on the same conception of short period equilibrium his theory fitted naturally into Keynes' scheme and became absorbed into it in the subsequent development of the *General Theory*' (Robinson 1952, 159). In addition to this, her earliest in a long line of published claims that Kalecki anticipated Keynes (see Robinson 1964, 1971, 1976, 1977), Robinson also wrote a letter to Kalecki in September 1936 (reproduced in Patinkin 1982, 95)) which may be interpreted as support for Kalecki's claim of anticipating the *General Theory*.[7]

Since the mid-1960s many others have noted that Kalecki may have anticipated Keynes, for example Shackle (1967, 127), Dobb (1973, 221), Eshag (1977a, 1-2) and Blaug (1978, 696), while Feiwel's book *The Intellectual Capital of Michal Kalecki* (1975) has been prominent in advancing Kalecki's claims. Chapter 1 of part 1 of Feiwel's intellectual biography is entitled 'The Kalecki-Keynes Revolution: Independent Discovery of the *General Theory*' and in this chapter Feiwel (1975, 27) claims that Kalecki 'discovered all the basic components which entered also into Keynes' analytical system.'

Revisionism

After the publication of Feiwel's intellectual biography, intellectual dissent coalesced. In a neglected review, Solow (1976) rejects Feiwel's arguments for reasons similar - albeit less developed - to those later advanced by Patinkin (1982). Solow argues that Kalecki's pre-1936 work concentrates on the investment cycle (like Klein, Solow uses Kalecki's 1935 *Econometrica* article as a reference point) and this work 'discusses only casually and briefly the process by which this [equilibrium between saving and investment] comes about through changes in output, employment and prices' (Solow 1976, 1334). Solow argues that for Kalecki to have built his 1935 *Econometrica* article into a theory of output determination 'requires another link, which is provided by Kalecki's theory of output shares' which, as far as he is aware, is provided only in his later 1938 *Econometrica* article.

In another review essay of Feiwel's book, Frazer (1976) argues that there are more differences between Keynes and Kalecki than Feiwel allows. Characterising Keynes's theory as being built up from basic building blocks of 'aggregate demand and supply, liquidity preference, and investment demand', Frazer (1976, 1163) argues that

Kalecki's analysis lacked a consumption function, had no theory of liquidity preference, and therefore is at some distance from Keynes's theory.

In discussing Kalecki's mathematical business cycle models in the context of the *General Theory*, Samuelson (1981, 368) suggests that 'Kalecki's determinate equations for the determination of profits by the level of investment comes the closest to duplicating the Keynesian system' and suggests that if he 'had made explicit his latent notion that the total of non-profit incomes are in a determinate relation to the total of profit' Kalecki would have discovered the theory of effective demand. In a later article discussing multiple discovery of the *General Theory*, Samuelson (1991, 398-9) supports the position that effective demand, which he accepts Kalecki may have discovered, and in a wider sense the IS-LM model, are the essentials of the Keynesian system. This is basically Patinkin's argument, to be examined below.

Despite odd murmurings of dissent, by the early 1980s scholarly opinion had concluded that Kalecki did independently discover many of Keynes's important contributions. All this changed with the publication of Don Patinkin's *Anticipations of* the *General Theory?* (1982) which presents a detailed study concluding that Keynes's book was not an instance of multiple discovery, either by Kalecki or anyone else.[8]

Patinkin (1982, 16-18) suggests that in order to discuss multiple discovery of a scientific theory one must first define its major innovation, described as the 'central message'. If both scientists have the same central message at about the same time, one can speak of multiple discovery. How does one identify the central message? Sometimes, Patinkin indicates, it is made more or less explicit by the author. In the frequent absence of such precision, one searches for an indication of the central message in terms of the title of a work, in terms of presentation of the main theme early in the work, and by repetition of the theme throughout the work. In addition, the context of other work by, and contemporary commentaries on, the author's work can help in identification (Patinkin 1983, 82-5).

According to Patinkin the *General Theory*'s central message was Keynes's theory of effective demand. For Patinkin the essence of effective demand is summarised in the 45° diagram, the key features of which, to paraphrase, are threefold: first, intersection of the expenditure/income equality with the function relating expenditure to income determines the level of output; second, disequilibrium between expenditure and income causes an output and not a price change; third it is output changes that clear the goods market. The role of output variations in clearing the goods market, Patinkin claims, is Keynes's central message and as such represents what others would have had to achieve in order to anticipate the *General Theory*.

As Patinkin (1982, 11) points out, 'there is obviously more to the *General Theory* [than effective demand]' and he then goes on to define what he views as two other major innovations that came out of the *General Theory*, Keynes's general equilibrium treatment of the goods and money market (or aggregate demand) and integration of this with the short-period marginalist theory of prices (or aggregate supply). In other words, Patinkin (1982) argues that a major innovation of the *General Theory* was the IS-LM/AS-AD model.

Patinkin uses his definition to reject Kalecki's claims for discovery of the *General Theory*. He examines Kalecki's work published prior to 1936 in order to ascertain whether it contains the central message of effective demand, asserting that '[t]he main basis for... [the] claim is Kalecki's Polish monograph *Proba Teorii Koniunktury*' [*Essay on the Business Cycle Theory*]. He concludes that the central message of the *Essay on the Business Cycle Theory* and Kalecki's associated publications in *Revue d'Economie Politique* and *Econometrica* is an analysis of investment and profit cycles. The basic content of the *Essay on the Business Cycle Theory* was also presented by Kalecki to the Econometric Society Conference at Leyden in 1933, and his *Econometrica* article drew comments from Frisch and Holme (1935) and Tinbergen (1935) which focus on his business cycle theory rather than on effective demand.[9]

Patinkin (1982, 71) acknowledges that 'Kalecki does in effect discuss the Keynesian equilibrating mechanism' in his 'The Mechanism of the Business Upswing' (1935c),[10] which was 'published in a Polish semi-governmental weekly devoted to economic commentary and reports [*Polska Gospodarcza*]', but suggests that 'this theme of "unemployment equilibrium" receives little if any attention in Kalecki's professional writings during the pre-*General Theory* period. And, lest I be misunderstood, let me emphasise that my point here is not that this theme appears in his non-professional writings but that it appears *only* there' (Patinkin 1982, 72, original emphasis).

Patinkin (1982, 85) compares Kalecki's article to one 'an economist would present, say, in a *Newsweek* column and which did not have a counterpart in his scientific writings.' Because Kalecki's 1935 article is not published in a professional journal, it is not regarded by Patinkin as central to his scientific contribution.

Professional and Non-Professional Publications

Patinkin contends that for a message to be central it should be included in a scientist's professional writings, arguing that if scientists do not address their output to the scientific community the ideas cannot be central to their work. Thus Patinkin proposes a two-step criterion along the following lines. First, determine the central message of a piece. Second, establish whether the work was central to a scientist's concerns. The second step, Patinkin suggests, is decided on the basis of whether the scientist published the work in a professional journal.

Objections to the distinction between professional and non-professional publications have already been raised by Sawyer:

> Patinkin (1982, especially pp. 72, 85) argues that ideas expressed only in non-professional journals are not to be counted as part of an author's central message. This would seem reasonable for someone who regarded themselves as primarily a professional economist with easy access to professional journals. In conversation Jerzy Osiatynski (editor of Kalecki's *Collected Works*) has suggested that Kalecki considered himself primarily a socialist economist rather than an academic economist, and could well have published his important ideas in socialist journals rather than academic ones. Further in Poland there was at the time only one academic journal on economics, which was generally rather orthodox (though it did publish Kalecki's review of Keynes (1936)). (Sawyer 1985, 208-9 n6).

Sawyer's suggestion that as a socialist Kalecki may have published important ideas in a socialist journal does not stand up in the case of the article to which Patinkin refers, because *Polska Gospodarcza* was 'a Polish semi-governmental magazine devoted to economic commentary and reports... published with the support of the Ministry of Industry and Trade as well as the Ministry of Finance and other government ministries' (Patinkin 1982, 71, n20).[11] The Polish government of the 1930s certainly could not have been characterised as socialist. While Sawyer's argument may have some validity for some of Kalecki's articles, it does not for the one to which both he and Patinkin refer.

Sawyer more circumspectly hints that Kalecki may have experienced difficulties in getting his revolutionary articles accepted in *Ekonomista*, a publication that he describes as a 'rather orthodox' journal. The suggestion that ruling paradigms shut heretical or revolutionary ideas out of accepted professional discourse has some plausibility in economics. Given the lack of knowledge about acceptance criteria for this journal during the 1930s, and given the language barrier, it is difficult to discern the nature of *Ekonomista*, orthodox or otherwise. However, strong indirect evidence exists against this latter suggestion of Sawyer. In addition to publishing Kalecki's review essay on the *General Theory*, *Ekonomista* published two articles by Kalecki, one in 1933 entitled 'On Foreign Trade and 'Domestic Exports' and another in 1934 entitled 'Three Systems'. In addition, *Ekonomista* published a four page criticism of 'Three Systems' by A. M. Neuman and Kalecki's rejoinder (Kalecki, 1990, 482-6), as well as a four-page review by

Kalecki's friend and colleague Ludwik Landau of *Essay on the Business Cycle Theory* (editorial note, Kalecki 1990, 443). On the available evidence *Ekonomista* could not stand accused of not publishing Kalecki's work.

Commenting on Sawer's suggestion that as a socialist economist Kalecki may have had different publication criteria, Bhattacharjea and Raghunathan (1988, 1392 n24) briefly question Patinkin's distinction between professional and non-professional publications on the grounds that Kalecki was not a modern economist. They suggest that 'Kalecki is unlikely to have had the same attitude towards his articles in the Polish *Socialist Review* that a contemporary economist might have towards his column in *Newsweek.*' Again, like Sawyer, Bhattacharjea and Raghunathan do not point out that the disputed article (the 1935 *Polska Gospodarcza* article) was not published in a socialist journal.

Feiwel (1989) provides an alternative explanation of why Kalecki may not have made the distinction between professional and non-professional publications. He suggests that, to get a complete picture of Kalecki's contribution to macroeconomics prior to 1936, one must consider 'the articles published in non-academic journals, especially those he later selected for translation in the 1966 edition [Kalecki 1966]'. Kalecki, according to Feiwel, was not an academic economist. He earned his living in part as an economic journalist, so there may have been pecuniary motives behind his publication decisions (Feiwel 1989a, 71).

Patinkin's distinction between professional and non-professional publications does not take into account a number of factors peculiar to Kalecki's historical circumstances (Chapple 1991). Kalecki was developing and publishing his ideas in a different time and place. He was not even an academic economist, being self-taught. He was not subject to modern economics instruction at a higher level, an instruction which imparts a narrow set of mathematical and economic techniques and also socialises students into how to write academic papers and where to publish them as a mean of attaining status amongst the invisible college of fellow professionals.[12]

Comparing the context of Kalecki's 'The Mechanism of the Business Upswing' to something published in *Newsweek* or the business section of the *New York Times* is misleading. A comparison of the 1935 article with others published by Kalecki in professional journals at the same time reveals no differences in its degree of complexity, rigour or length.

Further evidence that the context of the 1935 article differs greatly from that of a *Newsweek* article is given by the fact that Kalecki republished the article in translation in his 1966 *Studies in the Theory of the Business Cycle, 1933 - 1939* and in his 1971

Selected Essays on the Dynamics of the Capitalist Economy, suggesting that he did not perceive any substantial difference (at least ex post) between the 1935 article and other 'professional' articles included in both books. That Kalecki does republish in translation papers that Patinkin compares to *Newsweek* articles suggests a difference in outlook between the modern professional Anglo-American economist and the pre-modern, self-taught Polish socialist. Kalecki also included the 1935 article in a booklet published in 1936 in Warsaw, *Mechanism Poprawy Koniunkturalnej* [The Mechanism of the Upswing].[13] This latter republication indicates that Kalecki's belief that the 1935 article was central to his work was not an ex post act prompted by publication of the *General Theory*, an interpretation which could be placed on it if it were only published in the 1966 and 1971 books.

Patinkin's conclusion that Kalecki's works before 1936 do not contain the *General Theory* hinges on the applicability of a distinction between professional and non-professional publications to the circumstances in which Kalecki found himself during the early to mid-1930s in Poland. It is up to Patinkin to present a case for a self-taught Polish socialist writing 60 years ago possessing identical publication criteria to a doctorial product of the modern Angle-American production line before he can reject Kalecki's claims for anticipation of the *General Theory* on the basis of the 1935 *Polska Gospodarcza* article.

Responses to Patinkin

The responses to Patinkin's work are interesting. In a review essay of Patinkin's book, Asimakopulos, an economist well-versed in Kalecki's economics, indicates that he regards Patinkin's arguments as largely convincing (Asimakopulos 1983, 522).[14] Bhattacharjea and Raghunathan (1988) also find themselves broadly in agreement with Patinkin's conclusions. Unlike Asimakopulos and Bhattacharjea and Raghunathan, the review essay of Patinkin's book by Osiatynski (1985), editor of Kalecki's *Collected Works*, concludes that Patinkin's analysis is misleading. Osiatynski acknowledges that Patinkin's assessment of the *Essay* as presenting a business cycle theory is correct, but argues that to understand Kalecki's theory one must reconstruct the basic elements of his model of short-period equilibrium as set out in the *Essay*. Once one does this reconstruction, Osiatynski (1985, 102) suggests, 'barring.... different institutional assumptions, the *Essay* contains.... the same theory of effective demand and the short period equilibrium as that of the *General Theory*'. Osiatynski also briefly reconstructs the model underlying Kalecki's 1933 'On Foreign Trade' and shows that it is consistent with his reconstruction of the theory of short-period equilibrium output in the *Essay*.

A weak point of Osiatynski's argument is that, while he demonstrates that Kalecki's model of short-period equilibrium differs from Keynes's (1936) only in its institutional specification, he does not argue that it was Kalecki's central message. Indeed, in arguing that 'much of Kalecki's theory had to be amputated or cut out of context in order to fit it into the comparative statics of the *General Theory*' (Osiatynski 1985, 109), he concedes that it was not.

In a later note, Osiantynski (1987) argues that in 'Three Systems' (Kalecki, 1934), an article not examined by Patinkin, Kalecki 'not only made the concept of short-period equilibrium central to his argument, but also introduced there a motion of "quasi-equilibrium" which is strikingly similar to Keynes' concept of "unemployment equilibrium"' (Osiatynski 1987, 259). This article is then briefly summarised by Osiatynski, who concludes that 'Kalecki's quasi-equilibrium contains, I believe, all the essential elements of the Keynesian unemployment equilibrium concept' (Osiatynski 11987, 260).

While Kalecki's (1971) claims for anticipating Keynes include his 1933 article 'On Foreign Trade and "Domestic Exports",' Patinkin elects to ignore this article because he considers that the assumption of a fixed share of profits in national income, which Kalecki uses to determine output, is ad hoc. Chapple (1991) argues that Patinkin's reason for neglecting this article is internally inconsistent, as assumptions underlying the Keynesian-cross model, which Patinkin uses to summarise Keynes's theory of effective demand, amount to assuming a fixed profit share. Chapple (1991) then demonstrates that Kalecki's article does contain an open economy theory of effective demand, a 'Keynesian' interpretation supported by Flanders (1989).

What do Kalecki's Collected Works Show?

The 1990 publication of volume one of Kalecki's *Collected Works* presents many of his important pre-1936 articles in full English translation for the first time. Not all this new information can be considered in depth here, but two important items deserve to be mentioned. The first of these items is Kalecki's *Essay on the Business Cycle Theory*. The second item is a 1934 article of Kalecki's, 'Three Systems', which, as has been seen above, Osiatynski (1987) summarises. What are implications of these two works for the question of anticipation of the *General Theory*?

Examination of the *Essay* in full translation allows a better assessment of its central message and of what Kalecki sees as its contribution to economics. The *Essay* opens with a summary of the main themes (Kalecki 1933a, 67-8). It is clear from his introduction that Kalecki seeks to explain the business cycle - regular fluctuations in the degree of capacity utilisation, investment, employment and 'social income' (national income). He draws both a comparison and a distinction between his theory of the business cycle and that of Aftalion. Kalecki argues that Aftalion's theory, like his, starts from an analysis of investment and an acknowledgment of the importance of the time it takes to construct investment goods. However, Aftalion's theory assumes continual full utilisation of capacity, while Kalecki suggests that in his theory capacity utilisation is variable and determined within the model. From the start Kalecki signals that his theory differs from that of Aftalion, and by implication makes a contribution to the literature, insofar as it provides a theory of variable capacity utilisation and of output determination. Thus the *Essay* is more centrally concerned with output than Patinkin acknowledges.

A complete analysis of the theory of output determination in the *Essay* is beyond the scope of this chapter.[15] However, the *Essay* provides a path- breaking integration of a theory of effective demand (the goods market in Kalecki's business cycle work clears through output variations) with a theory of investment. Investment plays a dual role in the *Essay*, functioning as both the driving component of effective demand and as a creator of productive capacity. It is this interaction, Kalecki believes, that gives rise to cyclical fluctuations in profits, investment, capacity utilisation and output. Thus the *Essay* presents the first 'Keynesian' model of the business cycle - three years before publication of the *General Theory*.[16] While Kalecki's central message is not a short-run static theory of effective demand, the incorporation of such a theory into his model of the business cycle shows that he came much closer to the *General Theory* than Patinkin acknowledges.

Now consider 'Three Systems', a piece of work which - unlike the *Essay* - presents the theory of effective demand in an explicitly short-period setting and develops an integrated treatment of the goods and money markets and aggregate supply.[17] Assuming a given capital stock, rising marginal costs and perfect competition, Kalecki compares a real sector model (system I) and a model combining both a monetary and a real sector with a perfectly flexible money wage (system II), with a model of unemployment 'quasi-equilibrium' arising out of hysteresis-style money wage adjustments (system III), setting out what in terms of assumptions, most behavioural relations,[18] and analytical conclusions is an IS-LM/AS-AD model.

Kalecki's 1934 'quasi-equilibrium' model is based on the following three simultaneous equations :

$$i = f(r, S) \qquad\qquad (2.1)$$

$$I = \varphi(r, S, p) \tag{2.2}$$

$$p = \eta(R, r, S) \tag{2.3}$$

which are solved for the three endogenous variables; the production of investment goods i, the real interest rate p and the level of employment r (S is given capitalists' consumption and R is the given supply of labour, where $r < R$). The first equation is a saving function, the second an investment function (together the IS curve) and the third a money market equilibrium condition (the LM curve) which incorporates the aggregate supply curve (since price changes induced by changes in the level of real output will alter the real money supply).

In addition to 'Three Systems' and the Keynesian model sharing common assumptions about a fixed capital stock, rising marginal costs and perfect competition, and a simultaneous equation approach to economic equilibrium, a number of other factors sustain an IS-LM/AS-AD interpretation. First, Kalecki states that his main aim is to provide a theory of output, investment and the interest rate under such assumptions. Since employment moves with output (and indeed replaces output in Kalecki's equations) this implies both a theory of employment and a concern to explain Keynesian aggregates. Second, a set of expenditure, money market and aggregate supply equations can be written down, embodying Kalecki's assumptions, which comprise an IS-LM/AS-AD system. Each of Kalecki's three quasi-equilibrium equations can be sensibly derived from an IS-LM/AS-AD model. In a fashion consistent with the Keynesian model, Kalecki is aware that to close system III and to generate a 'quasi-equilibrium' at below full employment requires a money wage equation.

Not only are the assumptions and model building consistent with IS-LM/AS-AD, but so too are the analytical conclusions. In system II, where money wages are fully flexible in the face of unemployment, interactions between labour, money and goods markets ensure that the only possible equilibrium is full employment, very much the conclusion of an IS-LM/AS-AD model with fully flexible money wages. And all Kalecki's analytical conclusions in system III regarding the impact of saving and investment shocks on output, employment, interest rates, investment (in the case of a saving shock) and real wages follow logically from a Keynesian model based on his assumptions.

There has been some controversy regarding interpretation of 'Three Systems'. Kriesler and McFarlane (1991) suggest that 'balance' was wrongly translated as 'equilibrium' in the English version of 'Three Systems,' thus casting doubt on the above interpretation. One way of checking Kriesler's and McFarlane's contention is to compare the wording in the 1934 article with Kalecki's Polish review of the *General Theory*, which discusses Keynes's theory of short-period equilibrium. As the Polish word for balance/equilibrium has the same root in 'Three Systems' as Kalecki uses for his 1936 discussion of Keynes's concept of short-period equilibrium, there are no grounds for their contention of mistranslation.[19]

A final indication of Kalecki's command of the Keynesian model can be found in his review of Keynes's book (Kalecki 1936a). The level of understanding exhibited in Kalecki's review, his criticisms of Keynes's theory of investment, and his generalisation of Keynes's model of effective demand to imperfectly competitive conditions, all provide further support for the conclusion that he had already independently discovered the Keynesian model (Harcourt 1991).

Conclusion

There has been an ongoing controversy on the relationship between Kalecki's pre-1936 macroeconomics and Keynes's *General Theory*. This literature has registered strong swings in opinion over the years. The initial consensus was that Kalecki had anticipated the revolutionary elements of Keynes's work. Dissent emerged, solidified by Patinkin, which saw opinion swing back to the revisionist conclusion that Kalecki did not anticipate effective demand as a central message. However, responses to the revisionist work and the publications of previously untranslated (or partially translated) work in volume one of Kalecki's *Collected Works* should seriously modify conclusions that Kalecki did not anticipate Keynes. Indeed, the balance of probabilities suggests that Kalecki anticipated both the theory of effective demand and the IS-LM/AS-AD model in his pre-1936 work. In addition, Kalecki integrated the theory of effective demand with a theory of investment, where investment functions as both the key element in determining effective demand and a creator of productive capacity, thus developing the first rigorous 'Keynesian' macrodynamic theory of the business cycle.

Ironically, Kalecki's 'Three Systems' is closer in two important ways to IS-LM/AS-AD than to the *General Theory* itself. First, system II's conclusion that, via interactions between the labour, money and goods markets, perfect money wage flexibility results in full employment equilibrium is also that of the neoclassical synthesis, not Keynes. Second, in system III unemployment results because of money wage stickiness - again the conclusion of the neoclassical synthesis. Kalecki's arguments are more consistent with 'imperfectionist' readings of Keynesian theory than with Keynes's theory itself.

The irony is that Kalecki is an icon of the post Keynesians, who see the IS-LM/AS-AD model as a bastardisation of Keynes, resulting from an incomplete break from his neoclassical teachers. Unlike Keynes, as a result of his Marxian heritage Kalecki is presumed free from such contamination. This creates a certain amount of unjustified resistance amongst some Kaleckian-inclined post Keynesians to acknowledging mainstream aspects of Kalecki's 1934 work, despite the fact that he criticises the stock-flow inconsistency of the equilibrium (or quasi-equilibrium) in 'Three Systems', pointing out its neglect of dynamic elements (Kalecki 1934a), 218-9), and does not follow up on this line of enquiry in later work, presumably because of the lack of dynamics.

Perhaps it is time that Kalecki received full credit from all economists for *all* his innovations prior to 1936.

Notes

1 See for example Eshag (1977b) and Sawyer (1985, chapter 9).

2 The chapter relies on Feiwel (1975), Patinkin (1982, 59-62), Sawyer (1985 chapter 9) and Osiatynski's editorial notes (Kalecki 1990, 463-467), supplemented by additional investigations, for documentation of the literature on Kalecki and the *General Theory*.

3 See for example Robinson (1977), Feiwel (1989a) and Kriesler and McFarlane (1991); see also Sawyer (1985), Osiatynski (1985), Asimakopulos (1988-9) and Bhattacharjea and Raghunathan (1988).

4 According to Sawyer (1985, 194, 209 n9), Kalecki's widow denies that Kalecki was ill in bed for three days, although she confirms that he may have felt sick. Shackle tells a similar story which supports Mrs. Kalecki's account in its details, indicating that Kalecki showed an immediate grasp of the *General Theory* on his arrival in England in 1936 because he had independently got there himself. Kalecki, apparently, was deeply disappointed at being forestalled. Shackle (1967, 127) writes: '"For three days I felt ill" he said to the present writer.'

5 According to both the bibliography presented in Feiwel (1975) and Kalecki's *Collected Works* (1990, 486), the second of these papers, 'On Foreign Trade and Domestic Exports,' dated 1934 by Kalecki, was published in 1933.

6 Zweig was at one time Professor of Political Economy at Kracow University and was later to write a history of economic thought entitled *Economic Ideas, A Study of Historical Perspectives* (1950). Despite his 1944 comments, and while containing twenty four references to Keynes, this book contains none to Kalecki, and makes no reference to Kalecki regarding Keynes's work. As with Schumpeter, the Cold War, McCarthyism and the anti-communist feelings of the time may have been influential in the lack of references.

7 While Patinkin (1982) dates this letter 1937, Asimakopulos (1988, 20 n1) suggests that 1936 is the correct date.

8 It is worth noting that his views have not changed substantially since 1982 (see Patinkin 1982, 1983, 1987, 1989, 1990a, 1990b).

9 Summaries of the Leyden Conference proceedings, including Kalecki's presentation which appears to have been in French, are provided by Marschak (1934) in English and Lutfalla (1934) in French.

10 The original Polish title of this article was 'The Essence of the Business Upswing' and it is under this title that it is translated in Kalecki's *Collected Works*. However, it was translated into English in 1966 as the 'The Mechanism of the Business Upswing.' As the latter is the title by which it is referred to in the English language literature, for the purposes of comparison the original English title will continue to be used here.

11 A more detailed description of this journal is given in the editorial notes to Kalecki (1990). Founded by the Polish Ministry of Industry and Commerce in 1920, *Polska Gospodarcza* was a weekly journal, published with the participation of the Treasury from 1924 and later with the assistance of the Ministry of Railways and the Ministry of Communication (editorial note, Kalecki 1990, 423).

12 For a revealing study of the current socialisation of graduate economics students in leading U.S. Universities see Colander and Klamer (1987).

13 Osiatynski (editorial notes, Kalecki 1990, 487, 490) refers to this collection of Kalecki's papers and mentions that it contains versions of his 1935 articles 'The Mechanism of the Business Upswing' and 'The Business Upswing and the Balance of Payments.' None of Kalecki's other articles are mentioned as being published in this booklet. In fact the booklet also reproduces a third article published in 1935 in *Polska Gospodarcza*, 'The German Experiment.' There is no introduction to the booklet.

14 Asimakopulos (1983) disputes Patinkin's contention that effective demand *alone* was Keynes's central message, arguing that effective demand in combination with a theory of investment volatility was the central message. However, a theory of investment volatility, unlike a theory where the goods markets clears via output variations, was not an original contribution of either Keynes or Kalecki: the ideas go back at least as far as Tugan-Baranovsky, Aftalion and J. M. Clark.

15 See Chapple (Chapple 1993) for such an analysis.

16 By Keynesian is meant a model where effective demand plays a central role. The post-1936 business cycle theories of Lundberg, Harrod, Samuelson and Kaldor can all be considered Keynesian in this sense.

17 While I believe that Osiatynski's (1987) analysis of this article is, in its essentials, correct, I do not believe that he fully appreciates all it contains. For a detailed discussion and dissection of Kalecki's's 1934 model and its equational structure, see Chapple (1995).

18 The major difference relates to consumption functions. For both Kalecki and Keynes consumption depends positively on income, with a propensity to consume between zero and one. However, for Kalecki this is because workers consume all their wages and the wage bill depends positively on national income.

19 I wish to thank Dr. Jacek Kracyzk of the Quantitative Studies Group at the Victoria University of Wellington for his discussions with me on the points contained in this paragraph.

References

Asimakopulos, A. 1983. 'Anticipations of the General Theory'. *Canadian Journal of Economics* 16(3), August : 517-30.

Asimakopulos, A. 1988. *Investment, Employment and Income Distribution.* London : Polity.

Asimakopulos, A. 1988-9. 'Kalecki and Robinson'. *Journal of Post Keynesian Economics* 11(2), Winter : 261-78.

Bhattacharjea, A. and Raghunathan, N. 1988. 'Keynes, Kalecki and the Question of Priority. *Economic and Political Weekly* 23 (27), 2 July: 1383-1393.

Blaug, M. 1978. *Economic Theory in Retrospect,* 3rd edition. Cambridge : Cambridge University Press.

Chapple, S. 1991. 'Did Kalecki Get There First? The Race for the *General Theory. History of Political Economy* 23(2), Summer : 243-61.

Chapple, S. 1993. 'Kalecki's Theory of the Business Cycle and the *General Theory.' History of Economics Review* 20, Summer: 120-139.

Chapple, S. 1995. 'The Kaleckian Origins of the Keynesian Model.' *Oxford Economic Papers,* forthcoming, July.

Colander, D, and Klamer, A. 1987. 'The Making of an Economist.' *Journal of Economic Perspectives* 1 (2), Fall: 95 - 112.

Dobb, M. 1973. *Theories of Value and Distribution Since Adam Smith.* Cambridge : Cambridge University Press.

Eshag, E. 1977a. Introduction to the Special Issue of Michal Kalecki Memorial Lectures. *Oxford Bulletin of Economics and Statistics,* 39(1), February: 1-6.

Eshag, E. 1977b. 'Kalecki's Political Economy : A Comparison with Keynes.' *Oxford Bulletin of Economics and Statistics.* 39(1), February: 79-86.

Feiwel, G. R. 1975. *The Intellectual Capital of Michal Kalecki.* Knoxville : University of Tennessee Press.

Feiwel, G. R. 1989. 'The Legacies of Kalecki and Keynes'. In Sebastiani 1989: 45-80.

Flanders, M. J. 1989. *International Monetary Economics, 1870-1960. Between the Classical and New Classical.* Cambridge : Cambridge University Press.

Frazer, W. 1976. 'Review Article : Keynes and Feiwel's Intellectual History of Kalecki'. *Southern Economic Journal* 43(3), October : 1161-1169.

Frisch, R. and Holme, H. 1935. 'The Characteristic Solutions of a Mixed Difference and Differential Equation Occurring in Economic Dynamics.' *Econometrica* 3(2), April : 225-239.

Harcourt, G. C. 1991. 'Review of *Collected Works of Michal Kalecki, Volume I: Capitalism: Business Cycles and Full Employment.' Economic Journal* 101 November (409), 1608-10.

Jonung, L. 1991. *The Stockholm School of Economics Revisited.* Cambridge : Cambridge University Press.

Kalecki, M. 1933a. *Proba Teorii Koniunktury.* Warsaw: ISBCP. As translated in Kalecki (1990) under the title *Essay on the Business Cycle Theory*: 65-108.

Kalecki, M. 1933b. 'O Handlu Zagranicznym i "Eksporcie Wewnetrznym." *Ekonomista* 33 (3): 27-35. As translated in Kalecki (1966) by Ada Kalecki under the title 'On Foreign Trade and Domestic Exports' 16-25.

Kalecki, M. 1934. 'Trzy Uklady.' *Ekonomista* 34 (3): 54-70. As translated in Kalecki (1990) under the title 'Three Systems' : 201-219.

Kalecki M. 1935a. 'Essai d'une Theorie du Mouvement Cyclique des Affaires.' *Revue d'Economie Politique* 2 (Mars-Avril): 285-305.

Kalecki, M. 1935b. 'A Macrodynamic Theory of Business Cycles.' *Econometrica* 3(3), July: 327-44. Reprinted in Kalecki 1990 : 120-38.

Kalecki, M. 1935c. 'Istota Poprawy Koniunkturalnej'. *Polska Gospodarcza* 16 (43): 1320-4. As translated in Kalecki (1966) under the title 'The Mechanism of the Business Upswing': 26-33.

Kalecki, M. 1936a. 'Pare Uwag o Teorii Keynesa'. *Ekonomista* 36 (3): 18-26. As translated in Kalecki (1990) under the title 'Some Remarks on Keynes's Theory': 223-232.

Kalecki, M. 1936b. *Mechanizm poprawy koniunkturalnej.* [The Mechanism of the Business Upswing]. Warsawa: Glowna Ksiegarnia Wojskowa.

Kalecki, M. 1938. 'The Determinants of the Distribution of National Income.' *Econometrica* 6(2), April: 97-112.

Kalecki, M. 1939. *Essays in the Theory of Economic Fluctuations.* London: Allen and Unwin.

Kalecki, M. 1942. 'A Theory of Profits.' *Economic Journal* 52(206-7), June-September: 258-267.

Kalecki, M. 1943. *Studies in Economic Dynamics.* London: Allen and Unwin.

Kalecki, M. 1954. *Theory of Economic Dynamics.* New York: Rhinehart.

Kalecki, M. 1966. *Studies in the Theory of Business Cycles*: 1933-39. Translated from the original Polish by Ada Kalecki. Oxford: Blackwell.

Kalecki, M. 1971. *Selected Essays on the Dynamics of the Capitalist Economy*, 1933-1970. Cambridge: Cambridge University Press.

Kalecki, M. 1990. *Collected Works of Michal Kalecki. Volume I: Capitalism, Business Cycles and Full Employment.* Edited by Jerzy Osiatynski. Translated by Chester Adam Kisiel. Oxford: Clarendon Press.

Keynes, J. M. 1936. *The General Theory of Employment, Interest and Money.* London: Macmillan.

Klein, L. 1951. 'The Life of John Maynard Keynes.' *Journal of Political Economy* 59(5), October: 443-51.

Klein, L. 1964. 'The Role of Econometrics in Socialist Economics'. In Kowalik et. al. 1964: 181-191.

Klein, L. 1966. *The Keynesian Revolution* (revised edition). New York: Macmillan.

Kowalik, T. 1964. *Problems of Economic Dynamics and Planning: Essays in Honour of Michal Kalecki.* Warsaw: Polish Scientific Publishers.

Kriesler, P. and McFarlane B. 1993. 'Michal Kalecki on Capitalism.' *Cambridge Journal of Economics* 17(1), March: 315-234.

Lange, O. 1939. 'Neoklasyczna Szkola w Ekonomi.' [The Neoclassical School of Economics]. In *Encyloeddii Nauk Politycznych,* Volume IV. Warsaw: Instytut Wydawniczy, Bibloteka Polsak: 23-35.

Lutfalla, G. 1934. 'Compte-rendu de la III Reunion de la Societe Internationale d'Econometrie.' *Revue d'economie politique* 44(3): 424-429.

Marschak, J. 1934. 'The Meeting of the Econometric Society in Leyden, September-October 1933.' *Econometrica* 2, April: 187-203.

Merton, K. 1957. 'Priorities in Scientific Discovery.' *American Sociological Review* 22(6), December: 635-59. As reprinted in Merton 1973: 286-324.

Merton, R. K. 1973. *The Sociology of Science: Theoretical and Empirical Investigations,* edited and introduced by Norman Storer. Chicago: Chicago University Press.

Osiatynski, J. 1985. 'Don Patinkin on Kalecki and Keynes.' *Oeconomia Polona* 12(1): 95-104.

Osiatynski, J. 1987. 'Unemployment Equilibria: A Note on Kalecki's and Keynes' Approach.' *Oeconomia Polona* 14(2): 259-62.

Patinkin, D. 1982. *Anticipations of the General Theory? and Other Essays on Keynes.* Oxford: Blackwell.

Patinkin, D. 1983. 'Multiple Discoveries and the Central Message.' *American Journal of Sociology.* 89(2), September: 306-23.

Patinkin, D. 1987. 'Keynes, John Maynard.' In *The New Palgrave. A Dictionary of Economics.* London: Macmillan: 19-41.

Patinkin, D. 1989. 'Michal Kalecki and the *General Theory.*' In M. Sebastiani ed. 1989. *Kalecki's Relevance Today:* 25-44. New York: St. Martin's Press.

Patinkin, D. 1990a. 'In Defense of IS-LM.' *Banca Nazionale del Lavoro Quarterly Review* 172: 119-34.

Patinkin, D. 1990b. 'On Different Interpretations of the *General Theory.*' *Journal of Monetary Economics* 26(2), October : 205-43.

Phelps Brown, E. 1937. 'Report of the Oxford Meeting, September 25-29, 1936.' *Econometrica* 5(4), October: 361.83.

Robinson, A. 1947. 'John Maynard Keynes 1883-1946.' *Economic Journal* 57(225), March: 1068.

Robinson, J. 1952. *The Rate of Interest: and Other Essays.* London: Macmillan.

Robinson, J. 1964. 'Kalecki and Keynes.' In *Essays in Honour of Michal Kalecki*, Warsaw, PWN. Reprinted in J. Robinson, *Collected Economic Papers Volume IV*. Oxford: Blackwell, 1965: 92-99.

Robinson, J. 1966. Introduction to Kalecki 1966: vii-xii.

Robinson, J. 1971. 'Michal Kalecki.' *Cambridge Review* 93(2204), October: 1-14. Reprinted in Joan Robinson, *Collected Economic Papers Volume IV*. Blackwell, Oxford: 1973, 87-91.

Robinson, J. 1976. 'Michal Kalecki: A Neglected Prophet.' *New York Review of Books* 23(3), 4 March : 28-30.

Robinson, J. 1977. 'Michal Kalecki.' *Oxford Bulletin of Economics and Statistics 39(1)*, February : 7-17. Reprinted in Joan Robinson, *Collected Economic Papers Volume V*. Oxford, Blackwell, 1979: 184-196.

Samuelson, P. A. 1981. 'Bertil Ohlin (1899-1979).' *Scandinavian Journal of Economics* 83(3): 355-71.

Samuelson, P. A. 1991. 'Thoughts on the Stockholm School and on Scandinavian Economics.' In Jonung 1991: 391-407.

Sawyer, M. 1985. *The Economics of Michal Kalecki*. London: Macmillan.

Shackle, G. L. S. 1967. *The Years of High Theory*. Cambridge: Cambridge University Press.

Schumpeter, J. A. 1939. *Business Cycles: a Theoretical, Historical and Statistical Analysis of the Capitalist Process*, 2 volumes. New York: McGraw-Hill.

Solow, R. M. 1976. 'Review of *The Intellectual Capital of Michal Kalecki: A Study in Economic Theory and Policy* by Feiwel, G.' *Journal of Economic Literature* 13(4), June: 1331-35.

Tinbergen. J. 1935. 'Annual Survey: Suggestions on Quantitative Business Cycle Theory.' *Econometrica* 3(3), July: 241-308.

Zweig, F. 1944. *Poland Between the Wars*. London: Secker and Warburg.

Zweig, F. 1950. *Economic Ideas. A Study of Historical Perspectives*. New York: Prentice-Hall.

3 MICROFOUNDATIONS: A KALECKIAN PERSPECTIVE

Peter Kriesler

'Well! I've often seen a cat without a grin', thought Alice: 'but a grin without a cat! It's the most curious thing I ever saw in all my life' (Alice in Wonderland)

I would like to thank Dr. G. C. Harcourt, Professor R. Rowthorn and Dr. M. Landesmann of the University of Cambridge, Dr. L. Mainwaring of the University of Cardiff, Professor P. D. Groenewegen of the University of Sydney, Dr. P Reynolds of Staffordshire University, Dr. J. Osiatynski, the editor of Kalecki's Collected Works, Dr. C. Freedman of the University of New South Wales, Dr. Jan Toporowski of South Bank University, Dr. E. Da Fonseca of the University of Sao Paulo, Brazil, Dr. Peter Riach of De Montford University and the late Professor A. Asimakopulos for their helpful comments. The paper was given at the ESRC Political Economy workshop in 1991 and I would like to thank the participants, especially Professor V. Chick of University College, London for their helpful comments, A very early draft of this paper was unfortunately published in M. Sebastiani, *Kalecki's Relevance Today* (1989).

Introduction

Like the relationship between the grin and the cat, the relationship between macroeconomic and microeconomic theory has left many puzzled. Over the last few decades there has been much debate as to the nature of the relation between microeconomics and macroeconomics, the so called problem of microfoundations. In particular, the question of how one moves from analysis at the level of the individual or of the firm to analysis of the economy as a whole, has invited much controversy. The discussion about 'microfoundations' has been about the exact way in which the microeconomics fits in with the macroeconomic theory for which it is the foundation. Not surprisingly, there is a strong relationship between the type of theory being examined and the relationship posited between the microfoundations and the macrotheory. In particular, the problem seems to be greatest for neoclassical theorists, for whom the tranquil waters of microeconomic equilibrium bear a strong contrast to the swiftly moving currents of macroeconomic unemployment. As noted in the Palgrave entry on 'macroeconomics: relations with microeconomics': 'The lack of clear connection between macroeconomics and microeconomics has long been a source of discontent among [neoclassical] economists. Arrow called it a "major scandal" that neoclassical price theory cannot account for such macroeconomic phenomena as unemployment' (Howitt 1987, 273).

It is important to note that this problem is more severe for neoclassical economics than it is for either classical or post Keynesian economics. Some reasons for this are considered in the next section, which is a brief historical survey on the relation between microeconomics and macroeconomics in the work of classical, neoclassical and some Marxist and post Keynesian economists. These views are then compared with Kalecki's contribution to the problem of microfoundations. It will be shown that the way in which micro and macro theories are interrelated in Kalecki's analysis is similar to the classical approach, while differing from the others discussed. In particular, for Kalecki, neither theory dominates nor forms a constraint on the other. Rather than any form of hierarchical relationship, the two theories lie side by side (so to speak), and both give information which the other cannot give, while the interrelation of the two yields further information not obtainable from either in isolation.

Historical Perspectives

The classical economists treated micro and macro interdependently, without being aware of any distinction between them. Both Ricardo and Marx, for example, moved fairly easily between these levels of analysis. Ricardo talks, at the microeconomic level, of tendencies towards uniform rates of profits, the determinants of distribution and investment, and discusses profit and wage rate differentials, which are then related to the macroeconomic discussion of economic growth. Similarly, Marx moves between discussion of changes in investment and technical progress, the labour process and the role of the reserve army of the unemployed, at the micro level, and problems with realization of the surplus, with economic growth and with overproduction, at the macroeconomic level. In other words, the distinction was not an operative one for either the classical economists or for Marx

As is now well known, the marginal revolution changed the focus of economic analysis away from the classical concerns with accumulation and growth towards questions of optimal allocation. As a result, the emphasis shifted towards analysis of individuals and firms isolated from the rest of the economy. It is with the work of Jevons and Walras that the establishment of what we now call microeconomics came to occupy the central stage in the study of economics. As a result, economics focused on either the analysis of individual markets (à la Walras and Marshall) or of individual exchange (à la Edgeworth). Value theory developed into the analysis of market-clearing price, and became synonymous with the whole of economics, though a minor role was still reserved for the analysis of disturbances originating from the monetary sector.

The great contribution of both Keynes and Kalecki was to challenge this conception of economics, and to restore a role for macroeconomic analysis, albeit with quite different emphasis, via the argument of 'fallacy of composition'. It was Keynes who formalized the distinction in economics between micro and macro in a memorable passage in the *General Theory*:

> The division of economics between the theory of value and distribution on the one hand, and the theory of money on the other is, I think, a false division. The right dichotomy is, I suggest, between the theory of individual industry or firm and of the rewards and the distribution between different uses of a *given* quantity of resources on the one hand, and the theory of output and employment *as a whole* on the other hand (Keynes 1973, 293; emphasis in original).

The formal separation of macroeconomics from microeconomics was the result of the (bastard) Keynesian 'neoclassical synthesis', which dominated mainstream economics until the mid-1970s.Under this view, the pre-Keynesian position of competitive harmony was analyzed at the microeconomic level, while the Keynesian insight of the possibility of the persistence of unemployed resources was analyzed at the macroeconomic level. 'The subject was split into two parts; Keynes was safely corralled in the section called "macro economics" while the main stream of teaching returned to celebrate the establishment of equilibrium in a free market. This section of the theory was described as "micro economics"' (Robinson 1979, 91).

Apart from objections by the odd outsider, such as Joan Robinson, the incompatibility of these two positions was, over that time largely ignored. It was the recognition of this incompatibility, and the effort to achieve harmony between the two branches of mainstream economics, which became referred to as the quest for microfoundations.

Most economists associated with 'neoclassical' general equilibrium deny any separate identity for macrotheory, which is perceived as being some sort of aggregate of micro relations: '[T]he microeconomic general equilibrium view would implicitly deny that aggregate *theorizing* could provide any significant insight that was *logically* unattainable from a more rigorous disaggregative approach' (Weintraub 1979, 7; emphasis in original).

Economists in this tradition, if they attempt to 'do macroeconomics', do so by deriving 'macroeconomic' results - such as non-market clearing equilibria - in general equilibrium models. In other words, the search for 'microfoundations' is reduced to an attempt to generate so-called macroeconomic results, in particular the existence of unemployment, in microeconomic models. By denying legitimacy to any 'holistic' approach they reject the criticism, made by both Keynes and Kalecki, that there is a fallacy of composition involved in drawing macro conclusions from micro theory. The underlying assumption behind this approach is that microeconomic theory is fundamental, while macroeconomic theory is only relevant when derived from it. This sort of dismissal of macroeconomics is found most often in the works of general equilibrium theorists. For example Hahn, in a book surprisingly called *Equilibrium and Macroeconomics*, writes:

> I am a reductionist in that I attempt to locate explanations in the actions of individual agents. ... My conviction that [this] is the right approach is pretty strong. For instance, although I have no difficulty with the idea of class I have not been able to give meaning to 'class interest' of the actions of a class until these interests and actions have been located in the individual members. Again I am quite prepared to accept that 'the whole may differ from the sum' but it seems only comprehensible when one starts at the level of the individual (Hahn 1984, 1-2).
>
> 'Macroeconomics is different from microeconomics'. If it is then I for one do not know what it is. It can hardly be the case that models which look on the world as if it were a single firm, a single household, and a single good thereby create some new kind of economic
> theory. ......

In our present state of knowledge, macroeconomics is simply the project of deducing something about the behaviour of such aggregates as income and employment from the microtheory which we have. The whole enterprise of giving microfoundations to macroeconomics is therefore misnamed. If macroeconomics before this enterprise was innocent of microeconomics it is not easy so see that it was anything at all. (*ibid*, 311).

The debate has also been taken up by some non-mainstream economists. As a result, we can identify a second approach to the question of the relationship between microeconomic and macroeconomic theory, most clearly associated with economists working within either the Marxist or the post Keynesian tradition. These economists see major constraints derived from the macro level binding and limiting the actions of individual units at the micro level. In other words, macroeconomic phenomena, such as the level of aggregate demand and unemployment, place constraints on the activities of individual firms and agents:

[These economists] consider macroeconomics to have been cut free by Keynes, from standard microeconomic analysis and consequently the way is open to them to reconstitute microtheory to support explicit Post-Keynesian analysis. From such a perspective the problem of 'what microfoundations for macroeconomics?' becomes an extrapolation of macroeconomic reasoning back to the behaviour of individual units (Weintraub 1979,13).

In this type of analysis, it is the macroeconomic theory which is seen as, in some sense, fundamental, with the microeconomic analysis having to conform to it.

We can take these two cases as extreme reference points. The first sees macroeconomics as a pure aggregation from the micro, with no new information resulting from the aggregation that is not already in the micro-theory. On the other hand, the second view can be characterized as regarding the micro as a pure disaggregation from the macro, with the macro imposing constraints on the behaviour of individual agents. In the next section it will be argued that Kalecki's analysis represents a significant break from both of these positions, and a return to the perspective of the classical economists.

The Kaleckian Approach

Background

Over the thirty years of his English writings on microanalysis, Kalecki significantly modified his analysis of pricing and distribution from the original English version in 'The Determinants of Distribution of National Income' (1939), to the final version in the posthumously published 'Class Struggle and Distribution of National Income' (1971). Despite these changes, there are certain features common to all versions of the analysis. Kriesler (1987) identified the stimulus for the modifications to the theory in Kalecki's attempting to improve the incorporation of the analysis of the firm and of imperfectly competitive industries into his analysis. However, further reasons for this were also suggested. In particular, it was argued that Kalecki was attempting to formulate the models in such a way as to make the determination of the shares of wages and profits in the national income independent of the level of output, and the determination of gross profits independent of both prices and relative shares. In many ways this division corresponds to a micro/macro distinction. In particular, the analysis of distribution is derived on the basis of the behaviour of individual firms, so it can be considered as microeconomic. On the other hand, the level of gross profits cannot be determined by aggregating the behaviour of individual units. This is because (as is shown below) there is a fallacy of composition involved in adding the behaviour of individual capitalists to derive their 'aggregate class' behaviour: what is true for capitalists as a class will not be true for individual capitalists (and vice versa). This justifies our calling this analysis macroeconomic. Kalecki was attempting to make his micro and macro theories independent of each other. This is apparent in his concern to remove the influence of industrial composition from the microanalysis and the determination of the wage share. It was the difficulties with achieving this independence which partially explain Kalecki's efforts at reformulating the analysis.

The purposes of this section are firstly interpretive, to attempt to logically reconstruct some possible reasons for this constant change, and to understand why Kalecki had this overriding concern with making the two types of analysis independent; and secondly normative, in that it attempts to draw some more general implications from Kalecki's analysis.

As we are primarily concerned with understanding what Kalecki was trying to do, rather than what he succeeded in doing, the problems with and the limitations of his analysis of pricing and distribution will not be considered. Rather, attention will be focused on what may be called Kalecki's 'pure' model. That is to say, we proceed on the basis that

Kalecki was able to achieve the independence of pricing and distribution from the level of output, and of gross profits from pricing and distribution, for which he was striving.

At this stage two limitations to our argument should be noted. Firstly, we consider only Kalecki's writings from 1938 on. An important omission is his 1933 paper 'Outline of a theory of the business cycle'. In that paper there is a footnote reference to a relation between aggregate production and profit per unit of output due to the role of overheads. However, this relation is not referred to elsewhere in his English writings, where the main determinant of 'the relative share of gross capitalist income and salaries in the aggregate turnover' is the average mark-up (Kalecki 1938, 102). In the early works, manual labour's share is determined by the average mark-up and the relative price of raw materials (Kriesler 1987, 37), while in the later works 'changes in the industrial composition of value added' are introduced as an additional determinant (Kalecki 1954, 29). The second limitation is that we are only concerned with Kalecki's 'pure' model - that is, a model of a closed economy with no government and in which workers do not save. The reason for concentrating on this simple model is that it highlights the underlying relations. When the model is made more complex by, for example, introducing government, workers' savings and an open economy, these basic relations become obscured.

In order to understand the relation between the micro and the macro analysis in Kalecki's works, it is useful to concentrate on those writings which incorporated both, in particular, his three books on capitalist economies: *Essays in the Theory of Economic Fluctuations* (Kalecki 1939), *Studies in Economic Dynamics* (Kalecki 1943) and *Theory of Economic Dynamics* (Kalecki 1954). In the preface to the first of these volumes, Kalecki states that: 'These essays, though formally independent, nevertheless constitute a whole. Each of them treats a problem which is interesting in itself, but at the same time it prepares the ground for the succeeding essays. In particular the first five essays lead up to the sixth, which contains a theory of the business cycle' (Kalecki 1939, 10).

The order in which subjects are presented for analysis in this book is significant, and it is the same order as in his other two books, in English, on capitalist economies cited above. All commence with the microeconomic analysis of pricing in the manufacturing sector, and of the determination of the relative share of manual labour in national income. They then consider the determinants of aggregate variables such as the total profits and level of national income, the rate of interest and investment, before culminating in a discussion of the business cycle. The sequence is important because it reveals Kalecki's microanalysis as a stage in the development of his theory of business cycles, which (as the quotation above also indicates) was his main interest. In other words, the role of the microanalysis has to be understood in terms of its contribution to the analysis of the business cycle, and, therefore to the macroanalysis.

The role of the macroanalysis

To understand the role of the macroanalysis, it is appropriate to consider its clearest statement, in a pamphlet which Kalecki published in Polish in 1939 entitled *Money and Real Wages*. Kalecki's analysis starts by isolating the two main assumptions in what he describes as 'the Classical Theory of Wages', but is more usually described as 'neoclassical' theory. These are, firstly, the assumption of perfect competition and of the so called 'law of increasing marginal cost', and secondly 'the assumption of a given price level or a given value of the aggregate demand' (Kalecki 1936b, 40). Although Kalecki immediately signals skepticism about the appropriateness of the law of increasing marginal costs, it is initially accepted for the sake of the argument. Its effect, Kalecki notes, is that rises in employment must be associated with a decline in real wages. With money wages given, aggregate output and employment can only increase if the price level also increases, causing real wages to fall. 'Thus from the "law of increasing marginal costs" follows the inverse relationship between production and the real wage' (*ibid.*, 42).

Causality, however, runs from the increase in employment to the reduction in real wages and not vice versa. According to Kalecki, the arguments favouring decreasing money wages in order to increase employment rely on an assumption of a given level of aggregate demand. If this is the case, then a reduction in money wages will lead to an increase in production due to increased profit margins, with prices initially stable. This will eventually cause prices to fall, as the same aggregate money demand is now spread over more goods. At the same time, marginal costs will rise due to the increase in output. Equilibrium is restored when marginal costs are, once again, equal to their respective prices. At this new equilibrium, provided wages have fallen more than prices, production and employment are greater than at the old equilibrium, and real wages are lower (*ibid.*, 43). Kalecki was extremely critical of the basic assumption of this analysis, calling it 'totally unfounded', because over the business cycle both the general price level and aggregate money demand 'are subject to violent swings'. (*ibid.*, 43).

Kalecki then examined the effects of a reduction in money wages, still assuming perfect competition and rising marginal costs, but dropping the assumption of a given price level and of a given level of aggregate demand. The model reflects a closed economy in which capitalists save part of their income and workers spend all their income on consumption. Kalecki represented the national income of this system as follows:

INCOME	EXPENDITURE
Income of Capitalists	Investment
Wages	Workers' consumption
	Capitalists' Consumption

where investment is defined as the sum of purchases of new fixed capital goods and the change in inventories.

Because workers do not save, their consumption equals their wages. By equating the income and revenue sides of the national income, it follows that:

Capitalists' Income = Investment + Capitalists' Consumption.

Given the above assumptions, workers cannot change the level of their consumption without changing the wage share. Capitalists, however, are not constrained by their income, as they can increase (or reduce) their consumption and investment above (or below) their present income by drawing on (or paying off) credit or reserves. This equation can, therefore, be interpreted as showing that the income of capitalists as a class will adjust to their expenditure, because aggregate production will reach the level at which the gross profits derived from it will equal capitalists' consumption plus investment.

As Kalecki notes: 'Therefore the capitalists as a class determine by their expenditure their profits and in consequence aggregate production' (Kalecki 1939a, 45). Kalecki demonstrates this result by reformulating the analysis using Marx's reproduction schemas. The economy is divided into three sectors, producing investment goods, capitalists' consumption goods and workers' consumption goods respectively. In sector 3, which produces workers' consumption goods, the output is partly consumed by workers from that sector, while the surplus output is consumed by workers in the other two sectors. Wages in sectors 1 and 2 are, therefore, equal to the profits received in sector 1. Schematically this can represented as follows, with O_i (i=1,2,3) being the output of Sector i, I_i its investment, W_i its workers' consumption, and C_i the consumption of its capitalists:

$$O_1 = I_1 + C_1 + W_1 = I_1 + I_2 + I_3 \qquad (3.1)$$

$$O_2 = I_2 + C_2 + W_2 = C_1 + C_2 + C_3 \qquad (3.2)$$

$$O_3 = I_3 + C_3 + W_3 = W_1 + W_2 + W_3 \qquad (3.3)$$

where $I_i + C_i$ correspond to the profits in the ith sector. From the above it is easily shown that:

$$I_3 + C_3 = W_1 + W_2 \tag{3.4}$$

Some implications of Kalecki's use of these schemas can now be examined. Consider the effects of an increase in investment caused, for example, by an improvement in entrepreneurial confidence. This leads to an increase in output, employment and wages in sector 1. In turn, this increases workers' consumption which boosts production in the wage goods sector (sector 3). If capitalists' consumption remains unchanged, aggregate production will expand until profits increase by the same amount as the increase in investment. Any increase in capitalists' consumption will further increase profits and production.

This demonstrates that the main result of the macroanalysis is to show that aggregate profits are determined by the expenditure decisions of capitalists as a class. It is important to realize that, although this is true at the aggregate level, it does not follow at the level of individuals. If any individual capitalist increases his/her expenditure, then the increase in profits will not necessarily accrue to him/her, but will rather go to another capitalist. This is why we have called the analysis 'macroanalysis'. For capitalists as a class, any increase in expenditure will lead to an equal increase in total profits, although this is unlikely to be true for individual capitalists.

The Micro/Macro Link

Having outlined the role which the macroanalysis serves for Kalecki, in order to understand the link with the microanalysis, it is important to consider the role of the latter. The main function of the microanalysis was to provide the other crucial link in the determination of the level of economic activity. The clearest statement of this is in *Studies in Economic Dynamics* (Kalecki 1943). After deriving the determinants of pricing and distribution, Kalecki, in the third essay ('A Theory of Profits'), assigns the microanalysis a crucial role:

> [These] factors...will affect not real profits but the real wage and salary bill and consequently the national output. If, for instance degree of market imperfection or oligopoly increases, and, as a result, so does the ratio of profits to wages, real profits do not change, but the real wage bill falls, first, because of the fall in real wage rates, and secondly, because of the consequent reduction in demand for wage goods, and thus of output and employment in the wage-good industries... [Mark ups] increase,

but the national output falls just so much that, as a result, the real total profits remain the same. However great the margin of profit on a unit of output, the capitalists cannot make more in total profits than they consume and invest (Kalecki 1943, 50).

This passage is of great importance in understanding the link between Kalecki's micro and macro analysis. Gross real profits are determined by the capitalists' consumption and investment decisions. With total profits, capitalists' consumption and investment determined in real terms, so too are the levels of output and employment in the investment goods sector (sector 1) and the capitalist consumption goods sector (sector 2). Therefore the microfactors which determine the distribution of income will act through real wages, and hence influence the level of national output via their impact on the wage goods sector (sector 3). Changes in these microfactors, such as changes in the degree of monopoly, therefore, cannot affect gross profits, but they will influence employment and output in the wage goods sector. So an increase in the mark up increases profits in the investment and capitalist consumption sectors, at the same time reducing wages in those sectors. The subsequent reduction in demand for wage goods reduces output and employment in that sector, and also reduces profits. The reduction in profits in the wage goods sector is equal to the increased profits in the other two sectors, so that total profits remain unchanged. In other words, the main function of the macroanalysis was to explain the determination of total profits, while the main function of the microanalysis was to determine the wage share in national income. The two together determined the level of national income

Joan Robinson has often stressed this important point: 'The most important point in Kalecki's analysis is the demonstration that the overall rate of profit cannot be raised by raising the degree of monopoly. A higher proportion of profit margins leads to lower real wages and lower utilization of plant, not to a higher overall total profit' (Robinson 1969, 261). In her subsequent tribute to Kalecki in the *Oxford Bulletin of Economics and Statistics*, the importance of this argument is emphasised:

> There are two elements in Kalecki's analysis, the share of profit in the product of industry is determined by the level of gross margins, while the total flow of profits per annum depends upon the total flow of capitalists' expenditure on investment and consumption. In this way, Kalecki was able to weave the analysis of imperfect competition and of effective demand together and it was this that opened up the way for what goes under the name of post-Keynesian economic theory (Robinson 1977, 13-14).

This analysis represents Kalecki's version of the paradox of thrift. Recall that, for Keynes, the paradox of thrift was an example of the fallacy of composition, whereby any individual can increase his or her savings by their increasing marginal propensity to save. However, if the entire community attempts to increase its savings in the same way, without changing investment levels, all that happens is that the increase in marginal propensity to save reduces equilibrium income to the level where total savings is again equilibrated with the unchanged level of investment. So what is true for the individual is not true for the economy as a whole. Similarly with Kalecki's analysis of the role of the mark up. Any individual capitalist can increase their profits by increasing their mark up. However, if capitalists as a class attempt to increase total profits by increasing the average mark up, without changing their total expenditure, then, although this will increase their share of output it will not increase total profits. Rather, output and employment will fall, so that capitalists will have a larger share of a smaller output, with total profits unchanged. So, what is true for capitalists as individuals is not true for capitalists as a class. This explains why we have called this aspect of Kalecki's analysis macroeconomic.

We see from this the basis of Kalecki's interrelation of micro and macro analysis. The macroanalysis is important for determining gross profits, but it is in combination with the microanalysis that the level of real wages, output and employment corresponding to those gross profits are determined. The microanalysis plays a pivotal role in the determination of the level of output. The macro and the micro analysis each tell part of the story, and it is only through their interrelation that the whole account emerges.

In this way it can be seen that the micro and the macro analyses, as was stated earlier, lie side by side, exisiting interdependently, that is, on an equal footing. Some things are determined at the micro level, largely independent of what is happening at the macro level. This was reflected in Kalecki's attempt to develop models of pricing and distribution which were independent of the level of output. Similarly, some things are determined at the macro level, largely independent of pricing and distribution. Both influence each other, and from their interrelation something different from either is determined: the level of aggregate output. Alternatively, we could say that, for Kalecki, the microanalysis and the macroanalysis give different information about the working of the economy, and the integration of the two gives additional information about the state of the economy and where individual units find themselves. The microanalysis of pricing and distribution determines the share of profit and wages in national income, the macroanalysis of investment and of intersectoral flows determines gross profits, and together they determine the level of output. This is in contrast with neoclassical general equilibrium economists, for whom macroeconomic phenomena are merely some sort of aggregate outcome of microeconomic relations. It is also in contrast to some post Keynesian analysis, where the micro-relations are derived from a backward extrapolation of the macro, so that the question really becomes one of finding '*the macro foundations of microeconomics*' (Crotty 1980, 23; emphasis in original). In Kalecki micro and macro stand side by side, with important feedbacks between them. Kalecki (following Marx and the classical economists) treated micro and macro issues interdependently, without really distinguishing between them.

As has been stressed, this does not imply that Kalecki regarded them as being of equal importance. It has already been observed that the microanalysis was mainly a step towards the development of the theory of output and business cycles. This explains some of the specific features of his analysis. As the editor of his *Collected Works* has observed: 'The immediate impulse for the formulation of the degree of monopoly theory of income distribution seems to have been the need to find analytical tools which make it possible to investigate cyclical and secular changes in wages and profits as components of national income' (Osiatynski 1979, 340). An example of this is Kalecki's discussion of changes in the degree of monopoly over the trade cycle, which has important implications for changes in the level of output in the economy as a whole. A further example of this is his concern with manual labour's share in the output of the industrial sector. This is important for the determination of workers' consumption, which Kalecki assumes to be equal to their income. The residual share of gross output will accrue to salaries and to profits, which provide the basis for capitalists' consumption. Their differential impact on effective demand explains the importance of the distinction between the income of manual workers, who consume all their income, and that of capitalists, who clearly do not. Part of capitalists' income will be saved, and used in the financing of investment, though, investment is not constrained by profits due to the difference in the constraints they face. Capitalists, unlike workers, are not bound in their expenditure decisions by their current income and can be treated as if they had a monopoly on credit institutions. For all these reasons, Kalecki's differential treatment of wage and non-wage incomes is an important analytical device. The implications of this for the level of effective demand, and hence for the explanation of fluctuations in output, are obvious.

Kalecki's approach to the question of microfoundations has some important implications. Although micro and macro questions may sometimes be regarded as separate areas of study, nevertheless there are fundamental interrelations. In particular, the analysis of the economy as a whole determines the position in which individual firms find themselves. Kalecki's method is, in many ways, similar to that of Ricardo and of Marx discussed above, in treating micro and macro side by side. The study of the behaviour of firms is, to an extent, independent of the analysis of macrophenomena, although there are important (dialectical) interrelations which form an equally important area of study.

An Important Modification

So far discussion has proceeded under the assumption that the independence of microanalysis and macroanalysis is achievable. As I have argued elsewhere (Kriesler 1987), this is not the case for Kalecki's analysis. In other words, the previous discussion must be modified so as to allow for some influence of the level and composition of output on the determination of prices and relative shares; and some influence of prices and distribution on the determination of aggregate profits. In particular, when analyzing the effects of a reduction on wages, Kalecki describes the fall in output of sector 3 relative to sectors 1 and 2. If the degree of monopoly of sector 3 is different from that of the average, then this change in output will change the average degree of monopoly, which will, in turn, lead to changes in the share of wages in total output. This will have further ramifications on employment, depending on which direction the microfactors have gone. In other words, the sectoral change in output resulting from a change in the real wage will influence distribution independently, via the microanalysis, therefore having second round effects on total output. In addition, once overheads are incorporated into the analysis, unless it is assumed that they accrue only to capitalists, changes in output will lead to changes in the share of profits.

Nevertheless, the general implications of Kalecki's approach need not be modified substantially. Rather, a return to the classical method of analysis by stages is suggested, once again emphasizing the similarity in method of Kalecki and the classical economists. First one considers (say) the microanalysis, which is determined by the 'degree of monopoly' with output constant. At the next stage, gross profits are determined by the expenditure decisions of capitalists, which are themselves determined by past decisions, with prices and distribution held constant. These, together, determine the level of output, which is then used to modify the previous analysis of pricing and distribution. This iterative process will continue until either the system's solutions result in stable outcomes for all the processes, or some dynamic can be determined. This approach was used elsewhere by Kalecki, where he separates the analysis into a number of logically and sequentially separate stages, with his analysis of taxation being a good example (Kalecki 1937).

According to Roncaglia this type of framework:

> represents a decision to analyze each particular problem separately, one at a time, isolating one from the other. The assumptions and methods of analysis need not necessarily be the same for each and every problem. It is necessary to choose, for each particular problem, only those variables most relevant to the analysis of the problem at hand, leaving aside those factors which, as Ricardo says, lead only to 'modifications' in the analysis, but not to changes in the substance of the analysis (Roncaglia 1978, 22).

In conclusion, it should be noted that this suggested modification will not affect the nature of the micro/macro relation within a Kaleckian framework. In fact, it clarifies the nature of the causal link, and places it in a framework of historical time. There is a definite logical sequence in which relations are determined, similar to the casual link identified by Pasinetti (1974, 44) in the works of Ricardo and Keynes. Kalecki's original link, with the microanalysis determining the share of profits, the macroanalysis the total value of profits, and the two determining the level of output; simply needs to be modified to allow for feedbacks from each level of analysis. These feedbacks stress the interrelations between the levels of analysis which underlie Kalecki's work.

Notes

1 See, for example, Harcourt (1977) and Weintraub (1979).

2 See Sardoni (1987), particularly chapter 4. Note his conclusion that 'Marx's micro-framework ... reaches analytical conclusions partly inconsistent with reality' (p.5).

3 Compare Meek (1968, 191): 'Marx, like Smith and Ricardo, made no distinction between macroeconomics and microeconomic analysis.' See also robinson (1977a, 4-5).

4 Discussion of Kalecki's contribution is postponed until the next section.

5 Sardoni argues that 'Keynes's analytical results .... are founded on a micro-framework that proves to be either unrealistic or inconsistent' (1987, 6). In chapter 8 Sardoni engages in a Kaleckian critique of Keynes's micro-foundations.

6 See, for example, Hahn (1984,2) and Harcourt (1977, 375-376, 380).

7 See Keynes (1973), Preface to the French Edition (especially xxxii, xxxiii) and chapter 19; Kalecki (1939a); Robinson (1951, 135) and Harcourt (1987).

8 See, for example Crotty (1980, 23) and Harcourt (1980, 27).

9 See, for example, Harcourt (1981, 9) and Pasinetti (1974, 118).

10 In Kriesler (1987) I attempted to trace the development of Kalecki's analysis of pricing and distribution and its relation to his analysis of output and employment, concluding that Kalecki was unable to capture his basic insights in a satisfactory model. See also Osiatynski (1992).

11 See also Osiatynski (1992).

12 Our approach is similar to the method of rational reconstruction in Wong (1978, 11-20). That is, we have attempted to 'reconstruct hypothetically the problem-situation in the context of which the theory was proposed.' This is not an attempt to 'delve into Kalecki's subconscious' but rather it is an attempt to reconstruct the problem which it is reasonable to argue that Kalecki was trying to solve.

13 Compare Asimakopulos (1983, 1-3, 8-13) and Rowthorn (1981).

14 The collection, *Selected Essays on the Dynamics of the Capitalist Economy (1933-70)* (Kalecki 1971) mainly reprints selections from these or other previously published essays.

15 This was translated into English and Published in the final two chapters of *Studies in the Theory of the Business Cycles 1933-1939*. The paper with the same name which appears as the third essay in *Essays in Economic Fluctuations,* and which was referred to in the last paragraph, is substantially different.

16 Reprinted from the *Economic Journal* (Kalecki 1942).

17 Mott stresses the role of '*changes in* rather than *the level of* the degree of monopoly' for changes in aggregate demand (Mott 1992, 117; emphasis in original).

18 In Kriesler (1987) two roles were the distinguished for the microanalysis. It was argued that in Kalecki's earlier works, the role of the microanalysis was to explain the inflexibility of the distribution between wage and non-wage income in the face of changes in the level of aggregate demand, while in Kalecki's later works the microanalysis was seen as playing an important role in the determination of the level of economic activity. However, the current paper does not distinguish these roles, as it can be seen that the two are, in fact, variants of the same idea.

19 That is not to say that they are of equali importance for the analysis of output and of trade cycles, which is clearly not the case.

20 For an excellent discussion of these issues, see Marglin (1984, 126.).

21 I am indebted to Jerzy Osiatynski for these observations. See also Osiatynski (1979, 339-340).

22 Similar comments are made in Robinson (1977a).

23 For further discussion of this 'procuedure by separate logical steps', see Pasinetti (1974, 297) and the description of partial equilibrium analysis as a similar process in Rogers (1989, 184).

References

Arestis, P. & Chick, V. Eds. 1992. *Recent Developments in Post-Keynesian Economics*. Elgar: Aldershot.

Asimakopulos, A. 1983. 'A Kaleckian Profits Equation and the United States Economy, 1950-82'. *Metroeconomica* 35(1-2), June: 1-27.

Crotty, J. 1980. 'Post-Keynesian Theory: an Overview and Evaluation" *American Economic Review, papers and proceedings* 70(2), May: 20-25.

Garegnani, P. 1983. 'The Classical Theory of Wages and the Role of Demand Schedules in the Determination of Relative Prices'. *American Economic Review, papers and proceedings* 73(2), May: 309-313.

Garegnani, P. 1984. 'Value and Distribution in the Classical Economists and Marx.' *Oxford Economic Papers* 36(2), June: 291-327.

Hahn, F. 1984. *Equilibrium and Macroeconomics*. Oxford: Blackwell.

Harcourt, G.C. 1980. 'Discussion of Appraisals of Post-Keynesian Economics'. *American Economic Review, papers and proceedings* 70(2): 27-28.

Harcourt, G.C. ed. 1977. *The Microeconomic Foundations of Macroeconomics*. London: Macmillan.

Howitt, P. 1987. 'Macroeconomics: Relations with Microeconomics' in J. Eatwell, M. Milgate, & P. Newman, eds. *The New Palgrave* Vol. 3, London: Macmillan, 273-6.

Kalecki, M. 1933. 'Outline of the Theory of the Business Cycle; reprinted in Kalecki 1971.

Kalecki, M. 1937. 'A Theory of Commodity, Income and Capital Taxation' reprinted in Kalecki 1971.

Kalecki, M. 1939a. *Essays in the Theory of Economic Fluctuations.* London: Alen and Unwin.

Kalecki, M. 1943. *Studies in Economic Dynamics.* London: Allen and Unwin.

Kalecki, M. 1954. *Theory of Economic Dynamics.* London: Allen and Unwin.

Kalecki, M. 1969. *Studies in the Theory of Business Cycles: 1933-1939.* Oxford: Blackwell.

Kalecki, M. 1971b. 'Class Struggle and Distribution of National Income;. *Kyklos 24* (1): 1-9. Reprinted in Kalecki 1971: 156-164.

Keynes, J.M. 1936. *The General Theory of Employment, Interest and Money.* London: Macmillan. Reprinted in 1973.

Kriesler, P. 1987. *Kalecki's Microanalysis: the Development of Kalecki's Analysis of Pricing and Distribution.* Cambridge: Cambridge University Press.

Marglin, S.A. 1984. 'Growth, Distribution and Inflation: a Centennial Synthesis'. *Cambridge Journal of Economics* (2), June: 115-144.

Meek, R.L. 1967. 'The Place of Keynes in the History of Economic Thought". In Meek, *Economics and Ideology and other Essays.* London: Chapman and Hall.

Mott, T. 1992. 'In What Sense Does Monopoly Capital Require Monopoly? An Essay on the Contribution of Kalecki and Steindl.' In J. Davis, ed. *The Economic Surplus in Advanced Countries.* Aldershot: Elgar: 114-29.

Osiatynski, J. 1979. 'Michal Kalecki's Theory of Income Distribution'. *Oeconomica Polona* 3: 339-358.

Osiatynski, J. 1992. 'Price and Monopoly in Kalecki's Theory.' In Arestis and Chick (1992) 82-94.

Pasinetti, L. 1974. *Growth and Income Disbrituion.* Cambridge: Cambridge University Press.

Robinson, J. 1951. *Collected Economic Papers, Volume I.* Oxford: Blackwell. Reprinted 1960, 1961.

Robinson, J. 1969. 'A Further Note'. *Review of Economic Studies* 36(106), April: 160-262.

Robinson, J. 1977. 'Michal Kalecki on the Economics of Capitalism'. *Oxford Bulletin of Economics and Statistics* 39(1), February: 7-18.

Robinson, J. 1977a. 'What are the Questions?' Reprinted in Robinson 1979a: 1-31.

Ribonson, J. 1979. 'The Disintegration of Economics'. Reprinted in Robinson 1979a: 90-8.

Robinson, J. 1979a. *Collected Economic Papers, Volume V.* Oxford: Blackwell).

Rogers, C. 1989. *Money, Interest and Capital.* Cambridge: Cambridge University
    Press.
Roncaglia, A. 1978. *Sraffa and the Theory of Prices.* Chichester: Wiley.
Rowthorn, R. 1981. 'Demand, Real Wages and Economic Growth.' *Thames Papers
    in Political Economy.*
Sardoni, C. 1987. *Marx and Keynes on Economic Recession: the Theory of
    Unemployment and Effective Demand.* Bridghton: Wheatsheaf.
Sawyer, M. 1920. 'On the Origins of Post-Keynesian Pricing Theory and
    Macroeconomics.' In Arestis and Chick 1992; 64-81.
Weintraub, E. 1979. *Microfoundations.* Cambridge: Cambridge University Press.
Wong, S. 1978. *The Foundations of Paul Samuelson's Revealed Preference Theory.*
    London: Routledge and Kegan Paul.

4 KALECKI'S THEORY OF PRICES AND DISTRIBUTION

Peter J. Reynolds

Introduction

This paper assesses the role of the 'degree of monopoly' in Kalecki's theory of pricing and income distribution. We begin by examining Kalecki's theory of prices, focusing on the meaning and role of the 'degree of monopoly'. We then discuss Kalecki's degree of monopoly theory of distribution and consider some alternative interpretations of the degree of monopoly, prior to considering the importance of this concept for Kalecki's macroeconomics. This leads us to consider three main areas where post Keynesian economists, despite declaring superficial sympathies with Kalecki's work, have either misunderstood, misrepresented or inadequately developed Kalecki's analysis. We consider the extent to which real wages are determined in the product rather than the labour market; relate Kalecki's theory of distribution to the 'neo-Keynesian' theories, as expressed in the Kaldor - Pasinetti equations; and discuss alternative interpretations of the role of the degree of monopoly in the long run.

I am grateful to John King and Iraj Seyf for comments on an earlier draft.

Pricing

Chapter one of *Theory of Economic Dynamics* begins as follows: 'Short-term price changes may be classified into two broad groups: those determined mainly by changes in cost of production and those determined mainly by changes in demand. Generally speaking, changes in the prices of finished goods are "cost-determined" while changes in the prices of raw materials inclusive of primary foodstuffs are "'demand-determined"' (Kalecki 1954,11). This distinction has been taken up by subsequent Kaleckian and post Keynesian economists and plays a key role in our understanding of the inflationary process.[1] Nevertheless, most of Kalecki's writing on prices - and all of what follows here - is concerned with the prices of finished goods.

Kalecki (1940) set down a model of 'pure imperfect competition', in which, under the assumption that an industry contains many firms, '[i]n short-period equilibrium the equality between the short-period marginal cost ... and the marginal revenue ... must be fulfilled ....' (Kalecki 1940, 93). The implied objective is short-period profit maximisation, though later in the same paper Kalecki introduced the concept of the 'degree of oligopoly', along with the firm's lack of knowledge about the precise nature of its demand and marginal cost functions, each of which may lead to the short-period equilibrium conditions being violated. Although the same pricing model was incorporated in 'A theory of long-run distribution of the product of industry' (Kalecki 1941), we may follow Peter Kriesler in regarding these two papers as representing, 'disruptions to the continuity of the evolution of Kalecki's thoughts' (Kriesler 1987, 51). In *Studies in Economic Dynamics* (1943), Kalecki again focused on pricing under conditions of imperfect competition and oligopoly, though his approach was modified substantially in *Theory of Economic Dynamics* (1954), where he stated that, 'In view of the uncertainties faced in the process of price fixing it will not be assumed that the firm attempts to maximise its profits in any precise sort of manner' (Kalecki 1954, 12; 1971a, 44).

In the 1954 book, he presented the pricing equation,

$$p = mu + n\bar{p} \tag{4.1}$$

where p and u represent the individual firm's price and unit costs, and $\bar{p}$ represents the average price charged by firms in the industry. 'The coefficients m and n characterising the price fixing policy of the firm reflect what might be called the degree of monopoly of the firm's position' (Kalecki 1954, 13; 1971a, 45). By aggregating across all firms in an industry, rearranging and defining $k = \overline{m}/1-\overline{n}$, where $\overline{m}$ and $\overline{n}$ are appropriately weighted industry averages of m and n, we obtain:[2]

$$\overline{p} = k\overline{u} \tag{4.2}$$

Thus k is determined by the degree of monopoly.

Kalecki (1954, 17) lists those factors 'underlying changes in the degree of monopoly'. The first two are the extent of industrial concentration and the importance of advertising relative to sales. Then there is a discussion of 'the influence of changes in the level of overheads in relation to prime costs' and 'the significance of the power of trade unions'. If overheads should rise significantly in relation to prime costs in a depression, this will cause profits to be squeezed, and so there *may* arise tacit agreement between firms so as to protect profits (*ibid.*,17). On the other hand, in a footnote on the following page, Kalecki notes that 'This is the basic tendency: however, in some instances the opposite process of cut-throat competition may develop in a depression' (*ibid.*, 18n).[3] Powerful trade unions may have a constraining effect on mark-ups because 'A high ratio of profits to wages strengthens the bargaining position of trade unions in their demands for wage increases since higher wages are then compatible with 'reasonable profits' at existing wage levels' (*ibid.*, 18). If, after such demands were met, prices were again increased to maintain the profit margin, an inflationary spiral might develop, with adverse consequences for the firm's competitive position. The significance of trade unions in constraining the mark-up was returned to in Kalecki (1971b) where the role of trade unions in affecting income distribution was further analysed.

In the light of the above paragraph, how should we interpret 'the degree of monopoly'? One possibility is to follow Lerner (1934) and define the degree of monopoly as the difference between price and marginal cost, expressed as a ratio of price. Kalecki (1938a, 100) did refer to the degree of monopoly in this way. *Under the assumption of profit maximisation* it is a matter of elementary calculus to demonstrate that this is equal to the reciprocal of the elasticity of demand. Under such assumptions, 'it is not the degree of monopoly that determines the respective shares of wages and profits in the economy, but the price elasticity of demand' (Osiatynski 1992, 87). Defining the degree of monopoly as the *ex post* margin is not consistent with arguing that the margin *is determined by* the degree of monopoly. This would amount to saying that the degree of monopoly determines the degree of monopoly, which is not very helpful. In fact, as pointed out by Sawyer (1985, 29), the misdirected criticism that the degree of monopoly theory of distribution is tautological arises from such an interpretation, based on Kalecki's earlier writings. Yet, as argued by Osiatynski (*op. cit.*), this was not Kalecki's intention and, as discussed above, in his later work Kalecki explicitly did not assume profit maximisation.

Following Reynolds (1983) we prefer to use the term, 'degree of monopoly', to refer to those institutional and environmental influences which affect firms' pricing behaviour. On this interpretation, the ratio of price to prime costs is a *reflection* of the degree of monopoly, rather than its definition, and consequently the question of tautology does not arise.[4] From here we can proceed in either of two ways. We can regard the extent of industrial concentration, the ratio of advertising to sales and the other possible influences as structural characteristics of the individual industry and work within the static structure - conduct - performance paradigm, as is common in much of the industrial economics literature. Alternatively, taking an approach more akin to that adopted by Hayek (1948, 92-106), we might consider the degree of monopoly as a set of factors which hinder or counter the *process* of competition.[5] On this interpretation, a low degree of monopoly would be associated with very intense competitive pressures and a high degree of monopoly would imply that the competitive process was relatively weak.

It is worth examining the factors listed by Kalecki as 'causes of change in the degree of monopoly' in the light of these two perspectives (Kalecki 1954, 17). Kalecki suggested that 'The influence of the emergence of firms representing a substantial share of the output of an industry can be readily understood ... the firm can fix its price at a level higher than would otherwise be the case' (*op. cit.*, 17). This does seem to be consistent with the static approach, implying a monotonic relationship between the degree of concentration and the mark-up. However, there are at least two problems with this interpretation. Firstly, although the extent of concentration might be expected to affect the intensity of competition, a monotonic relationship with any specific measure of concentration is not assured. Whether the process of competition is more intense with, for example, two firms in the industry rather than three remains an open question. This will depend on how each firm responds (or is expected to respond) to a change (or expected change) in the behaviour of its rival(s), which in turn will be influenced by a host of historical, legal and other influences.[6] Secondly, at the extreme of 'perfect competition', all of the ingredients of the competitive process are effectively absent.

A high ratio of advertising to sales might suggest an industry approximating to the Chamberlinian large group case, where advertising is used to create perceived differences in products so that competition in advertising replaces competition in price. Thus an increase in competitive pressure is manifested *either* in terms of reduced mark-ups *or* via increased expenditures on advertising. If by the term, 'high degree of monopoly', we mean a less intense competitive process, then a high degree of monopoly may lead either to high mark-ups or to low expenditures on advertising. On this interpretation a high degree of monopoly, implying a weak competitive process, might be associated with either low or relatively high spending on advertising. For a *given* degree of monopoly this would lead us to expect a negative association between mark-ups and the ratio of advertising to sales. Set against this, a high ratio of advertising to sales, by increasing perceived product differentiation, tempers the degree to which the firm is influenced by the pricing behaviour of its rivals, thereby increasing the degree of monopoly of the individual firm and alleviating the pressure to reduce mark-ups or even permitting higher mark-ups. We might think of the advertising / sales ratio as one of the institutional or environmental factors both affected by the intensity of the competitive process and in turn contributing to it.

As discussed above, Kalecki (1940, 1954) recognised that during a depression there may or may not be a rise in profit margins. This depends on whether the squeeze on profits causes the competitive pressures to intensify or whether there is tacit agreement to maintain or increase margins. There is more to the degree of monopoly than industrial structure. The latter is just one set of factors affecting the intensity of competition; the legal framework, affecting firms' propensity to collude, is another. Firms' expectations about the future, the psychology of the decision-takers and the internal organisation of the firm are all important in influencing how a firm responds to external circumstances, such as fluctuations in costs or demand. It is the sum total of all these factors which we refer to as the 'degree of monopoly', and it is changes and variations in the degree of monopoly which lead to changes and variations in the mark-up on prime costs. Reynolds (1984) and Mair, Reynolds, *et. al.* (1995) demonstrate that changes and variations in the degree of monopoly explain a large proportion of changes and variations in firms' mark-ups.

Pricing and distribution

Once the mark-up, or the ratio k, is determined, this can be used to derive the well-known degree of monopoly distribution equation for direct labour's share of value added in a particular industry. Hence we have a theory of distribution based on short-period considerations. The link between pricing and income distribution is straightforward and at its most transparent in a model of a vertically integrated closed economy. In such a model, wage costs are synonymous with prime costs, so that equation (4.2) can be rewritten as:

$$p = \frac{kwL}{x} \qquad\qquad (4.3)$$

where w, L and x represent the money-wage rate per worker, total direct labour input and output respectively. Prices are a mark-up on unit labour costs. Multiplying both sides of equation (4.3) by x gives:

$px = kwL$ (4.4)

Since wL represents total receipts to direct labour and px represents aggregate proceeds, which for a vertically integrated closed economy equal value added, direct labour's share of value added is wL divided by px, which can be obtained by rearranging equation (4.4) as follows:

$$\frac{wL}{px} = \frac{1}{k}$$ (4.5)

Labour's share of value added is equal to the reciprocal of the mark-up. For a non-vertically integrated economy, materials costs must be introduced, and direct labour's share of value added for the non-primary sector becomes

$w = 1/[1+(k-1)(j+1)]$ (4.6)

where j is the ratio of materials costs to wage costs.[7]

The implications for the real wage are worth exploring, which is most easily done via the concept of the 'product wage'. We define the real (product) wage as the receipts by an individual worker for producing one unit of output, using the price of the output as numeraire. Thus the real (product) wage is the money wage received by an individual worker divided by the value of the average product of labour. Consider again the equations for a vertically integrated closed economy: the real wage is w divided by px/L, which is exactly the same as equation (4.5) for labour's share of value added. Both labour's share and the real wage are equal to the reciprocal of the mark-up.

The model is extended to include both direct and indirect labour by Asimakopulos (1975). The equation is unaffected by 'opening' the economy, provided that j is interpreted as the ratio of wages costs to all materials costs, regardless of source. The important point to acknowledge is that income distribution is determined by firms in the process of price-setting. The factors determining price-setting are therefore responsible for determining income distribution.

Alternative Interpretations of the Degree of Monopoly

Peter Riach has argued that '... to the extent that monopoly power is exercised we would logically expect that in the long-run this would be directed towards obtaining a higher rate of return on capital rather than a high ratio of profits to sales proceeds...' (Riach 1971, 53). A similar 'Kaleckian' model is set out by Asimakopulos (1975). In Asimakopulos's model, complete vertical integration in industry is assumed, so that there are no raw material inputs and direct labour costs are the only prime costs. A price leader sets the price, taking particular account of the expected return on capital. Asimakopulos follows Kalecki in assuming that the degree of monopoly is *reflected* in the mark-up over unit prime cost, but argues that what it 'makes possible and *protects*' (my emphasis) is the rate of profit on capital earned by existing firms in the industry. 'It is thus the realised rate of return on investment which is a reflection of the degree of monopoly' (*op. cit.*, 315). According to Asimakopulos, the mark-up is designed to cover both overhead costs and an expected rate of return, or profit, on capital. This expected rate of profit includes both what is expected to be a 'normal' rate of return on industrial investment and any additional return due to the degree of monopoly.

This interpretation of the degree of monopoly, whereby it is 'reflected in expected rates of return on investment ...', 'pervades the work of Asimakopulos, who also points out that 'Joan Robinson's reformulation of Kalecki's pricing equation (Robinson 1969) makes use of an expected rate of return on investment' (Asimakopulos 1975, 315 n.5). In both the Riach and Asimakopulos analyses the mark-up on prime costs is set with reference to the expected rate of return on capital. In fact, Asimakopulos is quite explicit that 'provision for such returns becomes formalised in their mark-ups in the guise of some target rate of return' (*op. cit.*, 320).

Cowling and Waterson (1976) present a 'Kaleckian' model based on an industry consisting of *n* firms, each pursuing independent short-period profit maximisation but taking account of the expected reactions of its rivals. The model predicts a precise relationship between mark-ups on the one hand and the industry price elasticity of demand, the Herfindahl measure of industrial concentration and the individual firms' reaction coefficients (sometimes referred to as the 'conjectural variation' term) on the other.

Even in the 'Kaleckian' sub-class of mark-up pricing models considered above, there is an important difference in the role played by the degree of monopoly. In the Kalecki and Cowling models, the degree of monopoly has a direct influence on and is reflected in the mark-up, without any reference to long-run rates of return on either investment or capital. In the Riach and Asimakopulos interpretation, the degree of monopoly may affect the mark-up, but this comes about via its effect on the rate of return on investment. In the Riach approach, although the degree of monopoly is reflected in the mark-up, its role in the long run is to protect the rate of return on capital. Asimakopulos's interpretation to some extent lies between these two approaches, since it is the realised rate of return on investment which reflects the degree of monopoly, but provision for such returns enters into the pricing process via the target rate of return.

Let us investigate the implications of Asimakopulos's interpretation. Suppose that the degree of monopoly increases in a particular industry. This permits a higher rate of return on investment in that industry, so that further investment will be forthcoming in anticipation of that higher return. In Asimakopulos's analysis, since the oligopoly price leader is now pursuing a higher rate of return, this will be reflected in the target rate of return, which the price charged is intended to realise. Once the investment has been completed, the actual price charged, as distinct from the price which was expected before the investment was laid down, will depend on the institutional environment in which the firm operates. If this is exactly as had been anticipated, then the price charged will be exactly that which permits the firm to achieve its target rate of return. However, any change in the environment will necessitate a revision of the mark-up, so that the target rate of return may or may not be achieved. The observed mark-up will be a result of the institutional environment during the pricing period (which we interpret to include the effect on anticipated future sales of any price change). Certainly, for a mark-up to persist which yields rates of return higher than could be achieved elsewhere in the economy would require that there were some barriers to entry into that particular industry.

In this respect there is a similarity between Asimakopulos's views and those of Riach. However, for Riach to argue that to the extent that monopoly power is exercised it is *directed* towards obtaining a higher rate of return presupposes that monopoly power is legitimately interpreted to mean entry barriers. The existence, for example, of high degrees of industrial concentration would be associated with high entry barriers, which dissuade capital from entering a particular industry, leading to the existence of high profit rates *in that industry*. In Cowling's analysis it is industrial concentration *per se*, via its effects on the way in which firms respond to the actions of other firms in the industry, which is important in setting the mark-up. The difference between these two approaches to the degree of monopoly, whereby it is seen as the immediate influence on firms' pricing decisions, as in Kalecki and Cowling, or via long-run rates of return, as in Riach and Asimakopulos, becomes very important once one adopts a macroeconomic perspective. If the only role for the degree of monopoly is to enable rates of profit to be higher in some industries than in others, then there is no role for any notion of the degree of monopoly at the macroeconomic level.

Income Distribution, Profits and the Level of Income

As argued above, Kalecki provided a microeconomic theory of pricing and income distribution. This formed a critical part of his theory of the business cycle, appearing in one form or another in *Essays in the Theory of Economic Fluctuations* (1939), *Studies in Economic Dynamics* (1943) and in the form set out above in *Theory of Economic Dynamics* (1954). To appreciate its role, we now set out Kalecki's theory of profits.

Begin with the national accounting identity:

$$\Pi + W \equiv GNP \equiv I + C_w + C_c \tag{4.7}$$

where Π, W, GNP, I, C_w and C_c refer to aggregate profits, wages, gross national product, investment, workers' consumption and capitalists' consumption respectively. The simplifying assumption that workers do not save reduces equation (4.7) to:

$$\Pi = I + C_c \tag{4.8}$$

Kalecki argued that, since capitalists have discretion over how much they spend or consume but not over how much they earn, it is the right-hand side of equation (4.8) which determines the left hand side. Capitalists' consumption is assumed to depend on their income, that is profits, expressed as

$$C_c = q\Pi + A \tag{4.9}$$

where A is autonomous consumption and q is the capitalists' propensity to consume. Kalecki did introduce lags into the model; but we here focus on the static solution to the pair of equations, (4.8) and (4.9), which is given as:

$$\Pi = (I + A)/1\text{-}q \tag{4.10}$$

The *level* of profits, in aggregate, is determined by capitalists' investment and consumption decisions. Since the *share* of profits in value added is determined by the degree of monopoly, '[t]he national output will be pushed up to the point where profits carved out of it in accordance with the "distribution factors" are equal to the sum of capitalists' consumption and investment' (Kalecki 1954, 47).

We restate equation (4.10) and summarise the Kaleckian model as follows:

$$\Pi = (I + A)/1\text{-}q \tag{4.10}$$

$$\Pi + W = Y \tag{4.11}$$

$$w = W/Y = 1/[1+(k\text{-}1)(j+1] \tag{4.12}$$

$$k = f \text{(degree of monopoly)} \tag{4.13}$$

Equation (4.10) determines profits, equation (4.11) is an accounting identity, equation (4.12) is equation (4.6) restated, and equation (4.13) states that the mark-up is determined by the degree of monopoly. There are four equations/identities, allowing us to solve for the four unknowns, k, W, Π and Y.

The relationship between micro and macroeconomics in Kaleckian analysis is of interest and has been elaborated by Kriesler (1989), Osiatynski (1992) and by Kriesler and Arestis in this volume. Microeconomic factors are responsible for pricing and for determining direct labour's share of value added. The theory of profits is essentially macroeconomic, and it is the interplay between these two sets of factors which determines the level of national income.

The structure of the Kaleckian model has been outlined before.[8] Yet there are at least three aspects and implications which are not universally appreciated, and these are now considered.

Determination of the Real Wage

If in the face of changes in costs, or in any of the degree of monopoly factors, firms adjust their prices instantly, then the ratio of price to unit prime costs and consequently the distribution of income is entirely determined by firms. The act of setting the mark-up simultaneously determines the real wage, most transparently demonstrated for a vertically integrated economy. Under these conditions, the real wage is determined in the product market rather than the labour market. This result is often referred to as one of the key features of post Keynesian economics.[9]   Furthermore, one of the main policy recommendations of a significant group of American post Keynesians is for a tax-based incomes policy, the supporting theory for which is predicated on a mark-up approach to pricing.[10]   A critical assumption both for the result that real wages are determined in the product market and for the case in favour of tax-based incomes policies is that prices are adjusted instantly following a change in wage costs. This also underlies Kalecki's very important paper, published posthumously (Kalecki 1971b), where he argues that if trade unions are to have any effect on the distribution of income it must be via their effect on firms' pricing decisions.

Consider a vertically integrated economy in which prices are set every January 1st and money wages are set every July 1st. In setting prices, firms aim for a mark-up of 25%. Each year workers secure a 10% increase in money wages. Immediately after the new prices are set, $p = 1.25w$, implying a real (product) wage of $1/1.25 = 0.8$. That is to say, workers receive 80% of value added and capitalists receive 20%. On July 1st, money wages increase by 10%, so that the real (product) wage becomes 0.88 and workers achieve 88% of value added, a situation which lasts for six months. Averaged over the year, the real (product) wage is 0.84, corresponding to a wage share of 84%. When firms set prices they determine the real wage for six months. Then, when money wages are set, the real wage is determined, as a result of settlements in the labour market, for another six months.

Whether real wages are determined mainly in the product or in the labour market depends on the relative speeds with which prices and money wages are adjusted, on whether prices are adjusted fully to reflect cost increases, and whether money wages are adjusted fully to reflect price increases. The effect of a change in money wages on prices determines whether or not a change in money wages leads to a change in real wages and has important consequences for employment theory, as discussed, for example in chapter 19 of Keynes's *General Theory* (Keynes 1973), and in a paper by Kalecki originally published in Polish in 1939 (Kalecki 1969). In the 1939 paper, Kalecki acknowledged that, under the assumptions of perfect competition, a fall in money wages would lead to a fall in prices by the same proportion. This result also formed an important part of the arguments in Kalecki (1938b) and (1971b). However, under conditions of imperfect competition 'some prices will prove to be "rigid" and thus will fail to decline in the same proportion as wages' (Kalecki 1969, 55).

The speed and extent to which prices are adjusted following a change in costs is an empirical matter. Sylos Labini (1979) used annual data for Italy, the US, UK, West Germany and Argentina from the early 1950s to the early 1970s to examine the price-cost relationship.[11] He found that in all cases except Argentina cost changes were only partially shifted onto prices, the proportion ranging from 74% in the UK to 93% in the US. Furthermore, whereas changes in materials costs tended to be passed on virtually in their entirety, changes in wage costs were only partially shifted to prices. The suggested reason is that materials costs tend to be shared by all international competitors, whereas this does not apply to wage costs. Changes to wage costs tend to be passed on only partially as price changes, the extent of the shift depending on the pressure of international competition. Furthermore, shifts in labour costs tend to be asymmetrical, with the degree of asymmetry varying between countries. In a subsequent study using UK data, Arestis confirmed that 'changes in the prices of raw materials and labour costs are not fully compensated by rises in prices' (Arestis 1986, 356).

Two important implications of the result that prices do not adjust instantaneously concern first the contention that the only way in which trade unions can affect relative shares is via their ability to affect the mark-up, and second the case for a tax-based incomes policy - or its equivalent manifestation in the form of a counter-inflation tax. It is clear from the above that trade unions as a whole will also help to maintain their share by affecting the speed with which mark-ups are adjusted. For an individual firm, the variables of interest are the money wage in that particular industry and its own price, over which it has some control. From the perspective of an individual worker or union, the two variables of interest are the money wage in that particular industry and the aggregate price level. It is in the interests of workers as a whole to ensure first that money wages are adjusted rapidly in response to price inflationary pressures, and second that firms are discouraged from passing cost increases immediately onto prices. A number of advocates of tax-based incomes policy appear misguided in their statements that price controls are not necessary.[12] Appelbaum (1982) and Seidman (1983) both argue that price controls may improve the prospects of political implementation of TIP. But even if price controls are not necessary to reduce inflation, by placing all the onus on money wages these writers are weighting the dice against the interests of workers. Appelbaum (1982) expresses concern for the distributional implications of a 'wages only' TIP, especially via its effects on the secondary labour market. These concerns must become stronger when it is recognised that controlling prices but not money wages affects the *relative speed* with which prices and money wages can be adjusted and thereby, for the reasons outlined above, further biases the conflict over relative income shares against the recipients of wage income.

The Role of Savings Propensities

The post Keynesian theory of income distribution as expressed in most post Keynesian textbooks is not the degree of monopoly theory. Instead, it is a version of the model set out by Kaldor (1980), in which income shares are determined by the proportion of income invested and the relative savings propensities of capitalists and workers.[13] A simplified version of the model is when workers do not save, so that aggregate savings are equal to capitalists' savings. Setting aggregate savings equal to investment and restating the national accounting identity, the model is summarised as follows:

$$S = s\Pi \tag{4.14}$$

$$S = I \tag{4.15}$$

$$Y = \Pi + W \tag{4.16}$$

where S and s_c represent aggregate savings and the savings propensity of capitalists respectively, and the other terms are as defined above. By substitution and rearrangement, the profit share is given as

$$\Pi/Y = (1/s_c)(I/Y) \tag{4.17}$$

This model was referred to by Kaldor as 'Keynesian' because of the use of the condition that savings equals investment. Kaldor's response to criticism that the $S = I$ condition cannot be used to do two things at once was to suggest that the savings - investment equality be used to determine the level of income in the short run and the distribution of income in the long run.

The Degree of Monopoly in the Long Run

The question arises as to what exactly is the relationship between the 'Keynesian' and 'Kaleckian' theories of distribution. According to Kaldor, there are four potential constraints which may prevent his model from working. The third of these is that 'there may be a certain minimum rate of profit on turnover - due to imperfections of competition, collusive agreements between traders, etc., and which we may call m, the 'degree of monopoly' rate' (Kaldor, 1980, 233). From Kaldor's perspective, the degree of monopoly appears as a form of short-period constraint, which might prevent the economy from being on its full-employment steady-state path. This seems remarkably similar to the orthodox neoclassical view that it is price rigidities which prevent economies from reaching their long-run full-employment positions.

Kalecki argued that there may be a deficiency of demand in the long run, just as there is in the short run. There is not an automatic tendency to full employment in the long run. Indeed, one of Kalecki's most-quoted statements is that 'the long-run trend is but a slowly changing component of a chain of short-period situations' (Kalecki 1971a, 165).

For this reason, we do not require a separate long-run theory of distribution.

Instead Kalecki offered us a theory of distribution based on short-period considerations. Specifically, the distribution of income depends on firms' pricing decisions, whereby the ratio of price to prime-costs, k, is determined. Kalecki (1954, 19) was explicit that the ratio need not necessarily change in the long run. To the extent that changes in technique caused, for example, by technological change, have any effect on the relation between price and unit costs, he argues that this occurs 'only to the extent to which they influence the degree of monopoly' (*ibid.*). Kalecki acknowledges that this contradicts generally accepted views. In particular, 'It is usually assumed that as a result of increasing intensity of capital ... there is of necessity a continuous increase in the ratio of price to unit prime cost' (*ibid*). This view is based on the assumption that greater capital intensity automatically leads to a rise in profits plus overheads. This need not be the case. Profits plus overheads do not necessarily rise as the value of capital rises. Kalecki's argument is not that income distribution must remain constant, nor even that it is unaffected by changes in the capital to output ratio. Rather, it is that to the extent that changes in the capital to output ratio do affect direct labour's share then this must be by affecting those factors which influence the mark-up. In other words, changes in capital intensity affect income distribution only via their effect on those institutional / environmental factors which Kalecki referred to as the degree of monopoly.

Kalecki supported his argument with data relating to United States manufacturing for the period 1899 - 1914. This shows that despite a rise in the 'Ratio of real fixed capital to production' of 31 per cent, the 'Ratio of proceeds to prime costs' changed from 133 to 132 per cent. The long-run constancy of the ratio of proceeds to prime costs for various countries has since been well documented, for example by Weintraub (1959, 1978) and Hotson (1968). Despite the dramatic technological progress of the early and mid-twentieth century, Weintraub was able to refer to time-series data for the gross business product for the United States economy and observe that 'The series in K is something really to behold, never moving up by more than 9% or down by more than 6%' (Weintraub 1959, 26).

We now re-examine the Kaldor model in the light of the above considerations. Kaldor's distribution equation (4.17) is nothing other than equation (4.10) - Kalecki's profits equation - divided by Y, but under the assumption of zero autonomous consumption by capitalists. But, in the long run, the level of income remains undetermined. According to Kaldor,

> The interpretative value of the model ... depends on the 'Keynesian' hypothesis
> that investment, or rather, the ratio of investment to output, can be treated as

an independent variable, invariant with respect to changes in the two savings propensities s_p and s .... This, together with the assumption of 'full employment', also implies that the level of prices in relation to the level of money wages is determined by demand: a rise in investment, and thus in total demand, will raise prices and profit margins, and thus reduce real consumption, whilst a fall in investment, and thus in total demand, causes a fall in prices (relatively to the wage level) and thereby generates a compensating rise in real consumption. Assuming flexible prices (or rather flexible profit margins) the system is thus stable at full employment (Kaldor 1980, 229 - 230).

The system of equations (4.14 - 4.16) is sufficient to determine only three of the variables, W, Π, Y and S. Kaldor's model is short of an equation. This is effectively provided by assuming full employment, or formally, $Y = \bar{Y}$. In effect, the Kaldor model consists of the simple demand-side macroeconomic equations of 'bastard' Keynesian economics, along with the neoclassical assumption that the economy, in the long-run, will be at full employment. In what sense does this provide a *theory* of income distribution?

Consider the effect of an increase in s_c. *Prime facie* one might consider that by reducing the value taken by the right hand side of equation (4.17), this would lead to a fall in Π/Y. However, standard short-run Keynesian theory suggests that the increased savings will cause a fall in demand, reducing the level of income. The profit share rises solely as a result of the fall in income. Furthermore, one might anticipate a further fall in investment if the level of investment is affected by changes in income. A change in any of the terms on the right hand side of equation (4.17) brings forces into play which move the economy away from full employment and thereby violate one of the assumptions of Kaldor's distribution theory.

Now compare Kaldor's model with that of Michal Kalecki. In the Kaleckian version we again have the demand-side macroeconomic equations, but interacting with the microeconomic conditions of price determination. The mark-ups established by firms, in conjunction with their investment decisions, serve to determine both the level of income and its distribution.

Joan Robinson also offered a reconciliation of the 'Keynesian' and 'Kaleckian' distribution theories:

> The proposition that the share of profits in income is a function of the ratio of investment to income is perfectly correct, but capacity and the degree of monopoly have to be brought in to determine what income it is that profits are a share of, and investment is a ratio to (Robinson 1960, 149).

This is very close to the conclusion reached above in recognising that both the micro (Kaleckian) and macro (Keynesian) factors have a role to play in determining the *level* of income. However the formalisation of the model, as in equations (4.10) - (4.13), clarifies that provided excess capacity exists, it is the degree of monopoly that determines direct labour's share.[14] This is not to say that Kaldor's equation (4.18) does not hold. Of course it does. It simply tells us what the relationship between these variables must be if the economy is to be in equilibrium, in the sense that savings and investment plans are fulfilled and firms have adjusted their prices to attain the desired mark-ups in the face of the institutional and environmental influences upon them. Furthermore, the equation holds whether or not the economy is at full employment.

Conclusions

The 'degree of monopoly' is appropriately understood as referring to the various institutional and environmental influences on firms' pricing behaviour in those sectors of the economy where prices are determined by marking up prime costs. By setting prices, firms simultaneously determine the share of value added going to direct labour. Trade unions influence income distribution via their ability (a) to constrain the mark-ups which firms seek and (b) to secure increases in money wages at a rate which prevents firms from achieving their desired mark-ups over time.

The famous Kaldor-Pasinetti equations, relating the profit share to savings propensities and the investment - output ratio, are interesting expressions of the relationship between these magnitudes which must hold if an economy is to be on a particular steady-state growth path. They do not provide a theory of income distribution in that they do not explain the causes of changes in income distribution.

Notes

1 See e.g. Reynolds (1987).

2 $\bar{m}$ is the average of m weighted by total costs of each firm; $\bar{n}$ is the average of n weighted by respective outputs (Kalecki 1954, 16 n 1).

3 The circumstances which may give rise to each case were previously discussed in Kalecki (1940, 101). In the earlier paper Kalecki argues that a necessary, though not sufficient,

condition for cut-throat competition to develop is a dispersion in the levels of prime costs facing the different firms. Strong firms might then attempt to improve their relative position by driving weaker firms from the industry.

4 See Asimakopulos (1975, 314-5); Kalecki (1971a , 168).

5 For a discussion of different concepts of competition, see Auerbach (1989).

6 In a number of models, reputedly in the Kaleckian tradition, originating from Cowling and Waterson (1976), this is captured by a 'conjectural variation' term. However, a problem with such an approach is that the term is treated as a constant.

7 This is the well-known equation derived in Kalecki (1954, 28).

8 See, for example, Reynolds (1987) and the paper by Arestis in this volume.

9 See, for example, Kenyon (1978); Appelbaum (1979); Sawyer (1989, 356).

10 The original proposal was by Wallich and Weintraub (1971); see also Weintraub (1978, part 3).

11 The exact periods differed according to data availability and were: Italy 1951-75; US 1948-76; UK 1954-73; West Germany 1953-73; Argentina 1955-72.

12 Weintraub (1981), for example, argued that the control of prices is superfluous and plagued with many difficulties, such as how to deal with price rises accompanying changes in product specification.

13 See, for example, Arestis (1992, 133-7).

14 This does not mean that the level of demand has no part to play in income distribution. It has a role in allocating the non-direct-labour share between profits and overheads. As the level of economic activity increases, overheads may be spread more thinly, so that the share of output accruing to profits increases, while direct labour's share remains unchanged.

References

Appelbaum, E. 1979. 'Post-Keynesian Theory: The Labour Market.' *Challenge* 21(6), January/February: 39-47.

Appelbaum, E. 1982. 'The Incomplete Incomes Policy Vision.' *Journal of Post Keynesian Economics* 4(4), Summer: 546-557.

Arestis, P. 1986. 'Wages and Prices in the UK: The Post-Keynesian View.' *Journal of Post Keynesian Economics* 8(3), Spring: 339-358.

Arestis, P. 1992. *The Post-Keynesian Approach to Economics: An Alternative Analysis of Economic Theory and Policy.* Aldershot: Elgar.

Asimakopulos, A. 1975. 'A Kaleckian Theory of Income Distribution.' *Canadian Journal of Economics* 8(3), August: 313-333.

Auerbach, P. 1988. *Competition: The Economics of Industrial Change.* Oxford:

Blackwell.

Cowling, K. and Waterson, M. 1976. 'Price-Cost Margins and Market Structure.' *Economica* 43(171), August: 267-74.

Hayek, F. 1948. *Individualism and Economic Order.* Chicago : University of Chicago Press.

Hotson, J. 1968. *International Comparisons of Money Velocity and Wage Mark-ups.* New York: Kelley.

Kaldor, N. 1980. 'Alternative Theories of Distribution.' In N. Kaldor, *Essays on Value and Distribution*, 2nd ed. London: Duckworth.

Kalecki, M. 1938a. 'The Determinants of Distribution of the National Income.' *Econometrica* 6(2), April: 97-112.

Kalecki, M. 1938b. 'The Lesson of the Blum Experiment.' *Economic Journal* 48(189), March: 26-41.

Kalecki, M. 1939. *Essays in the Theory of Economic Fluctuations.* London: Allen and Unwin.

Kalecki, M. 1940. 'The Supply Curve of an Industry Under Imperfect Competition.' *Review of Economic Studies* 7, February: 91-112.

Kalecki, M.1941. 'A Theory of Long-Run Distribution of the Product of Industry.' *Oxford Economic Papers* (old series) 5, June: 31-41.

Kalecki, M. 1943. *Studies in Economic Dynamics.* London: Allen and Unwin.

Kalecki, M. 1954. *Theory of Economic Dynamics.* London: Allen and Unwin.

Kalecki, M. 1969. *Studies in the Theory of Business Cycles.* Oxford: Blackwell.

Kalecki, M. 1971a. *Selected Essays on the Dynamics of the Capitalist Economy.* Cambridge: Cambridge University Press.

Kalecki, M. 1971b. 'Class Struggle and Distribution of National Income.' *Kyklos* 24(1) : 1-9 (Reprinted in Kalecki 1971a).

Kenyon, P. 1978. 'Pricing in Post-Keynesian Economics.' *Challenge* 21(3), July/ August: 43-48.

Keynes, J. M. 1973. *The General Theory of Employment, Interest and Money.* Collected Writings VII. London: Macmillan.

Kriesler, P. 1987. *Kalecki's Microanalysis.* Cambridge: Cambridge University Press.

Kriesler, P. 1989. 'Methodological Implications of Kalecki's Microfoundations.' In M. Sebastiani, ed. *Kalecki's Relevance Today.* London Macmillan: 121-141.

Lerner, A. P. 1934. 'The Concept of Monopoly and the Measurement of Monopoly Power.' *Review of Economic Studies* 1, June: 57-175.

Mair, D., Reynolds, P. J. et.al. 1995. 'Kalecki's Degree of Monopoly Revisited.' Mimeo.

Osiatynski, J. 1992. 'Price and Monopoly in Kalecki's Theory.' In P. Arestis and V. Chick, eds. *Recent Developments in Post Keynesian Economics.* Aldershot: Elgar: 82-94.

Reynolds, P. J. 1983. 'Kalecki's Degree of Monopoly.' *Journal of Post Keynesian*

Economics 5(3), Spring: 493-503.

Reynolds, P. J. 1984. 'An Empirical Analysis of the Degree of Monopoly Theory of Distribution.' *Bulletin of Economic Research* 36(1), May:59-84.

Reynolds, P. J. 1987. *Political Economy: A Synthesis of Kaleckian and Post Keynesian Economics*. Brighton: Wheatsheaf.

Riach, P. 1971. 'Kalecki's Degree of Monopoly.' *Australian Economic Papers* 10(16) June: 50-60.

Robinson, J. 1960. *Collected Economic Papers. Volume Two*. Oxford: Blackwell.

Robinson, J. 1969. 'A Further Note.' *Review of Economic Studies* 36(3): 260-2.

Sawyer, M. C. 1985. *The Economics of Michal Kalecki*. London: Macmillan.

Sawyer, M. C. 1989. *The Challenge of Radical Political Economy: Radical Alternatives to Neoclassical Economics*. Brighton: Harvester-Wheatsheaf.

Sylos Labini, P. 1979. 'Prices and Income Distribution in Manufacturing Industry.' *Journal of Post Keynesian Economics* 2(1), Fall:3-25.

Seideman, L. S. 1983. 'Keynesian Stimulus Without Inflation.' *Journal of Post Keynesian Economics* 6(1), Fall: 39-46.

Wallich, H. and Weintraub. 1971. 'A Tax-Based Incomes Policy.' *Journal of Economic Issues* 5(2), June: 1-19.

Weintraub, S. 1959. *A General Theory of the Price Level, Output, Income Distribution and Economic Growth*. Philadelphia: Chilton.

Weintraub, S. 1978. *Capitalism's Inflation and Unemployment Crisis*. Reading, Mass. : Addison: Wesley.

Weintraub, S. 1981. 'A Prices and Incomes Policy.' In D. Crane, ed. *Beyond the Monetarists*. Toronto: Lorimer: 67-89.

5 KALECKI ON THE TRADE CYCLE AND ECONOMIC GROWTH

Malcolm Sawyer

Introduction

The purpose of this chapter is to review Kalecki's contribution to the understanding of the business cycle and to growth, and to relate his contribution to other works in these areas. The phenomenon of the business cycle was central to Kalecki's economic analysis of capitalism and his discovery of the importance of aggregate demand for the level of economic activity was undertaken in the context of cyclical fluctuations. His earliest and some of his last writings were concerned with cycles and growth, and involved a continuous search for an improved understanding of these issues.

Kalecki's analysis of capitalism had four features which are particularly relevant for this chapter. First, the level of economic activity is strongly influenced by the level of aggregate demand: capitalism is demand- rather than supply-constrained. Second, and related to the first, unemployment is a general characteristic of capitalism, and even at the top of the business cycle there is rarely full employment.[1] Third, he made little use of equilibrium analysis and from the beginning (in 1933) his theorising of the role of aggregate demand was within a business cycle framework. Fourth, the key ingredient driving aggregate demand is investment expenditure rather than consumer expenditure.

The generation of cycles is closely linked to investment, which itself is set by a form of accelerator mechanism. It should be noted that Kalecki's formulation did not link investment decisions to changes in output *per se*, but rather to variables such as changes in the rate of profit which tend to be correlated with output. Further, he argued that investment decisions were linked with both the level of economic activity and changes in economic activity, as will be illustrated below. Indeed, Kalecki viewed 'the determination of investment decisions by, broadly speaking, the level and the rate of change of economic activity' as the *pièce de résistance* of economics (Kalecki 1968, 263). But economic activity (and changes therein) is relevant through its impact on savings and profitability, and not because it creates the requirement for a larger capital stock to produce a higher level of output.[2] He argued that 'it would appear to be more realistic to base the acceleration principle on the grounds suggested above than to deduce it from the necessity of expanding capacity in order to increase output. It is well known that large reserve capacities exist, at least throughout a considerable part of the cycle, and that output may therefore increase without an actual increase in existing capacities. But whatever the basis of the acceleration principle may be, it is inadequate not only because it does not take into consideration the other determinants of investment decisions examined above, but also because it does not agree with the facts. In the course of the business cycle, the highest rate of increase in output will be somewhere close to the medium position. This, however, is unrealistic' (*ibid.*, 285)

Kalecki (1971, 167) made 'drastic simplifications to concentrate the attention of the reader on the most essential issues without, however, throwing out the baby along with the bath-water', and in his analysis of the business cycle these drastic simplifications included the use of a closed private economy in which workers' savings are zero. It is indicated below that there are a range of other forces involved in the business cycle which appear to be complimentary with Kalecki's approach. It should be noted that the analyses presented below all refer to a closed private sector economy, and in doing so I am largely following Kalecki's approach. This is, of course, not to say that foreign trade and government activity have no effect on the business cycle but rather that the purpose of this exercise is to isolate the workings of the private domestic economy and the underlying causes of the business cycle. Any specific business cycle will, of course, be influenced by the behaviour of the traded sector (exchange rates, demand in the rest of the world etc.) and of the government sector as well as by random factors.

Kalecki's analysis of cycles omits a range of forces which feature in other analyses of the business cycle. Some of these other forces would be consistent with Kalecki's analysis and indeed could with some advantage be integrated into that analysis. But other forces would be alien in spirit, if not directly inconsistent with Kalecki's approach. It will be evident from the discussion below that Kalecki in effect assumed a passive monetary system which would provide credit on demand which would permit expansion to occur (further discussed in Dymski, this volume).[3] But it is clear from his other writings that he acknowledged that banks could choke off any prospective expansion through an unwillingness to lend and/or by raising interest rates (on loans) in response to any increased demand for loans (to finance investment expenditure). '[T]he possibility of stimulating the business upswing is based on the assumption that the banking system, especially the central bank, will be able to expand credits without such a considerable increase in the rate of interest. If the banking system reacted so inflexibly to every increase in the demand for credit, then no boom would be possible on account of a new invention, nor any automatic upswing in the business cycle. For then there would be a change only in the structure of investments made, not in their volume. Investments would cease to be the channel through which additional purchasing power, unquestionably the *primus movens* of the business upswing, flows into the economy' (Kalecki 1990, 489). Further, his analysis could be seen to reflect his conception of the Polish (and other) economies in the inter-war and early post-war period. Thus it would not be inconsistent with the analysis of Kalecki to introduce brakes on expansion which arise from an unwillingness of the banks to finance that expansion. The approach of post Keynesian authors, notably Minsky (e.g. Minsky 1982) focusing on financial instability would add a further dimension, namely that there can be disturbances in the financial system which adversely effect the real economy.

The conflict between wages and profits lies at the heart of the Goodwin analysis (Goodwin 1967, 1982) of the business cycle. In his approach, savings out of profits determine investment, and high rates of accumulation raise employment levels and then real wages. This reduces profitability and accumulation, followed by a fall in real wages, which then re-stimulates accumulation. Goodwin's analysis generated a self-perpetuating cycle, and does deviate from Kalecki's approach in the important respect of not involving an independent investment function. But the influence of profits on investment, and the struggle over income shares, are fully consistent with the ideas of Kalecki.

Whilst these two sets of ideas would, at least at a general theoretical level, not be inconsistent with the general thrust of Kalecki's approach to economic analysis[4], the recent dominant literature on business cycles would be. The cycle in new classical macro-economics has two specific features. First, the cycle is around a level of full employment, and hence sometimes involves over-employment and other times under-employment. Kalecki (cf. quote in note 1 below) clearly thought that full employment was not even always achieved at the top of the cycle. Second, the cycle is driven by expectational mistakes over prices, and Kalecki's approach pays little regard to the role of prices or to expectational mistakes.[5]

It could be said that Kalecki's approach was a fixprice one. First we note that Kalecki made tthe distinction between cost-determined and demand-determined prices, with the former predominant in the industrial sector and the latter in the primary goods sectors. Prices are not rigid, but rather cost-determined; prices move in response to cost changes but are little affected by demand variations. Over the course of the trade cycle, prices and wages may well vary, both in absolute and relative terms. But Kalecki did not see those price movements as having any significant effect on the course of the trade cycle. In effect, it is permissible to work in real terms.

However, in other work Kalecki suggested that the price-cost margin and the degree of monopoly may vary counter-cyclically : 'there is a tendency for the degree of monopoly [and thereby the price-cost margin] to rise in the slump, a tendency which is reversed in the boom', though this is only the basic tendency and there can be price cutting in the depression. Kalecki, though, argued that "gross profitability is at each moment determined by the mechanism of the business cycle" and that 'fluctuations of the share of gross profits in aggregate output during the trade cycle are independent of the wage struggle' (Kalecki 1990, 100). Essentially, real gross profits are determined by prior real investment decisions and hence are not affected by changes in money wages. However, in an open economy 'wage reductions or increases will unquestionably cause a shift in the distribution of social income between capitalists and workers' (*ibid.*, 101).

Although Kalecki's early work on the business cycle was undertaken in the context of a stationary economy followed by modification of the equations to bring in the trend, he later regarded this as unsatisfactory. He argued that '[b]y this separation of short and long-run influences I missed certain repercussions of technical progress which affect the dynamic process as whole. I shall now try to avoid splitting my argument into these two stages as much as I shall try to avoid applying the approach of moving equilibrium to the problem of growth' (Kalecki 1991, 435-6). Below, I discuss first Kalecki's approach to the 'pure' business cycle so as to highlight the forces generating the cycle, and then proceed to consider growth with cycles.

Technical Issues

A fully satisfactory theory of the business cycle must include mechanisms which generate change and which lead to continuous fluctuations that neither die away nor explode. Kalecki struggled with the technical problem of finding a mathematical formulation which would generate self-perpetuating cycles. He sought to overcome it in a number of different ways. His first attempt was to assert that the values of the key parameters in his model were such that the solution to the equation describing the time path of investment was indeed a stable (non-explosive, non-dampening) cycle. But this requires a precise relationship between the empirical values of these parameters, and there is no particular reason to think that the relationship would hold (and indeed slight changes in one or more of the parameters would disturb the relationship). Kalecki (1935a) initially adopted this approach, but was sharply criticised for doing so by Frisch and Holme (1935) and soon dropped this approach.[6] The multiplier-accelerator model developed by Samuelson (1939) generated a second-order difference equation which faces the same difficulties, and indeed it was argued that for the key parameters were likely to generate explosive cycles. The 'solution' to this difficulty advanced by Hicks (1950) was to subject the cycle to 'ceilings' and 'floors', so that, for example, output continues to rise until it hits the 'ceiling', after which output growth slows and then output falls. Kalecki rejected this approach since 'there is no confirmation for the theory that the "ceiling" is usually reached in the boom' (Kalecki 1954, 139)

A second attempt arises from arguing that the solution of the business cycle equation is generally a damped one, but that the cycle is kept going by various exogenous shocks. Kalecki (1954, chapter 13) argued by means of elementary simulations that random shocks acting on the underlying business cycle equation could generate a roughly constant cycle. There is the crucial difficulty with this approach, which Kalecki recognised, that if the shocks are in some sense large then the time path of output or investment is largely determined by the shocks rather than by the underlying business cycle equation.

The technical resolution to these difficulties was found (within economic analysis) by Kaldor (1940), whose model appeared 'to generate self-sustaining cycles without the need for rigid specifications of parameters and the use of time lags and initial shocks' (Chang and Smyth 1971) when he introduced non-linearities into the investment and savings equation and shifts in those functions through changes in the capital stock.[7] Following the pioneering analysis of Goodwin (1967), it is now clear that non-linear equations can generate (under certain conditions) limit cycles, which are self-perpetuating cycles towards which the actual cycles tend.[8] Kalecki did not incorporate this mathematical advance into his work, and his analysis remains incomplete in the sense that his model has not been shown to be capable of self-perpetuating cycles.[9] However, he did allow for variations in some of the key parameters of his equations which were not formally analysed but could help to generate perpetual cycles: one specific case is discussed below

Kalecki's Analysis of the Business Cycle

The central feature of Kalecki's explanation of the business cycle is the influence of investment on economic activity, and hence the determinants of investment.[10] Steindl

(1981) identifies three versions by Kalecki of the trade cycle, each of them having a different view of the determinants of investment, and this categorisation of Steindl is followed here.[11] In particular, Steindl observes that there are differences in the ways through which profits influence investment and the impact of the size of the existing capital stock on investment. However, Kalecki's different approaches can also be divided into those which are 'pure' cycles (that is involve, on average, zero growth) and cycles-with-growth. The discussion in this section concentrates on the 'pure' cycles case, and the discussion of cycles-with-growth is postponed until the following section.

Kalecki built in to his analysis the equality between savings and investment (in the context of foreign trade and the government budget being in balance). Investment decisions are assumed to be implemented in full though not immediately. This implementation can be assumed because of the acknowledgement of a lag between the decisions and the actual investment expenditure and that credit expansion permits the investment decisions to be financed. No distinction was drawn by Kalecki between desired and actual savings or, equivalently, between *ex ante* and *ex post* savings. Hence savings are generated by the level of investment, but there is no consequent effect if the actual savings deviate from desired savings (for the level of income, profits etc.). There is also no lag between consumption (and savings) out of profits and the receipt of profits.

Version 1

Kalecki's first theorising on the trade cycle[12] also forms the basis of the claim that he anticipated Keynes in a number of key respects.[13] [14] It will be clear that investment expenditure plays a key role in the generation of the business cycle: ('[t]he business cycle theory presented here is one which starts from investment processes and pays special attention to the time of construction of capital equipment' (Kalecki 1990,67).

The first part of Kalecki's exposition deals with the relationship between gross profits and capitalists' expenditure. This gives:

$$P = \frac{C+A}{1-q} \tag{5.1}$$

where P is gross profits, q is the propensity to consume out of profits, A is gross accumulation,[15] and C is the constant part of capitalists' consumption. The derivation of this equation assumes zero savings by workers, and the instantaneous equality between gross accumulation (A) and savings out of profits. This equation contains Kalecki's equivalent of the multiplier, and is a relationship which occurs without lags (apart from that between accumulation and investment decisions). Aggregate inventories are assumed to remain constant throughout the cycle, and then gross accumulation is equal to the production of capital goods. The distinction is drawn between investment orders (denoted by I), production of investment goods (A) and deliveries of finished equipment. There is a simple lag between orders and deliveries, but the recognition of the lag makes it reasonable to assume that the demand for investment (the orders) is fulfilled by supply (the deliveries).[16] Investment orders (relative to the size of the capital stock) depend on anticipated net profitability, which in turn is seen to be influenced by actual gross profitability (rate of profit) and the interest rate. Since (as discussed below) the interest rate is taken to vary with the rate of profit, and using equation (4.1) to substitute for profits, yields an investment equation which in its linearised form is :

$$\frac{I}{K} = m\frac{C+A}{K} - n \tag{5.2}$$

where m and n are shown by Kalecki to be positive. This forms the basis of the mechanism of the cycle, which runs as follows. An increase in investment orders leads to a rise in production of investment goods (accumulation) which further stimulates investment activity. However, at some stage the capital stock (K) begins to rise, and this initially slows down and then reverses the increase in investment orders.

Equation (5.2) involves the gross capital stock (K) and gross investment (I) which, minus replacement needs, is the derivative of K. Manipulation (see Kalecki 1990, 82-3) eventually yields:

$$J'(t) = \frac{m}{v}[J(t) - J(t - v)] - nJ(t - v) \tag{5.3}$$

where J is the deviation of investment from its average level, J' its derivative, and v is the average period of construction of investment goods. This is a mixed difference-differential equation for which there may be many solutions. Kalecki sought to establish that there is one solution for which the amplitude remains constant. 'This case is especially important because it corresponds roughly to the real course of the business cycle'. He then argued that, with that condition satisfied, the other parameters of the model are such that a regular cycle of around 10 years would be generated which conforms with the general pattern of the time of a cycle of the order of 8 to 12 years in length.[17](Frisch reports them as $m = 0.95, n = 0.121, v = 0.6$). Frisch (1935) argued that '[t]he imposition of the condition that the solution shall be undamped is in my opinion not well founded. It is more correct, I think, to be prepared to accept any damping which the empirically determined constants will entail and then explain the maintenance of the swings by erratic shocks' (Kalecki 1990, 447). But Frisch and Holme do show that Kalecki's contention that there was at most one root giving a period longer than v was correct.

In this approach, profitability in the investment equation appears as a proxy for future profitability. Apart from the obvious point that current profitability may not be a good guide for future expected profitability, two other points can be made. First, Kalecki assumed that the rate of interest is an increasing function of gross profitability, and '[t]his assumption ... may be maintained only so long as (i) i is a "market" rate, i.e. we leave aside interventions of the central bank; and (ii) there is no crisis of confidence when, during the depression, the rate of interest rises' (Kalecki 1990, 74). Second, the relevant index of future profitability could be seen as the incremental rate of profit, which may or may not be well proxied by the average current rate of profit.

Kalecki gradually moved away from the idea of the influence of future profitability on investment to the influence (operating through finance) of current profitability. In Kalecki (1937) he had introduced the 'principle of increasing risk', which strongly suggests that the volume of profits influences the availability and cost of both internal and external finance. He argued that investment decisions will be an increasing function 'of the difference between the marginal [*prospective*] rate of profit and the rate of interest' (Kalecki 1991, 306) with the long-term rate of interest as the relevant one but assumed constant. The marginal rate of profit is determined by the level of national income and the stock of capital equipment.

Version 2

The second version of Kalecki's approach to the business cycle (identified by Steindl with Kalecki, 1943) makes this influence of the availability of finance clearer ('the inflow of new gross savings ... push forward the barriers set to investment plans by the limited accessibility of the capital market and "increasing risk"' (Kalecki 1991, 164) and also expresses the idea that previous additions to the capital stock have an adverse impact on current investment decisions.[18] In addition it brings in the demand prospects facing firms into the investment decisions. The firm's financial resources are based on its current savings, though, in Kalecki's terms, there is 'incomplete re-investment': that is, additional savings generate some additional investment but on a less than one-for-one basis. In this model, as is generally the case with the work of Kalecki, a range of simplifying assumptions and approximations are made. The basic equation for investment decisions is:

$$D_{t+w} = R_t + (1-c)\left(NI_t - s_t\right) + a\,\frac{dP_t}{dt} - bNF_t \qquad (5.4)$$

where D refers to investment decisions, R to replacement investment, NI to total net investment and NF to the net addition to fixed capital equipment, s to rentiers' savings and P to profits. Kalecki argued that this equation contains some of his previous modelling and the accelerator model (where $b = 0$, $c = 1$) as special cases. He then proceeded to make a range of further assumptions and approximations (e.g. that investment in inventories averages out at zero over the cycle) to reach his final equation. But since the final equation does not throw any further light on the cyclical mechanism, those further approximations need not detain us here. Instead attention is focused on the influences on investment decisions in equation (4.4). These influences are threefold. First, the term $(1 - c)(NI_t - st)$ relates to the availability of internal finance, bearing in mind that the equality between total savings and total investment is accepted and that workers savings are zero: hence the second term refers to total savings minus rentiers' savings. Second, the term $a.\ dP/dt$ reflects the influence of increased profits on investment, with a 'by no means a constant, but a positive coefficient susceptible to various types of changes and reflecting, *inter alia*, the influence of changes in the prices of investment goods' (Kalecki 1991, 166). Thirdly, previous investment has an explicitly negative effect on current investment decisions, with b positive but not necessarily constant.

The variations in a are seen to play a role in the perpetuation of the cycle. At the beginning of the recovery Kalecki argued, 'the coefficient a may be assumed here very high. The entrepreneurs know that "the recovery is on". The change in profits is therefore an inducement to them, not only because the rate of profit as calculated on the basis of current profits has increased, but also because they anticipate a further considerable rise in profits in the near future, (Kalecki 1991, 172). As the recovery proceeds, the value of a declines as entrepreneurs become less optimistic about further rises in profits. As the cycle moves into a downturn, the value of a increases, meaning that as profits decline there is the prospect of further falls, and so the impact of declining profits on investment is strengthened.

Version 3

The first two versions were explicitly developed for a static economy, though Kalecki did often proceed to discuss how a trend could be introduced. This partly reflected his intention to develop a theory of the cycle without dealing with a range of other matters (which is reflected in the simplifying assumptions which he made). In the third version (Kalecki 1968), he returned to the 'continuous search for new solutions in the theory of investment decisions' (Kalecki 1971, viii). But his approach to the modelling of investment has a number of novel features.

Kalecki's discussion of investment decisions draws on the idea of looking at the parts of (existing) profits which are 'captured' by new investment. At the aggregate level, there is a rearrangement of profits between firms as well as some change in the level of profits. Kalecki then related the level of investment in a particular year to the rate of profit generated on that investment. The function $I(\Pi)$ relates investment to the rate of profit, where the first derivative of I is negative. The nature of this function is that it relates the level of investment to the rate of profit which that level of investment yields. The direction of causation in this function runs from the level of investment to the rate of profit, and the negative relationship reflects competition between firms. Kalecki postulated two aspects of this function. The first is that any new investment captures only a small proportion of the total increase in profits in a year, with the old equipment capturing the remainder. The profit accruing to the new equipment is taken as a proportion n of the change in profits ΔP. The second aspect arises only from technical progress, which leads to new machines which are more productive than old ones, and the real costs of operating old machines rises through the introduction of new machines and the consequent increases in productivity and real wages. The profit on the old machines falls and is in effect transferred to the new machines. The profit yielded by old machines falls each year by a proportion α of real labour costs. The proportion α will be larger, the greater the increase in productivity from technical progress. Real labour costs are equal to output (Q) minus profits (P) (both expressed in real terms), and hence from this second source the profits gained by new equipment will be $\alpha(Q - P)$. Thus the following equation is arrived at:

$$I(\pi) = \frac{n\Delta P + \alpha(Q - P)}{\pi} \tag{5.5}$$

Kalecki then portrays investment decisions as dependant on entrepreneurial savings, the difference $I(\pi) - I$, and the stimulus from innovations. The resulting equation for investment decisions, in conjunction with a growing stimulus from innovations, is used to generate a growth cycle, and some cycles are further discussed in the next section.

Growth and the Cycle

Whilst the early versions of Kalecki's theory of the business cycle explicitly dealt with a stationary economy, the later versions incorporated the trend as well as the cycle. The consideration of the trend introduces two new elements. The first new element concerns the determinants of the trend and its relationship with the growth of the labour force. Kalecki saw that technological change was an essential ingredient in the growth process. In the absence of technological change, net investment would eventually grind to a halt, and, as will be seen below, Kalecki in effect added on to the investment function a term which indicated the effect on investment induced by technology. It is also, of course, the case that rises in productivity come predominantly from technological change. Kalecki's approach does not include any consideration of the labour market: real wages are set by the relationship of prices to wages through the degree of monopoly, and employment is determined by the level of economic activity and demand. Hence there is no reason to think that the growth of employment will match the growth of the labour force, and so perpetually rising or falling unemployment may result, a point which is further discussed below. The second new element concerns the generation of growth and the determination of the trend. In a simple neo-classical growth model the rate of growth is set by the exogenous growth of the effective labour force (growth of labour force plus growth of technology), and the growth of output converges onto that exogenous rate. In Kalecki's approach, the rate of growth (of the capital stock, and also implicitly of output) is determined within the model, as will be seen below.

Kalecki's last paper (Kalecki 1968) on the topic of cycles and growth begins with some statements on the underlying nature of his approach which differ sharply from the orthodoxy. He argues that the analysis of the short-run and the long-run has to be integrated, which to some extent, he suggests, is a criticism of his own earlier work where 'I started from developing a theory of the "pure business cycle" in a stationary economy, and at a later stage I modified the respective equations to get the trend into the picture. By this separation of short-period and long-run influences I missed certain repercussions of technical progress which affect the dynamic process as a whole' (Kalecki 1971, 166). But it is also a criticism of the 'Keynesian' (neo-classical synthesis) approach in which demand factors were seen to determine short-run movements over the business cycle, whilst supply-side factors set the long-run growth path (along with full employment).

Another important ingredient of his approach is summarised in the oft-quoted statement that 'the long-run trend is but a slowly changing component of a chain of short-period situations; it has no independent entity' (Kalecki 1971, 165). This laconic statement, on which Kalecki did not elaborate, can be interpreted as undermining the predominant equilibrium approach to economic analysis whereby there is a long- period equilibrium around which the economy fluctuates or towards which the economy tends and which is unaffected by the short period movements of the economy. The clearest example of this is the neo-classical growth model where the equilibrium growth rate is the 'natural' rate of growth (i.e. the exogenously given growth of the effective labour force) towards which the 'warranted' rate (equal to savings propensity divided by the capital-output ratio) tends through movements in the capital-output ratio. A further example would be the Sraffian/neo-Ricardian approach where the prices of production, based on an equalised rate of profit, are centres of gravity for market prices. Kalecki's statement could be read as saying that the economy cannot be modelled in terms of a long-run equilibrium which can be identified (without consideration of the short-run or path to the equilibrium) and a short run adjustment mechanism by which the economy moves towards the long-run equilibrium. Rather the short-run situation and its evolution has to be examined, and from this the long-run can be built up (as something akin to the average of the short-run or the trend through successive short-run situations).[19]

Some interesting (and largely ignored) features of Kalecki's approach to growth can be seen from considering his 1954 model, which has four basic equations. The first is the equality of savings and investment ($S = I$). The second is the relationship between previous investment and current profits:

$$P_t = \frac{I_{t-\omega} + C_t}{1-q} \tag{5.6}$$

where P is profits, and q the propensity to consume out of profits. The third is the relationship of output (O) to profits which, is derived from the equation for the wage share in gross private sector income:

$$O_t = \frac{P_t + B_t}{1-\alpha} + E_t \tag{5.7}$$

where E is real aggregate indirect taxes, while α and B govern the movements in the wage share.[20]

The fourth equation is that for investment:

$$I_{t+\theta} = \frac{a}{1+c} S_t + b\frac{\Delta P_t}{\Delta t} + e\frac{\Delta O_t}{\Delta t} + d_t \tag{5.8}$$

where S refers to savings and d to 'developmental' factors (e.g. innovations) which stimulate investment. The coefficient a reflects the influence of savings, and c the effect of changes in the capital stock on investment decisions in the initial investment equation. The first three terms, whilst slightly different from the previous formulations, reflect familiar influences on investment. The final term represents the stimulating effect on investment of a stream of innovations. Innovations can be broadly interpreted 'to include kindred phenomena, such as the introduction of new products which require for their manufacture new equipment, the opening up of new sources of raw materials which make necessary new investment in productive and transportation facilities etc.' (Kalecki 1991, 334).

These equations can now be combined to yield an equation for the evolution of investment:

$$I_{t+\theta} = \frac{a}{1+c} I_t + \frac{1}{1-q} \left(b + \frac{e}{1-\alpha} \right) \frac{\Delta I_{t-\omega}}{\Delta t} + L_t + d_t \qquad (5.9)$$

where the term L_t is defined as:

$$L_t = \frac{1}{1-q} \left(b + \frac{e}{1-\alpha} \right) \frac{\Delta C_t}{\Delta t} + \frac{e}{1-\alpha} \frac{\Delta B_t}{\Delta t} + e \frac{\Delta E_t}{\Delta t} \qquad (5.10)$$

The movement in investment is decomposed into two elements, which can be identified as the trend or long-run movement, labelled y_t, and the cyclical element, labelled i_t. The long-run movement is defined as the variable which satisfies the equation:

$$y_{t+\theta} = \frac{a}{1+c} y_t + \frac{1}{1-q} \left(b + \frac{e}{1-\alpha} \right) \frac{\Delta y_{t-\omega}}{\Delta t} + L_t + d_t \qquad (5.11)$$

The equation for the cyclical element is then achieved by the subtraction of (5.11) from (5.9), which gives:

$$i_{t+\theta} = \frac{a}{1+c} i_t + \frac{1}{1-q} \left(b + \frac{e}{1-\alpha} \right) \frac{\Delta i_{t-\omega}}{\Delta t} \qquad (5.12)$$

Equation (4.12) provides the business cycle equation. Our focus here is on the long-run equation (4.11), for this is the one which relates to the growth process. The 'driving force' in this equation comes from L_t and d_t and it is necessary to consider their determinants. It can be seen from equation (4.10) that L_t depends on changes in C, B and E, which Kalecki postulated, as a working hypothesis, vary proportionally with the long-run level of investment (and so with the level of income). Hence L varies proportionally with $\Delta y/\Delta t$, albeit with a lag so that $L_t = \sigma \Delta y_{t-\omega}/\Delta t$.

The economy would be stationary in the absence of innovations.In those circumstances, investment would be constant and equal to depreciation of the capital stock (which he takes as βK), and $\Delta y_{t-\omega}/\Delta t = 0$. With those substitutions, equation (4.10) would yield $d = (1 - n)\beta$, where n is used to denote $a/(1+c)$, and this gives one component of the development factor term. The other component comes from the impact of a stream of innovations on investment, which Kalecki took to be proportional to the capital stock, or γK, where K is a measure of the capital stock. Hence we have:

$$d_t = n\beta K_t + \gamma K_t \tag{5.13}$$

Denoting $(1/1-q).(b + e/1-\alpha) + \sigma$ by m, and making the necessary substitutions, we arrive at:

$$y_{y+\theta} = ny_t + m \frac{\Delta y_{t-\omega}}{\Delta t} + (1-n)\beta K_t + \gamma K_t \tag{5.14}$$

Denoting the growth of (gross) investment by v, approximating $(1/y_t) (\Delta y_{t-\omega}/\Delta t)$ by v, and with $y_{t+\theta}/y_t$ equal to $1 + \theta v$, the equation for the growth rate is given by

$$1 + \theta v = n + mv + \frac{(1-n)\beta + \gamma}{\beta + v} \tag{5.15}$$

which is a quadratic in v which may have none, one or two roots of interest. This equation provides the growth rate of investment (and by implication that of output). In the case where $m < \theta$, one root is negative whilst the other is positive. When the inequality is reversed, there will be two roots (which possibly coincide) or no real roots. When there are two roots, the smaller has the property that the development factor influences growth positively whilst the larger involves the development factor influencing growth negatively.

This equation for the growth rate of investment is of interest in at least two related ways. First, there is no reason to think that this essentially demand-side determined rate of growth (of investment) will be consistent with a constant level of employment or with full employment. Second, the growth rate depends on a range of parameters which reflect the behaviour of enterprises: for example n $(=a/1+ c)$, where a is the 're-investment factor' and c the effect on investment of past growth of the capital stock. There is no pre-determined or exogenously given growth rate which governs the growth of output or investment within the model. A clear contrast can then be drawn with the neo-classical model, where the growth of output is set by the 'natural' rate of growth (which equals the growth rate of the labour force in the simple case and that rate plus the rate of technical change in the more general case). In effect, Kalecki's analysis provides for an endogenous rate of growth, albeit one which rests on the stimulating effect of innovation on investment.

Kalecki (1962) is more clearly focused on growth, and represents some further modifications to the model just considered; its properties have been discussed by Gomulka et al (1990). In the discussion here, the formulation of Gomulka et al rather than Kalecki's own formulation is used.[21] The investment equation reads:

$$I_{t+1} = (a-c)I_t + \frac{bm_1}{h}(I_t - I_{t-h}) + bn \tag{5.16}$$

where K_t' is the 'trend' value of the capital stock, ϵ the stimulating effect of innovations, a, b, and c have similar meanings to those above, and m_1 and n_1 are coefficients from the consumption out of profits function.[22] Gomulka et al show that this can provide an equation for growth of the form:

$$g_{t+1} = \xi g_t + \frac{\eta}{h}(g_t - g_{t-h}) + \eta g_t g_{t-h} + \varepsilon \tag{5.17}$$

where $\xi = a + bn1 - c$ and $\eta = bm$. For constant growth (i.e. $g_{t+1} = g_t$) a quadratic equation in the growth rate g is obtained, of which the larger root can be shown to be unstable, and the smaller is $\frac{1}{2}\left[1 - \xi - (\{1-\xi\}^2 - 4\,\eta\epsilon)^{\frac{1}{2}}\right]$. This growth rate is the demand-induced rate, and the influence of the innovation-induced investment parameter can be readily seen. Kalecki did not discuss the stability of this smaller growth rate, but Gomulka et al show that it may be unstable (it is stable only if $h > \frac{2\eta}{}$). Gomulka et al argue that Kalecki's investment equation should be modified, essentially because the trend rate of profit included therein (and equal to n_1) did not make allowance for the impact of innovation-induced investment on profits, and that the trend rate of profit should be $m_1 g_t + n_1$. With that substitution made, eqaution (4.16) has the slight change that c is now equal to $bm_1 g_r$. This yields the following equation:

$$g_{t+1} = ag_t + \frac{bm_1}{h}\left(g_t - g_{t-h}\right) + bm_1 g_t\left(g_{t-h} - g_t\right) + \epsilon \tag{5.18}$$

which has just one solution for balanced growth of $\epsilon/(1-a)$, which is stable under conditions essentially similar to those identified for the smaller of the growth rates above.

However, as Gomulka et al argue, the growth rate g of the capital stock and of output does not bear any particular relationship to the growth of the labour force. Signifying the growth of productivity which arises from innovations as λ (where it is assumed that the ratio K/Y is constant along the trend growth path), then the growth of employment would be given by $g - \lambda$. If that rate is less than the growth of the labour force then there is ever-increasing unemployment; otherwise unemployment declines towards zero. In the latter case, full employment would be reached. The economy then becomes supply constrained, and growth is determined by the growth of the labour force. Although Kalecki did not discuss this aspect of his theory, the following points can be made. First, the growth of the labour force is not determined by the growth of population but varies with changes in the participation rate: over a range the growth of the labour force adjusts to the growth of labour demand. People may be pulled into or ejected from the labour force. Second, the trend growth rate in Kalecki's model will, of course, change with any variation in the underlying parameters of the model, and different eras may well display different parameter values. In some eras, the trend growth rate may involve employment growing faster than the labour force whilst others may involve the reverse. In addition the eras in which the employment rate is rising may not last long enough for full employment to be achieved.

Kalecki's growth model (see Kalecki 1968) can also be used to analyse capacity utilisation. His model suggests that the trend degree of capacity utilisation depends on three factors: positively on the rate of depreciation, and on the maximum rate of growth of a function which depends on consumption out of profits and the stimulus to investment from innovations; and negatively on the degree of monopoly.

Nature of Growth under Capitalism and Differences with Socialism

A number of features of the nature of growth under capitalism as perceived by Kalecki stand out from the above discussion. Kalecki saw his own analysis as showing 'that long-run development is not inherent in the capitalist economy' (Kalecki 1991, 337). He viewed innovations as the "most important promoter of development". Writing in 1954, and to some degree echoing Steindl (1952), he thought that 'a decline in the intensity of innovations in the later stages of capitalist development results in a retardation of the increase in capital and output' (*ibid.*, 337). He also saw a rising degree of monopoly and rentiers' savings, through their adverse effects on consumer expenditure and investment, as leading to a slowing-down of the long-run rate of growth. Unemployment obviously rises when the growth of output falls short of the growth of productivity plus the labour force, but 'this is not likely to set forces to work which would automatically mitigate the rise in unemployment by inducing a higher rate of increase in output'.

One feature which is not readily evident from the above focus on algebraic formulations is that 'the rate of growth at a given time is a phenomenon rooted in the past economic, social and technological developments rather than determined fully by the coefficient of our equations as is the case with the business cycle. This is, indeed, very different from the approach of purely "mechanistic" theories (based frequently on such fallacious *a priori* assumptions as a constant degree of long-run utilisation of equipment), but seems to me much closer to the realities of the process of development. To my mind future inquiry into the problems of growth should be directed not towards such semi-autonomous magnitudes as $A(t)$ and $B(t)$ [capitalists consumption and impact of innovations on investment] but rather towards treating also the coefficients used in our equations ... as slowly changing variables rooted in past developments of the system' (Kalecki 1971,183). These variables include the degree of monopoly and responsiveness of investment to profitability, and this passage of Kalecki's belief is a clear indication that the trend rate of growth will evolve over time in response to changes in the underlying parameters.

Space does not permit a discussion of Kalecki's writings on growth under socialism.[23] (see though Toporowski, this volume) but some of the features of growth under capitalism can be highlighted by way of comparison. It is convenient to begin from Kalecki's equation for the rate of growth of output:

$$r = (1/m)(I/Y) - a + u \qquad\qquad (5.19)$$

where r is the rate of growth of output, m the productive effect of gross investment (which is labelled I), a the loss of production due to depreciation, and u the change in utilisation of productive capacity. This equation is effectively an identity, and as such holds under capitalism and under socialism. The differences, as seen by Kalecki, are under threefold. First, capitalist economies are viewed as demand-constrained whereas socialist economies are supply-constrained. Second, decisions over savings and investment are in the hands of the private sector (predominantly the capitalists) whereas under socialism those decisions are in the hands of the planners. Third, there may be more price flexibility under socialism than under capitalism, since in capitalism prices (relative to wages) are set by the relevant degree of monopoly, which may change with the industrial structure but is not flexible enough to restore balance between savings and investment at full employment.

Conclusion

Kalecki saw business cycles as an endemic feature of capitalism, and grounded his analysis of them in the movement of investment, which itself depended on the level and rate of change of economic activity. In this chapter I have suggested that, whilst Kalecki's analysis focuses on the role of demand, it could be broadened to include the role of monetary and financial factors and the struggle over income shares. Kalecki viewed the business cycle and growth being closely linked, and in both investment had a key role to play. Growth requires a stream of innovations for it to be maintained, but the rate of growth depends on a range of factors including the degree of monopoly and socio-political variables.

Notes

1 'A considerable proportion of capital equipment lies idle in the slump. Even on average, the degree of utilization throughout the business cycle will be substantially below the maximum reached during the boom. Fluctuations in the utilization of available labour parallel those in the utilization of equipment. Not only is there mass unemployment in the slump, but average employment throughout the cycle is considerably below the peak reached in the boom. The reserve of capital equipment and the reserve army of unemployed are typical features of capitalist economy, at least throughout a considerable part of the cycle' (Kalecki 1991, 311).

2 Kalecki (*ibid.*, 167) argued that the simple acceleration principle (which he took to be that the rate of investment decisions net of depreciation is proportional to the rate of change in profits) 'has been definitely disproved by statistical enquiries'. Further, he argued that the 'acceleration principle requires that the rate of investment decisions is highest when profits (or output) pass through their medium position in the cycle on the way upwards. The facts, however, show that most investment decisions are reached in a much more advanced stage of the boom'. Kalecki (1950; reprinted in 1991,. 191-202) sought to argue on the basis of the cyclical movements of output and investment that investment (more accurately investment decisions) were a function of both the level of output and its rate of change. However, he argued 'the high level of income [is] correlated [with] a high level of savings, and that the stream of new savings stimulates investment because it makes it possible to undertake investment without increasing indebtedness' (*ibid.*,.198).

3 This is subject to the caveat that 'there is ... [a] factor which is of decisive importance in limiting the size of a firm: the amount of entrepreneurial capital, i.e. the amount of capital owned by the firm. The access of a firm to the capital market, or in other words the amount of rentier capital it may hope to obtain, is determined to a large extent by the amount of its entrepreneurial capital. It would be impossible for a firm to borrow capital above a certain level determined by the amount of its entrepreneurial capital' (*ibid.*,.277). I would interpret this to mean that there is a distinct limit on a firm's ability to raise finance, but most firms most of the time are operating well below that limit, so that an expansion of investment demand is not generally financed-constrained. But retained profits have a significant influence on the availability of finance and thereby on investment decisions.

4. There may be an over-determinacy problem, which I have discussed in another context: see Sawyer (1995, chapter 6).

5. In one regard Kalecki could be seen as using adaptive expectations, in the sense that expectations of future profitability are based on current profitability. But there is no role for expectational mistakes in Kalecki's approach, and there is a sense in which firms' expectations as to current demand are realised.

6. The interchanges between Kalecki and Frisch (and others) over Kalecki's original analysis of the business cycle and other background material are reproduced in Kalecki *ibid*.,. 436-479.

7. Kaldor (1940) discussed Kalecki's model and criticised it on the grounds, inter alia, that 'with the theories of the Tinbergen-Kalecki type, the amplitude of the cycle depends on the size of the initial shock. Here the amplitude is determined by endogenous factors and the assumption of 'initial shocks' is itself unnecessary'. For further discussion see Kalecki (1990,.526-28). Kalecki (1990.175, n 49) that his approach has 'a certain affinity to that of Mr Kaldor. He obtained his results by examining a special case of my theory in the *Essays* which I have failed to consider. His theory is therefore based on the assumption of a particular shape of the functional relation between income and the rate of investment decisions; and it is difficult to advance any satisfactory a priori reasons for this shape being necessarily as he assumes. In my present theory the cycle is prevented from being damped down by variations in a (the coefficient of the infuence of profits upon the rate of investment decisions), and the pattern of these changes in variations seems to me much better founded than the shape of Mr Kaldor's curve'. Jarsulic (1994) views Kaldor (1940) as producing a synthesis of Kalecki and Harrod, and 'like Kalecki, he [Kaldor] assumed that financial constraints and changes in income distribution would provide a ceiling to the growth of demand, and that autonomous investment would prevent a collapse of demand'.

8. For a variety of approaches to the business cycle see, for example, Nell and Semmler (1991, part V), and for a convenient introduction see Jarsulic (1994).

9. See Goodwin (1989) for his views on Kalecki's approach.

10. In the presentation of Kalecki's analyses of the business cycle I have kept as close as possible to the original symbols, but have made some changes to avoid the same symbol being used for different concepts, as Kalecki's own use of symbols varied between different versions.

11. Kalecki presented many versions of his trade cycle theory, some of which are essentially similar.

12. This was initially published in 1933 in Polish. Partial translations were Kalecki (1935a) and (1935b), in French. Now fully translated into English in Kalecki (1990, 66-108).

13. For further discussion on the relationship between Kalecki and Keynes, see Sawyer (1985, chapter 9), and Chapple, this volume.

14. It may also benoted that Kalecki assumed for most of the analysis inthe1993 article that 'fre competition rules unhindered,'and thenconsideration two pages the implications of cartels. But it is significant that his theory of business cycless andof the occurrence of unemployment did not depend in any way on imperfect competion or the degree of monopoly.

15. It can be noted that initially Kalecki refers to A as savings, though almost immediately he indicates that 'A includes...all goods which are used in the reproduction and expansion of fixed capital as well as the increase in inventories. In the future. A will be referred to as gross accumulation.'

16. Note that Kalecki works out the relationship between orders, accumulation and deliveries in some detail in many of his papers on investment.

17. Post-war cycles have often been seen as closer to four years in length, though the experience of the 1980s in the US and UK does not readily confrom to that pattern.

18. For another discussion of Kalecki's second version see Sordi (1988).

19. Thus Kalecki would be more in line with the approach of Robinson (e.g. 1962, 1980) than Garegnani (1976) over the independent existence or otherwise of the long period. For a recent overview see Park (1994).

20. The wage share, which is total income minus profits divided by income, is taken as equal to a + B/Y, reflecting the degree of monopoly. From this, income can be derived as equal to $(P + B)/(1-\alpha)$, and output is equal to private secotor income plus indirect taxes, yielding eqn. (5.7) in the text.

21. These differences are relatively slight and concern the value of the trend rate of profit.

22. The consumption out of profits functions is $CP=pP + Q$, which yields $P=I/(1-c) + A/(1-c)$; m_1 is used for $1/(1-c)$ and $A/(1-c)$ is written as n_1K.

23. For Kalecki's writings on this see Kalecki (1972, 1933), and Sawyer (1985, chapter 11).

References

Chang, W. W. and Smyth, D.J. 1971. 'The Existence and Persistence of Cycles in a Nonlinear Model: Kaldor's 1940 Model Re-examined'. *Review of Economic Studies* 38(1), January: 37-44 .

Frisch, R. 1933. 'Propagation Problems and Impulse Problems in Dynamics'. In *Economic Essays in Honour of Gustav Cassel.* London: Frank Cass.

Frisch, R and Holme, H. 1935. 'The Characteristic Solutions of a Mixed Difference and Differential Equation Occurring in Economic Dynamics'. *Econometrica* 3(2), April: 225-39.

Garegnani, P. 1976. 'On a Change in the Notion of Equilibrium in Recent Work on Value and Distribution: a Comment on Samuelson'. In M. Brown, K. Sato and P. Zarembka (eds) *Essays in Modern Capital Theory.* Amsterdam: North Holland: 22-45.

Gomulka, S, Ostaszewski, A. and Davies, R.O. 1990. 'The Innovation Rate and Kalecki's Theory of Trend, Unemployment and the Business Cycle'. *Economica* 57(228), November: 525-40.

Goodwin, R. 1967. 'A Growth Cycle'. In C. H. Feinstein ed. *Socialism, Capitalism and Economic Growth.* Cambridge: Cambridge University Press: 54-8.

Goodwin, R. 1982. *Essays in Economic Dynamics.* London: Macmillan.

Goodwin, R. 1989. 'Kalecki's Economic Dynamics: a Personal View'. In Sebastiani 1989: 249-51.

Jarsulic, M. 1994. 'Business Cycles'. In P. Arestis and M. Sawyer eds. *The Elgar Companion to Radical Political Economy*. Aldershot: Elgar: 24-8.

Kaldor, N. 1940. 'A Model of the Trade Cycle'. *Economic Journal* 50(197), March: 78-92.

Kalecki, M. 1935a. 'A Macrodynamic Theory of Business Cycles'. *Econometrica* 3(3), July: 327-44.

Kalecki, M. 1935b. 'Essai d'une Theorie du Movement Cyclique des Affaires'. *Revue d' Economie Politique* 2.

Kalecki, M. 1949. 'A New Approach to the Problem of Business Cycles'. *Review of Economic Studies* 16(2): 57-64. Reprinted in Kalecki 1991: 191-202.

Kalecki, M. 1968. 'Trend and Business Cycles Reconsidered'. *Economic Journal* 78(310), June: 263-76. Reprinted in Kalecki 1971: 165-83 and in Kalecki 1991: 191-202

Kalecki, M. 1971. *Selected Essays on the Dynamics of the Capitalist Economy*. Cambridge: Cambridge University Press.

Kalecki, M. 1972. *Selected Essays on the Economic Growth of the Socialist and the Mixed Economy*. Cambridge: Cambridge University Press.

Kalecki, M. 1990. *Collected Works of Michal Kalecki Volume 1*. Ed. J. Osiatynki. Oxford: Clarendon Press.

Kalecki, M. 1991. *Collected Works of Michal Kalecki Volume 2*. Ed. J. Osiatynski. Oxford: Clarendon Press.

Kalecki, M. 1993. *Collected Works of Michal Kalecki Volume IV*. Oxford: Clarendon Press.

Minsky, H. 1982. *Can 'It' Happen Again?: Essays on Instability and Finance*. Armonk, N Y.: Sharpe.

Nell, E. J. and Semmler, W. eds. 1991. *Nicholas Kaldor and Mainstream Economics: Confrontation or Convergence*. London: Macmillan.

Park, M. S. 1994. 'Long Period'. In P. Arestis and M Sawyer, eds. *The Elgar Companion to Radical Political Economy*. Aldershot: Elgar: 249-55.

Robinson, J. 1962. *Essays in the Theory of Economic Growth*. London: Macmillan.

Robinson, J. 1980. 'Time in Economic Theory'. *Kyklos* 33(2): 219-29.

Sawyer, M. 1985. *The Economics of Michal Kalecki*. London: Macmillan.

Sawyer, M.1995. *Unemployment, Imperfect Competition and Macro-economics*. Aldershot: Elgar.

Sebastiani, M. 1989. *Kalecki's Relevance Today*. London: Macmillan.

Sordi, S. 1989. 'Some Notes on the Second Version of Kalecki's Business-Cycle Theory'. In Sebastiani 1989: 252-74.

Steindl, J. 1981. 'Some Comments on the Three Versions of Kaleckis Theory of the Trade Cycle'. In J. Los *et. alia* eds. *Studies in Economic Theory and Practice. Essays in Honour of Edward Lipinski*. Amsterdam: North Holland: 125-33. Reprinted in J. Steindl, *Economic Papers 1941-88*. London: Macmillan, 1990: 139-48.

6 KALECKI'S MONETARY ECONOMICS

Gary A. Dymski

The *real barrier* of capitalist production is *capital itself.* (Karl Marx 1967, III: 250)

Introduction

Kalecki and Keynes share honors for discovering the principle of aggregate demand. But whereas Keynes set out this principle in a static model expressed in Neoclassical language, Kalecki explored it in a disequilibrium dynamic model incorporating Marxian and Classical insights about class conflict and income distribution. Geoffrey Harcourt has characterized Kalecki's writings as 'the most profound of the twentieth century' (Harcourt, 1987). Nonetheless, Kalecki has exerted less influence than Keynes, even among heterodox economists.[1]

The author gratefully acknowledges the comments of Philip Arestis, Geoffrey Harcourt, John King, Edward Nell, Bob Pollin, and Howard Sherman on an earlier version of this paper. All remaining errors are the author's responsibility.

This essay examines Kalecki's monetary economics from a Post Keynesian perspective, and finds this neglect unwarranted. Kalecki's period approach to firms' microeconomic behavior sheds new light on the contemporary debate over the importance of finance constraints. Further, Kalecki's principle of increasing risk both foreshadows New Keynesian credit rationing models and also exposes limitations in the New Keynesian approach. Kalecki's investment/profit model suggests how real-sector forces can be integrated into Minsky's financial cycle model. Finally, Kalecki's conceptions of the links between micro and macro analysis, and between finance and power, are important for contemporary debates. In sum, Kalecki's monetary ideas suggest ways of bridging the gaps between what Harcourt and Hamouda (1992) call the three strands of Post Keynesian economics, and hence of countering these strands' fragmentation into mutually appreciative but non-intersecting discourses.[2]

Monetary Themes in Kalecki's Model of Capitalist Dynamics

Scholars are in broad agreement that Kalecki's monetary approach is underdeveloped (see, e.g., Kregel 1989; Kriesler and McFarlane 1993; Sawyer 1985a). Osiatynski observes:

> Kalecki's [monetary] assumptions require modification. On the one hand, changes in the supply of and the demand for finance capital are determined by factors which are not fully allowed for in his theory. On the other hand, those changes determine the investment decisions of the private sector in a more complex way than Kalecki has postulated. (Osiatynski 1986, 19; bracketed word is added)

We might add that monetary concepts seldom appear in Kalecki's mature writings; when they do, the author treats them sparingly. For example, in the various permutations of Kalecki's dynamic investment model, financial elements are incorporated only partially, and the banking system consistently plays a passive role.[3] But is this treatment, as Osiatynski suggests, due to the partial-equilibrium character of Kalecki's model,[4] or does it instead reflect disinterest in monetary phenomena - or even a judgement that these phenomena are second-order?

Kalecki's early writings on capitalist economies demonstrate his appreciation of monetary issues, and suggest that the paucity of monetary elements in his formal model(s) reflects a strategic choice. In 'The world financial crisis', written in 1931, Kalecki demonstrates his acute awareness of the causes and consequences of the collapse of financial asset prices, and of the loss of public confidence in banks and/or national currencies. In 'Mr. Keynes's predictions' (1932), Kalecki comments critically on Keynes' evocation of devaluation as a solution for the world financial crisis. Kalecki implicitly disagrees that the stabilization and realignment of financial prices will rescue the capitalist economies from their fatal flaw. Kalecki argues instead that a 'Reduction of wages during crises' (1932) is the real 'universal remedy' being applied by capitalist governments and ruling classes.

In the next three years, Kalecki formulated his investment/profit model of the business cycle. Interestingly, this model excludes the 'fatal flaw' which had preoccupied Keynes and other economists, and focuses instead on a neglected aspect of these dynamics: the class struggle over distribution.[5] Kalecki argues in his 'Essay on the business cycle theory' (1933) that since the interest rate varies pro-cyclically, it can be treated as an increasing function of the profit rate. This eliminates the interest rate as a variable and effectively removes financial considerations from the model. Kalecki warns that this simplification holds only if 'there is no crisis of confidence when, during the depression, the rate of interest rises' (Kalecki 1991a, 74) and if the central bank does not intervene. In a later chapter, 'The money market,' Kalecki discusses how banks first expand their credit in cyclical upturns, and then eventually increase deposit rates due to their decreasing liquidity (1991a, 93-98). In this chapter, Kalecki again discusses banking panics; he concludes that 'leaving out crises of confidence is crucial to our theory,' because allowing financial factors fuller scope would invalidate the stylized laws of motion of his dynamic model.

In a subsequent essay, 'A macrodynamic theory of business cycles' (1935), Kalecki again subsumes the short-term interest rate in the profit rate. This time he takes just a sentence to justify this simplification, and then notes that ignoring 'technical conditions in the money market' (1991a, 137), investment finances itself.[6] His 1939 essay, 'The theory of economic fluctuations,' makes the same simplifying interest rate/profit rate assumption. However, this essay includes two chapters devoted to monetary topics - one on the principle of increasing risk (first published in *Econometrica* in 1937) and another on the long-term interest rate - and thus incorporates, for the first time, all the monetary elements of his business cycle theory.

We will examine the monetary analysis in Kalecki's mature model in some depth, relying primarily on the 1954 *Theory of economic dynamics*. Not only did Kalecki make important refinements to his model in this volume, but he also emphasized therein the financial determinants of investment (Steindl, 1991). Kalecki's exposition unfolds in three parts: first, he examines the determinants of profits, especially investment spending; second, he discusses the determinants of investment, among which are anticipated and realized profits; and third, he interweaves these two elements into a business-cycle model driven by the two-way interactions of profits, investment, and output.

Kalecki begins with his price theory: firm prices constitute a markup over prime costs, whose size depends on the firm's degree of monopoly. This readily suggests a class theory of income distribution wherein *Gross investment = Gross profit + Capitalist consumption*. Kalecki observes that this relation is 'independent of the rate of interest which was customarily considered in economic theory to be the factor equilibrating the demand for and supply of new capital.' Contrary to the Quantity Theory view, 'in the present conception investment, once carried out, automatically provides the savings necessary to finance it' (1954, 50).

Kalecki then develops a model of output determination. In this model, capitalists' consumption behavior is based on lagged realized profit flows; profit flows are determined by lagged investment spending; and national output in any period is a determinate function of current profit flows. Kalecki's model contains an investment multiplier similiar to Keynes', except that lagged (not current) investment spending determines output. The level of output varies inversely with the markup and with capitalists' consumption propensity out of profits.

Kalecki next examines the determinants of interest rates. He argues that interest rates do not result from the interplay of the supply and demand for capital (loanable funds); instead, he proposes distinct explanations of the short-term and long-term interest rate. The short-term rate, in his view, is a function of the volume of transactions and of the supply of money (that is, the quantity of bank accounts and notes); and the supply of money is in turn determined by banking policy. Kalecki observes,

> It has been frequently assumed that velocity is constant, and this is indeed the cornerstone of the quantity theory of money. But it seems fairly obvious that the velocity of circulation in fact depends on the short-term rate of interest. Indeed, the higher the short-term rate the greater is the inducement to invest money for short periods rather than to keep it as a cash reserve. (Kalecki 1954, 73)

This treatment resembles Keynes' discussion of liquidity preference; but it is evident in context (1954, 74 n 1) that Kalecki's remarks pertain to corporate treasurers, not wealthowners (rentiers). Banks are envisioned as holding a supply of bills and bonds as well as of reserves (1954, 78); the supply of bank money and the short-term interest rate thus shift upward (downward) when banks buy (sell) bills and/or bonds. So the supply of money is endogenous.

The long-term interest rate, in Kalecki's view, is determined additively by two factors: the expected short-term rate; and the risk of loss due to differences between current and expected future long-term rates. Since long-term rates respond only partially to changes in short-term rates, they are more stable than short-term rates. 'Indeed,' Kalecki concludes, since 'the long term rate of interest ... does not show marked cyclical fluctuations, it can hardly be considered an important element in the mechanism of the business cycle.' (1954, 88)[7]

Kalecki now turns to his second central topic -- the determinants of investment. He again begins with the behavior of the non-financial firm. Because of Kalecki's markup theory of pricing, the question of how much any one firm invests is equivalent to the question of what limits any one firm's growth. He rejects scale diseconomies in production and the limitations of the firm's market, and instead proposes a third factor, 'the amount of the capital owned by the firm.' Kalecki argues that 'firms below a certain size have no access whatever to the capital market.' (1954, 92) But even firms above this size are finance-constrained due to what Keynes called 'lender's risk' (Keynes 1936, 144):

> The access of the firm to the capital market, or in other words the amount of rentier capital it can hope to obtain, is determined to a large extent by the amount of its entrepreneurial capital. ... Even if the firm should undertake to issue the bonds at a higher rate of interest than that prevailing, the sale of bonds might not be improved, since the higher rate in itself might raise misgivings with regard to the future solvency of the firm. (Kalecki 1954, 91-92)

And common stock cannot be issued indefinitely as a means of financing firm growth, since 'a joint-stock company is not a "brotherhood of shareholders" but is managed by a controlling group of big shareholders while the rest of the shareholders do not differ from holders of bonds with a flexible rate of interest. (*ibid.*, 93). Kalecki cautions that firm expansion may also be slowed by another financial factor, the 'principle of increasing risk.' This factor, which is akin to Keynes' 'borrower's risk,' exists because at least some capitalists are risk adverse and because profits are more variable, the more highly leveraged is any unit of capital.

These financial constraints explain why firms of a different size can coexist within any given industry; and 'It follows ... that the expansion of the firm depends on its accumulation of capital out of current profits' (*ibid.*, 92).

Kalecki then sets out an aggregate model of investment, wherein:

$$F_{t+\tau} = aS_t + b\frac{\Delta P_t}{\Delta t} - c\frac{\Delta K_t}{\Delta t} + d \qquad (6.1)$$

Here $F_{t+\tau}$ represents investment spending for fixed capital at time $t+\tau$, which is completely determined by a prior investment decision at time t. So in effect, period-t investment decisions are a linear function of S_t, gross savings, and the time rates of change of aggregate profits, P_t, and the capital stock, K. All four parameters (a, b, c, and d) are positive. Kalecki's discussion makes clear that financial factors affect the motion of equation (6.1) via coefficient a. The magnitude of a increases when firms borrow and leverage their retained earnings, but decreases when the size of firms' existing markets shrinks, when firms enter risky new markets (1991b, 289), and when rentiers fail to reinvest all the savings they are apportioned by firms.

Kalecki's conception of capitalist dynamics concludes by exploring the character of cyclical fluctuations; he argues that the parameters in equation (6.1) above will be less than one, and hence cycles will be damped. The economy does not settle down to a stationary path due to occasional stochastic shocks. Investment cycles thus arise endogenously -- capital, as Marx put it in the quote reproduced above, is the 'real barrier' to the growth of capital.

Kalecki performs several experiments with the dynamic, two-class model summarized in equation (6.1). One especially leads to an arresting result: in a no-trend economy, with zero (average) net investment and zero net savings, any positive net savings by salary earners and rentiers implies offsetting negative net savings by entrepreneurs. So, over time, the ownership of capital passes from entrepreneurs to rentiers, and investment becomes increasingly externally financed; but this implies a slowdown in investment spending, since external financing depresses entrepreneurs' investment plans. It follows that, if the trend growth rate is sufficiently slow, this ownership shift will occur, leading to more external financing and slower investment spending. This experiment is of interest because it reproduces aspects of the historical experience of the U.S. and the U.K. in the 1980s, and of Japan in the 1990s.

Kalecki's Vision and the Three Post Keynesian Economics

Kalecki's writings clearly foreshadow concepts that have subsequently become building blocks of both New and Post Keynesian economics; see the following section. Yet finance and monetary elements play a paradoxical role in his conception: they are repeatedly discussed, but have limited effects on the model's dynamic motion. That this treatment reflects Kalecki's design, as discussed above, does not resolve the problem.

To understand this paradox, and to grasp how Kalecki's monetary economics intersects with Post Keynesian economics, we turn to a schema suggested by Harcourt and Hamouda (1992). These authors identify three broad approaches within Post Keynesian economics. The first approach is the Sraffian; rooted in Marx and Ricardo, it focuses on the long period as a centre of gravitation. Distribution is crucial, but uncertainty is analytically insignificant, and ex ante/ex post tension unimportant. The long period framework makes financing invisible.

The second tradition is associated with Davidson. This approach regards the long period as being without meaning. Distribution is important for pricing behavior. Uncertainty is irreducibly present, and exerts independent effects on investment and saving behavior. Time is 'real'; it destabilizes linkages across time for complex processes, and introduces continual problems of stock/flow imbalance. Finance constraints may exist, but the supply of money is endogenous. Agents faced with uncertainty must devise means of overcoming its effects; chief among these means are credit contracts, which sometimes take a monetary form.

Interestingly, the third tradition identified by Harcourt and Hamouda is that of Kalecki and Robinson.[8] In this approach, the long period exists as a reference point, but may be unattainable; economic motion is primarily cyclical - that is, short-run.[9] Financing constraints can be important in cyclical dynamics. Uncertainty exists, and expectations and realizations typically differ. Distribution is crucial in pricing behavior and in economic dynamics.

So the first Post Keynesian approach uses a dynamic equilibrium model rooted in intertemporally stable parameters; the second, a 'real time' disequilibrium framework that denies the existence of intertemporal parameters; the third proposes a dynamic disequilibrium model governed by evolving intertemporal parameters.

These approaches suggest different monetary economics. Schumpeter's distinction between 'real' and 'monetary' analysis (Schumpeter 1954: 276; see also Rogers 1987) offers a useful way to characterize these differences. In a real analysis, all essential features of the economy - including money and financial assets - respond to real forces (technology, preferences, power); the volumes of money and nominal claims have no significant effect. In a monetary analysis, by contrast, money is not a neutral means of pricing and acquiring real goods, but 'affects motives and decisions . . so that the course of events cannot be predicted, either in the long period or in the short, without a knowledge of the behavior of money between the first state and the last' (Keynes 1973, 408-9).

The Sraffian approach clearly embodies real analysis, while Davidsonian analysis is preeminently monetary. But Kalecki's model combines elements associated with both approaches. This is the source of confusion. As in the Sraffian model, Kalecki postulates the existence of time-invariant parameters governing cyclical motion; but, as in the Davidsonian approach, Kalecki denies that long-period positions constitute a behavioral centre of gravitation.

Kalecki's formal cyclical model is 'real': it explains capitalist economies' essential laws of motion without allowing for feedback effects from variations in monetary stocks, prices, or flows. This is immediately evident on reviewing equation (6.1) above. Monetary factors simply form part of the parametric backdrop of cyclical motion. This construction disallows any behavioral reactions due to divergences between what was hoped for ex ante and what has happened ex post; agents treat future values as pre-given or at least probabilistically certain.

Finance constraints *can* be incorporated into logically consistent 'real' models, as long as the underlying preferences and technology are appropriately specified.[10] For example, in the well-known model of Diamond and Dybvig (1983) agents contend with microfounded finance constraints in an equilibrium setting.[11] Analyses of this sort are 'real' because the effect of shocks can be dampened or eliminated if they are properly anticipated ex ante.

But Kalecki's framework cannot be encompassed in a real analysis; his theoretical building blocks can be *consistently* combined only in a monetary analysis. Kalecki assumes a disequilibrium world; this implies a monetary analysis irrespective of any conditions imposed on preferences and technology. Further, a disequilibrium analysis like Kalecki's is inherently 'monetary' because agents seeking to carry value forward must rely on nominal assets whose real value is not predetermined within the system. That is, in a disequilibrium analytical world the Davidsonian conception of time and uncertainty is the only consistent approach.[12]

But as Kalecki developed it, his model is real and not monetary. One problem is his shallow treatment of uncertainty. Kalecki develops the conceptual basis of his cycle model as if it were deterministic; only when estimating it empirically does he reveal that his business cycle mechanism is disturbed by normally distributed shocks (Kalecki 1954, chapters 10-13); and these shocks appear, as error terms, without comment. But where do these shocks come from, and why do not agents react to the risks that continual shocks pose? At best, Kalecki's micro conception is an inappropriate underpinning for his macro model of monetary disequilibrium.[13]

His interest-rate theory is also untenable as a monetary analysis. Kalecki's notions that crises of confidence can be ignored, that 'short-term credit can be depended on to finance any expansion in step with output and sales' (1991b, 291), and that the long-term rate can be ignored because it does not vary cyclically, all avoid the problem of uncertainty.

The next two sections link Kalecki's structural model of investment cycles with the monetary (Davidsonian) Post Keynesian approach. This will allow a deeper appreciation of finance constraints and credit rationing, and will suggest links between Minsky's financial instability hypothesis and the 'real' factors stressed by Kalecki.

Kalecki's Monetary Micro Analysis

Kalecki's micro analysis touches on monetary themes in two areas: his treatment of finance constraints and his notion of increasing risk. We discuss these topics in order, and then briefly discuss other monetary aspects of his micro analysis.

Finance constraints

Kalecki explicitly included finance constraints in his model. Keynes did not, in the *General Theory*, but in subsequent articles clarifying his intentions in that volume, Keynes emphasized the importance of finance constraints.[14] Asimakopulos (1983) stimulated a prolonged debate among Post Keynesians when he examined these authors' conceptions of finance constraints and concluded that the fundamental Keynesian notion that 'investment precedes savings' might be incoherent because it the financing of investment.

Papers by Kregel and Davidson largely resolved the conceptual points at issue in this debate. Kregel observes that when finance constrains investment spending, the unavailability of loanable funds may be attributed to two very different causes: the lack of savings or the 'liquidity preferences of the banks' (Kregel 1986, 94). The first explanation suggests a 'real' limitation on investment, the second a 'monetary' one; and since a Kalecki/Keynes framework must embody monetary analysis, Kregel argues, it can admit finance constraints only of the second kind. Davidson clarifies matters further when he observes that 'bank-created (non-resource using) finance must be distinguished from the role of long-term financial markets which require the public to give up an amount of liquidity equal to real savings (i.e., unexercised income claims on resources) in the process of funding the investment.' (Davidson 1986, 101). Davidson cautions that 'the financial system ultimately can restrict accumulation because of a shortage of liquidity, even when idle resources and entrepreneurial `animal spirits' exist' (*ibid.*, 105n; and see *ibid.*, 108-110).[15] Pollin and Justice provide empirical support for these conclusions: they demonstrate that there are at best 'loose connections' (1994, 305) between savings and finance flows.[16]

This resolution affirms Kalecki's approach in building his model, since this model asserts both that finance constraints matter *and* that investment precedes savings.[17] Left unresolved, however, is a further question that has been little discussed in this debate: how important is it to incorporate finance constraints (and credit relations) explicitly in Keynes/Kalecki models?[18]

Kalecki's and Keynes's own writings illuminate this question. The defining characteristic of a Keynes/Kalecki macro model is that shortages of saving do not cause shortages of investment. The models developed by Keynes and Kalecki embody this notion differently, and have very different implications concerning the importance of explicitly including finance constraints.

Keynes in the *General Theory* develops his ideas in the context of a one-period, static framework. Investment is always self-financing in a framework of this sort due to two factors: (1) the investment multiplier has time to work itself out completely, so the savings required to finance investment are always endogenously generated; and (2) the tension between investment orders and investment spending (emphasized by Kalecki) disappears, and with it the need to worry about short-term financing, because the time needed for initiating investment is merely a fraction of the relevant analytical short period.

So clearly finance constraints cannot be meaningfully introduced (unless the period framework of the model is conceptualized differently, as we discuss below). What makes the analysis *potentially monetary* is, ironically, the lengthy time this one-period approach encompasses - a span extending from the implentation to the termination of any investment project. In effect, all the ramifications of the uncertainty about the future that Keynes emphasizes *may* affect agents' behavior through volatile investment and liquidity preference 'functions,' *if* the theorist chooses to recognize them.[19]

In Kalecki's model the emphasis is different, and consequently so is the monetary framework. Kalecki relies on an investment multiplier argument in his complete model of income determination. However, in the accompanying analysis of the determinants of investment, Kalecki makes it clear that his effective analytical period is short. Kalecki's short period is too short to allow for returns on investment projects with long payback horizons; the investment multiplier can hardly begin to work itself out before decisions must again be made. And from (short) period to period, economic agents are receiving stochastic shocks, which confront them with new sets of ex ante constraints. So Kalecki's deterministic approach centers on a prior step in the chain of events - that is, on how investment plans are converted into investment orders and thence into new in-place plant and equipment. And what breaks the connection between changes in savings and changes in investment at *this* stage of the investment cycle is banks' flexible lending capacity.

This short-period focus leads Kalecki to all but ignore uncertainty, as noted above. If it were always the case that the banking system could seamlessly accomodate non-bank units' credit needs at anticipated interest rates, Kalecki's finance constraints would never bind. What makes his analysis monetary (and not real) at this stage is the possibility of disequilibrium - rationing - outcomes in the markets for finance. And this possibility emerges because of (as Keynes puts it) banks' reluctance to become less liquid, *not* because of the spectre of uncertainty over investment projects' fate.[20]

This discussion suggests that whether finance constraints matter analytically depends on the relative weight given to two distinct phases: first, the period before investment goods are up and running; and, second, the period after the investment expenditures occur, during which multiplier effects are working themselves out. Figure 1 illustrates this point. This figure divides investment projects into five stages, from planning to full depreciation. Kalecki's investment-determinants model encompasses the middle three stages - the placement of investment orders, the delivery of investment goods, and their initial deployment. Keynesian investment-multiplier models ignore these planning/order/delivery stages, and instead encompass the last two stages, in which investment goods are put in place and used to exhaustion.[21]

When the fifth stage is excluded from any model, then the only goods that money can chase are those on hand; in this event, finance constraints are very likely to bind, and it is analytically crucial to describe explicitly the mechanisms for allocating credit - and hence for obtaining access to goods.[22] But as stage five is given more weight, finance constraints shrink in significance: more goods are produced within the analytical period, so income is generated endogenously, as is the pool of savings available to finance purchases. Thus finance is obtained to a larger and larger extent on income flows driven by the investment multiplier, and depends to a smaller and smaller extent on ex ante creditworthiness criteria independent of ex post income generation capabilities.

Figure 1 also sheds light on the effect of uncertainty on investment. The agents within a Post Keynesian model encompassing uncertainty will be aware of that uncertainty; so analysis must include at least stages (1) and (5) to be complete. A mechanical investment multiplier analysis, by contrast, would encompass only stage (5) and ignore stage (1).

This returns us to the question posed above - how crucial is it explicitly to incorporate finance constraints in a Keynesian model? The answer is, it depends on what a 'Keynesian model' is, and on the period analysis deployed. Models that acknowledge the impact of investment realizations can clearly qualify as Keynesian - in allowing for aggregate demand effects in a monetary analysis framework - without explicitly incorporating finance constraints. But in models that do not explicitly encompass investment realizations, finance constraints inject a Keynesian flavor, both because they embody the idea of demand constraints and because they demonstrate concretely the effects of Keynesian uncertainty within the short-period framework (even though the full effects of this uncertainty are felt in a stage excluded from analysis).[23]

Figure 1: A Schema of Investment, Finance, and Uncertainty

Investment project stages	(1)	(2)	(3)	(4)	(5)
Investment project stages	Investment plans	Investment orders	Investment good delivery	Investment goods initially used	Investment goods fully depreciated
Short-term finance (revolving fund)	Construction finance demanded by I-good producer	Construction finance supplied to I-good producer	Construction finance repaid by I-good producer	Working capital demanded, supplied to I-good user	Working capital finance paid off by I-good user
Long-term finance	Long-term finance investigated by I-good user	Long-term finance demanded by I-good user	Long-term finance supplied to I-good user		Long-term finance paid off by I-good user
Risk factors for lenders		Degree of liquidity in money market	Default risk on borrowers' projects	Liquidity and interest-rate risk on lenders' liabilities	
Risk factors for borrowers	Degree of default risk: willingness to increase leverage or decrease liquidity		Operational risks: wage levels	Operational risks: work effort, monitoring, output market conditions	

New Keynesian models

The short period in Kalecki's cycle model

Keynesian investment multiplier models

Increasing risk

Joan Robinson (1966) observed that Kalecki addresses a question unanswered by Keynes: why should investment remain limited if projects remain, not yet undertaken, that could return more than the rate of interest? It is not clear in Keynes; but Kalecki finds an answer in the firm's financial structure:

> the amount of finance that each individual enterprise will commit to investment is an increasing function of the prospective rate of profit, depending upon the ratio of borrowing to its own capital. Then, with any given distribution of capital amongst enterprises, there is a particular relation between the total amount of investment plans being drawn up at any moment and the level of prospective profits. (Kalecki 1991a, 338-9)

Tracy Mott (1990) points out that this principle of increasing risk foreshadows the New Keynesian microfoundational theory of credit markets. Indeed, Mott argues that the two approaches can be integrated: 'new Keynesianism gives microfoundations based ultimately on informational imperfections, which Kalecki did not bother to furnish, showing why rational, utility maximizing individuals would behave so as to give Kaleckian macroeconomic results (Mott 1990, 11). The structural similiarities between elements in Kalecki's model and in the New Keynesian credit-markets model are undeniable. And Kalecki's model would benefit in at least one particular from a New Keynesian insight: the notion that sticky interest rates may transmit and even magnify economic shocks. But Mott goes too far in appropriating the New Keynesian model as Kalecki's microfoundation. The two approaches are analytically distinct.

Kalecki's cumulative investment/profit cycles are anathema for New Keynesians; their rational expectations assumption leaves room only for inventory or time-to-build cycles, not the cumulative dynamic effects embodied in equation (6.1). More fundamentally, New Keynesian models focus exclusively on ex ante decision-making equilibria. They do not investigate ex post realizations and ignore the resulting stock/flow disequilibria which Kalecki insists are the essence of macroeconomic outcomes. Figure 1 shows that there is virtually no overlap between the investment stages that appear in New Keynesian and in Kaleckian models. Stiglitz (1992) observes that the firm's financial structure is endogenous within the New Keynesian framework. As a result, it makes no sense to discuss how finance constraints attributable to the firm's debt build-up would constrain its further investment spending; from the New Keynesian (stage 1) perspective, a rational firm's investment planning should encompass the entire period from the beginning to the end of any asset's lifespan.

Further, New Keynesian models are almost invariably real, not monetary. These models assume the credit market is in equilibrium, even if rationing occurs; and they are at best ambiguous about whether investment generates savings. This ambiguity arises because of the partial-equilibrium, representative-agent framework of New Keynesian models of the credit market. The supply of credit is assumed to be restricted; there is seldom any inquiry into whether this credit supply derives from bank liquidity, prior savings, or current savings. But since representative-agent models assume that agents receive endowments (savings) at birth, which they can then allocate over some lifespan, it is natural to assume that savings precede - that is, generationally constrain - investment.

This brings us to a final dissimiliarity between Kalecki's approach and the New Keynesian. New Keynesian models generally employ as little institutional detail as possible, since their aim is to demonstrate that small departures from Walrasian assumptions will yield significant differences in outcomes. Kalecki's model has a very different aim - to embody the institutional context of the real-world capitalist economy.[24]

In sum, while the metaphors of increasing risk and adverse selection are similiar, the analytical frameworks of Kalecki and the New Keynesians are very different, and so too are the uses of these metaphors in characterizing economic outcomes. This conclusion is of some relevance for the current debate over the relationship of the New and Post Keynesian economics. Some (Fazzari (1992), Fazzari and Variato (1994)) have claimed that asymmetric information is a more fundamental concept in a Keynesian approach than is Keynesian uncertainty; their argument is that the primary Keynesian result that financial structures matter and generate sticky prices follow solely when asymmetric information alone is introduced into an equilibrium framework. This assertion has met with resistance.[25] Kalecki's framework is also incompatible with Fazzari's assertion. Asymmetric information is *the* crucial analytical feature generating deviations from first-best outcomes only if the fundamental analytical reference point is a well-behaved (Walrasian) equilibrium. Kalecki's framework, of course, characterizes the economy as being fundamentally a dynamic disequilibrium system. Within *this* economy, increasing risk - due to what is today called asymmetric information - is an important factor constraining firms' behavior. But increasing risk arises because of agents' reaction to their ignorance within this dynamic disequilibrium; it is in no sense an equilibrium solution to a well-understood principle-agent equilibrium game. Agents in a Kaleckian world -- that is, in a Post Keynesian world - are affected by the principle of increasing risk precisely because they *cannot* solve problems posed by shifts in the environment and in other agents' intentions in any neat way.

Kalecki's Markup in a Monetary Light

We have observed that Kalecki's formal model is real, not monetary. From a monetary perspective, Kalecki's notion of the markup requires some deepening. For one thing, Kalecki argues that the level of the markup will increase with the degree of monopoly. But this in turn will reduce the level of financial fragility, in that the higher the markup, ceteris paribus, the more the cash flow to service debt obligations. A second modification in the markup concept is required if firms are transforming maturity (that is, financing long-term assets with short-term liabilities). For if they are, then liquidity risk is necessarily built into the markup. Then there are two options: either the markup becomes stochastic, and sensitive to financing expectations, or the markup remains deterministic *and* the firm's financing risk is being borne invisibly by other sectors (such as banking).

Financial Instability and the Kaleckian Business Cycle

The above sections have argued that Kalecki's model is incomplete because it includes real factors but ignores financial ones in characterizing the economy's disequilibrium dynamic motion. Ironically, the opposite holds true for Hyman Minsky's financial instability hypothesis (FIH). Minsky's model, like Kalecki's, is grounded in the behavior of a typical non-financial firm; but it abstracts almost entirely from 'real' variables. As Mullineux puts it, 'The FIH does not attempt to provide a complete theory of business cycles but concentrates instead on explaining speculative booms and subsequent crises' (Mullineux 1990: 62).

A union of Kalecki's with Minsky's perspectives can make each more complete: Kalecki's contribution to Minsky's model is to demonstrate the importance of feedback from real to monetary factors; and Minsky's contribution to Kalecki's model is to show the role of feedback from monetary to real factors.[26] There is space here only to discuss suggestively how this union might be approached.

Minsky's FIH is rooted methodologically in the Davidsonian strand of Post Keynesian economics. Minsky builds his cycle model on a 'two-price' construction, which formally resembles Tobin's 'q' theory of investment demand. Minsky makes 'q' conform with his disequilibrium cycle approach by adding to it Keynes' lender's and borrower's risk. Shifts in agents' expectations about future cash-flows - and hence in the magnitude of these risks - then account for cyclical turning points. His emphasis is entirely on the evolution of firms' financial positions. Firms shift from internal and toward external finance as an expansion proceeds, and hence from 'robust' to 'speculative' (and possibly to 'Ponzi') financial structures. The increasing burden of interest payments cuts into firms' cash flows. Minsky emphasizes that the upswing turns into downturn when a shock of some kind disappoints expectations and causes a downward expectational revision inconsistent with built-up financial positions. This account of the turning point neglects real-sector factors of the sort Kalecki emphasizes.[27]

Kalecki does not depend on a shock effect to generate cyclical momentum: rather, in his model exogenous shocks prevent damped oscillations from eventually yielding a steady state. But the oscillations themselves are due to structural forces within his model. Kalecki's real cycle model is summarized in equation (6.1) above. Investment varies directly with profit flows and with increases in profit flows, and inversely with increases in capital stock. Kalecki points to two factors that will convert any expansion into a slowdown: first, the endogenous evolution of the coefficient a on profit flows; second, the eventual 'flip' of the accelerator effects associated with coefficients b and c from growth-enhancing to growth-slowing. Kalecki's first factor, as he left it, is problematic. Kalecki suggests that a will decline due to two factors - rentiers' capture of a larger portion of profits and the riskiness of investment projects - which he does not link to cyclical forces. Indeed, Kalecki (1991b, 184-185, 335) describes trends in rentiers' control of savings as more important for secular trends than for cyclical fluctuation.

This is where Minsky's cyclical conception can help to complete Kalecki's. Minsky's notion of increasingly aggressive and fragile financing can explain the evolution of a in Kalecki's equation (6.1). Implicitly Kalecki's cycle anticipates a shift from internal to external financing as growth proceeds; and Minsky's FIH explains how rising external financing eventually derails expansion. Not only that, but, if the FIH holds, then the portion of (earned and unearned) income obtained by rentiers does play a role in cyclical dynamics. We can hypothesize a financial cycle dynamic of this sort: as recovery begins, financial asset prices rise, generating capital gains; these, in turn, make speculation profitable, shifting rentier funds out of 'productive' financing and raising asset prices further, even as production-based income flows weaken; weakening fundamentals force firms to take measures to keep asset prices up (by, for example, increasing their dividends). Innovations by financial intermediaries could stretch the supply of credit, allowing both more debt-financed investment and for increased leveraged purchases of financial assets.[28] However, eventually the tension imposed by the twin demands of maintaining *both* cash-flow and asset-price levels becomes too great, and a crisis ensues. Kalecki misses these Minskyian dynamics because the real-analysis grounding of his own cyclical model allows only for production-based income, not for capital gains.

What Kalecki can do for Minsky's FIH is integrate it into an account of production (surplus-extraction) processes. This integration can also make Minsky's cyclical account less dependent on expectational shocks; for, clearly, the cash flows (profits) that are needed in the FIH to service financial positions are reduced cyclically in Kalecki's model due to rising wages, a falling profit rate (as the base level of capital-in-place rises), or both. In effect, accompanying the firm's 'real' investment/profit cycle is a financial cycle, slightly mismatched with it in time, that initially amplifies and eventually undermines it.

But before this merger is sanctioned, the methodological tension between the Minsky's monetary framework and Kalecki's real framework must be addressed. It would seem that Kalecki's real approach must give way, since Minsky's financial fragility hypothesis requires a framework in which agents' financial decisions can have unanticipated real outcomes.

Kalecki on the Micro-Macro Link and on Power in Financial Relations

This section comments briefly on two further contributions of Kalecki's monetary economics to current debates: his treatment of the link between microfoundational and aggregate analysis; and his approach to the role of power in financial relations.

The Micro-Macro Link

In contemporary Neoclassical and New Keynesian analysis, two conditions must be met: aggregate behaviors must follow directly from axiomatically derived microfoundational behaviors; and the economy as a whole is understood as being in equilibrium. Kalecki's approach to microfoundational analysis is quite different. He works out a single firm's behavior, and then suggests aggregate dynamics corresponding to this behavior. In effect, he follows the first Neoclassical condition only loosely, and violates the second. As Kriesler (1989) observes, Kalecki did not privilege either the micro or macro levels of analysis as ontologically superior or methodologically prior, and his model moves seamlessly from one to the other level (see above). Davidson (for example, 1978) and Minsky, among others, handle the micro-macro link as Kalecki does.

New Keynesian economists have tried to conform with the first approach to the micro-macro link; but this puts them in an analytical double-bind. The deviations from first-best equilibria that New Keynesians postulate - due to asymmetric information in the labor or credit markets - cannot survive in an equilibrium that is too general.

New Keynesians have thus far largely managed this double-bind by setting their microfoundational models within partial equilibrium frameworks.[29] At the same time, they have used the dual Neoclassical criteria for the micro-macro link to criticize Post Keynesian models which implicitly take Kalecki's approach. Consider Stiglitz's (1992) criticism of the (Post Keynesian) idea that (aggregate) financial fragility can arise because, at the micro level, firms have burdensome debt levels which impede their investment spending. As we have seen, this idea is rooted in Kalecki's notion of increasing risk. Stiglitz argues that firm financial structure is endogenous in a well-specified model of firm decision-making: the firm, when planning its investment expenditures, should take into account how different financing structures will affect expected cash flows. In effect, firms choose their liability structures and cash-flow commitments - they are not constrained by them.

Stiglitz's critique, and implicitly his view of the micro-macro link, stands up only if one takes a very restricted view of the investment process as described by Kalecki. Stiglitz insists that models must embody ex ante equilibria - that is, in the context of Figure 1, they must encompass solely stage (1), the investment planning stage alone.

Clearly, it is difficult to introduce financial fragility if Stiglitz's approach to the micro-macro link is granted.[30] If instead Kalecki's approach to the micro-macro link is used, financial structures *can* consistently influence investment. Firm investment behavior can be viewed in a dynamic disequilibrium encompassing the entire multi-stage process of Figure 1. The time lags between investment-good orders, receipt, and deployment ensure that firms will at least sometimes have financial structures that are 'wrong' for their present circumstances. And the relentlessly dynamic context of investment requires that firms must invariably initiate new rounds of investment planning before returns are all in on previous rounds'. Using Kalecki's approach to the micro-macro link, one does not search for microeconomic behaviors that can conform with some conception of an aggregate equilibrium; rather, one seeks to describe plausible behaviors in the context of inevitable disequilibrium and dynamic flux.

Rentiers, Power, and Finance

As made clear above, one of Kalecki's legacies to economic theory is his emphasis on the distribution of wealth. As Mott (1990) observes, the existence of finance constraints on accumulation - Kalecki's theory of increasing risk -is essential for his distributional account of capitalist dynamics. Without them, every individual could be an entrepreneur. Kalecki himself was eminently aware of this link in his logic; of the relation between distribution and market power, Kalecki wrote:

The limitation of the size of the firm by the availability of entrepreneurial capital goes to the very heart of the capitalist system. Many economists assume ... a state of business democracy where anybody endowed with entrepreneurial ability can obtain capital for starting a business venture. This picture of the activities of the 'pure' entrepreneur is, to put it mildly, unrealistic. The most important prerequisite for becoming an entrepreneur is the *ownership* of capital (Kalecki 1954, 109).

Kalecki was acutely aware that market power spilled over into political control of policies that in turn reproduced the conditions required to sustain that market power. Kalecki's 'Political aspects of full employment' essay (Kalecki 1943) pointed out that full employment could not come about without creating conditions (upward wage pressure) that would undermine successful accumulation (that is, full employment itself).[31]

Kalecki's argument might be usefully extended to rentiers. For rentiers' economic interest, ceteris paribus, is in high-debt, low-inflation economic conditions. But these conditions are likely to lead to stagnation, as Kalecki showed in the 'experiment' summarized at the very end of section 2 above; and stagnation is antithetical to the interests of the industrial capitalists (represented in equation (6.1)). So tension will also arise, spilling over into the political sphere, between industrial capitalists and rentiers, the two claimants on the surplus produced by labor.[32]

Conclusion

Kalecki's distinctive approach is to view economic processes as structured, inherently dynamic disequilibria, in which decision-makers continually engage in further rounds of planning and commitment before knowing how previous decisions have worked out. This essay has shown that this approach is informed by a subtle and mature monetary conception.

Nonetheless, Kalecki purposely set financial factors into the background of his model of the business cycle. As a result, his writings treat monetary and financial dimensions of economic fluctuations in a bifurcated way: in describing aggregate dynamics, Kalecki does not consistently draw out the implications of the monetary factors he introduces at the microeconomic level. But such (micro) phenomena as increasing risk and credit-rationing arise because of the presence of fundamental uncertainty and real time, which in turn necessitate a *monetary* framework; so aggregate dynamics too necessarily involve monetary, and not just real, factors.

So Kalecki's framework is implicitly monetary. And when reinterpreted as such, this framework may offer a bridge between the different strands of Post Keynesian inquiry: a platform suitable for investigating interactions among real and monetary factors, and for examining the collision of micro behaviors with aggregate dynamics.

Notes

1 King's essay in this volume discusses some reasons for this neglect among American Post Keynesians. I would add one more. This trained engineer was preoccupied with questions of statistical measurement and empirical fit; and as such, Kalecki's writings show little sensitivity to methodological questions. This sensitivity became a necessity for later (Post Keynesian) economists engaged in debate with mainstream macroeconomists over such issues as the measurement of capital and the treatment of uncertainty.

2   This essay does not explore Kalecki's ideas on financial factors in developing economies; but see Fitzgerald (1993). Kalecki's two mature essays on this topic. 'The problem of financing economic development' (1954; reprinted in Kalecki 1993) and 'Problems of financing economic development in a mixed economy' (1963; reprinted in Kalecki 1993), both follow closely his monetary ideas as test are set out in the *Theory of Economic dynamics* (Kalecki 1954), which is the subject of section III below.

3   Throughout this essay, the terms 'monetary analysis' and 'monetary system' refer broadly to the entire complex of financial assets and markets, and not to money narrowly defined.

4   In his definitive study, Sawyer (1985a, 92) characterizes Kalecki's dynamic model as more a 'thought experiment' than a complete model.

5   All these early essays are reproduced in Kalecki (1991a). Kregel (1989) points out that Kalecki's truncated treatment of finance in the investment/savings linkage is explained by his primary interest in how changes in distribution might affect the level of profits.

6   While Kalecki purposefully ignored monetary considerations in these two essays, he remained a subtle monetary analyst. His 'The business cycle and inflation' (1932) and several subsequent essays (1991a, 147-200) demonstrate a grasp of the role of private and central bank credit inflation in the world economic crisis.

7   Kalecki would surely reconsider this conclusion in the wake of the far greater long-term (as well as short-term) interest-rate volatility in the period since 1954. Interestingly, it is precisely the relative stickiness of interest rates that has led to the New Keynesian reassessment of the importance of credit-market channel in cyclical volatility. See Dymski (1994) and Fazzari (1992) and the discussion in the section on Kalecki's's monetary micro analysis below.

8   Robinson's monetary approach resembles Kalecki's when she writes in her 1962 volume on capitalist dynamics. 'For purposes of our model [finance] is best treated, along with the 'animal spirits' of the firms, as an element in the propensity to accumulate of the economy' (Robinson 1962, 43). But elsewhere Robinson takes up monetary issues that Kalecki did not address, such as the significance of historical time for economic models.

9   While most of his work on capitalist dynamics distinguished trend from cyclical forces, Kalecki rejected this distinction late in his life; see 'Trend and the business cycle,' written in 1968, in Kalecki (1991b, 434-50).

10   See Dymski (1990).

11   The Diamond-Dybvig model offers a microfoundational rationale for why banks exist. In it, agents have available two technologies to generate consumption goods, one short-term and liquid, the other long-term, illiquid, and more productive. Agents may receive unobservable consumption shocks forcing them to prematurely liquidate their holdings of productive assets. No agent knows in advance who will die young; so in autarky all agents forego the more productive investment. Banks are large and know with certainty the proportion of their depositors will have consumption shocks; so banks can invest in the illiquid technology.

12   An assumption that uncertainty is characterized by probabilistic risk is difficult to sustain in a disequilibrium world. As Joan Robinson (1962) observes, agents who are off their demand or supply curves are not any longer in the same dimension of experience and expectation that gave rise to those curves. Calculating future expected values given the possibility that each conceivable disequilibrium outcome may lead to a new set of binding effective demand constraints etc., becomes an impossibly daunting task - even if one assumes that the numerical calculations can, in principle, be done.

13   Kalecki's treatment of uncertainty can be given a more sympathetic hearing. One could justify Kalecki's use of a deterministic framework as akin to assuming that, in the short-term, firms and individuals operate in ignorance. In effect, if agents are simply ignorant about the future, there is no meaningful way to predict future shocks. Abstracting completely from firms' expectations about their case flows suggest that firms *cannot* forecast them.

14   Keynes wrote that 'banks hold the key position in the shift from a lower to a higher scale of activity. ...The investment market can become congested through shortage of case. It can never become congested through shortage of saving.' (1937, 669) Keynes writes that 'nothing is more certain than that the credit or "finance" required by ex-ante investment is not mainly supplied by ex-ante saving' (*ibid* 664). Keynes suggests that finance has a two-stage role in investment: first, short-term finance must be obtained to initiate an investment, that is, for construction; second, the investment put in place must be financed by a long-term instrument. So Keynes argues that investment spending depends on banks' willingness to provide short-term finance, on the one hand, and on the prospects for converting this finance into a long-term issues, which depends on the level of long-term interest rates. Asimakopulos (1991, 109-115) discusses Keynes's ambiguous treatment of this matter.

15   Interestingly, Asimakopulos's original 1983 paper suggests a similar resolution: 'the achievement of a higher level of investment thus requires the banking system to become less liquid (to increase its current account liabilities, balances by IOUs from investing firms) and to maintain a less liquid position at least until the full multiplier has operated.' (Asimakopulos 1983, 225-6).

16   Pollin and Justice also find that interest rates sometimes rise when lending flows exceed savings flows. This is inconsistent with Kalecki's assertions about the stickiness and/or pro-cyclical behaviour of interest rates; however, Pollin and Justice observe that whether interest rates rise depends on institutional factors such as the occurrence or absence of financial innovations.

17   Kalecki observes of his own investment-savings equation (that is, (6.1) above) that 'investment, *once carried out*, automatically provides the savings necessary to finance it' (emphasis added; see above).

18 Messori's 1991 paper touches on this question. Messori's principal argument is that investment and production financing should be distinguished in Kalecki's framework. Messori also shows that the effect of finance constraints on real outcomes depends on whether the production of investment and consumption goods is conceptualized as instantaneous. This leads to a deeper point - within any model, a logically coherent treatment of the linkages among investment, saving, and finance is possible only if the model consistently accounts for the flow of time in economic processes. This insight is pursued further here.

19   Kregel (1976, especially the appendix) also concludes that Keynes is logically consistent in combining a 'shifting equilibrium' (here termed monetary analysis) with a static analytical framework. and Asimakopulos writes, 'The focus of attention in *The General Theory* on the stock demand for the holding of money is a logical outcome of the setting of its made in historical time, where the uncertain knowledge of future conditions cannot be ignored, and there is a role for money as a store of wealth' (Asimakopulos 1991, 86).

20   Sawyer (1985, 96) points out that banks' willingness to lend in a disequilibrium environment depends on their inherited positions, with these inherited positions in turn shifting from the end of one period to the beginning of another.

21   Kregel (1989) is certainly right in insisting that one should not overemphasize merely technical points of difference in comparing the contributions of Kalecki and Keynes. Periodization can be handled differently without altering the substantive analytical context; so the handling of basic substantive issues is of greater importance. Kregel (1994) has recently criticized Asimakopulos' approach to the finance/saving linkage on these grounds; in Kregel's view, Asimakopulos wrongly presumed that substantive causation (A causes B) necessitates temporal separation within a model (A precedes B).

22   This is the periodic framework developed by John (1981) in his defense of explicitly finance constraints in macroeconomic analysis.

23   It is interesting to note Kalecki's critique of Keynes's investment theory in light of this discussion (see Targeti and Kinda-Hass 1982, reproduced in Kalecki 1991a). Kalecki had two criticisms: first, Keynes's theory made no distinction between investment decisions and actual investment in the short period; second, Keynes assumes that a given state of expectations governs investment, but ignores the effect of investment realisations on expectations, and thus proposes static solution to a dynamic problem.

24   The treatment of financial intermediation and banking in New Keynesian economics emphasizes the requirements of equilibrium theory over institutional detail. In the Diamond-Dybvig model (see note 11), which Mullineux (190) wrongly regards as Post Keynesian, banking is not a firm or institution instead takes the disembodied form of an optimal contract. Of course, Kalecki too can be criticized for his inattention to bank behaviour.

25   Dymski (1994) counters that Keynesian uncertainty is not reducible to asymmetric information, and further than Keynesian uncertainty makes it impossible for agents to amass the amount and type of information they need to find well-behaved asymmetric-information equilibria. See also Crotty (1994).

26   Minsky has increasingly emphasized the importance of Kalecki's equation of investment with profits (see e.g., Minsky 1986). Minsky has not explicitly examined Kalecki's cyclical model in the context of his FIH. However, a letter dated November 19, 1974, from Minsky to Sidney Weintraub makes clear that Minsky was sympathetic to - and indirectly influenced by - Kalecki's framework; he wrote, 'within a cyclical perspective uncertainty becomes operational in the sense that myoptic (sic) hindsight determines the current state of Keynesian/Robinsonian Animal

Spirits: without a cyclical perspective uncertainty is more or less of an empty bag. I am indebted to John King for sharing a copy of this letter.

27 Asimakopulos (1991, 73-4) observes that Keynes *General Theory* contains two distinct and contradictory theories of the determinants of investment: the marginal efficiency of capital theory (Ch. 11), which proposes a rational calculus of the present value of cash flows; and the theory of unstable expectations in response to a fundamentally uncertain future. Minsky tries to combine these two theories into one. But since the cash-flow projections on which investment depends are shiftable, the effect is to make Minsky's investment theory entirely dependent on unstable, ungrounded expectations. Minsky's model is set out more fully, and this critique developed, in Dymski and Pollin (1992).

28 Speculation can be defined as buying an asset not for its long-run potential return, but for an anticipated short-term appreciation in its market price. Note that the dynamics set out here do not rely on irrational expectations; even if speculating units know that financial prices will eventually 'hit the wall,' competitive pressures to maximize returns in the very short run may keep them in the game (against their best longer-run judgement).

29 Of course- micro-macro consistency poses no problem in non-Keynesian models like the infinite-horizon and overlapping generating frameworks, in which agents begin and end in equilibrium. One of the few attempts to set a new Keynesian microfoundation within a general equilibrium is Greenwald and Stiglitz (1990), which *combines* asymmetric information microfoundations *with* an IS-LM framework. The fit is awkward at best, however, for example, the LM curve explicitly represents a 'money market,' and uses Walras' law to exclude the other representative financial market, the loanable funds market. The notion of just one market for loanable funds is, however, inappropriate unless all borrowers therein pose the same kinds of principal/agent problems for lenders. Such an assumption is inconsistent with modern theories of information and agency in financial markets and with institutional realities.

30 Difficult, but not impossible. While Minskian fragility is ruled out, financial structure can affect aggregate outcomes due to the effect of unanticipated price-level changes on the collateral pledged by borrowers seeking to signal their creditworthiness. That is, collapsing prices reduce the nominal value of collateral and trigger credit-market disequilibrium; overly variable prices make collateral value indeterminate and increase the 'cost of intermediation.'

31 See Sawyer (1985b, 157-158).

32 Epstein (1994) develops a model with some Kaleckian features that explores this political-economic tension over macroeconomic and monetary policies.

References

Asimakopulos, A. 1983. 'Kalecki and Keynes on finance, investment, and saving'. *Cambridge Journal of Economics* 7(3-4), September-December: 221-33.

Asimakopulos, A. 1985. 'The role of finance in Keynes's General Theory.' *Economic Notes*, Monte dei Paschi di Siena 3: 5-16.

Asimakopulos, A. 1991. *Keynes's General Theory and Accumulation.* Cambridge: Cambridge University Press.

Crotty, J. 1994. 'On the Relation Between Fundamental Uncertainty and Asymmetric Information in the Keynesian Tradition: the Uncertain Alliance Between New and Post Keynesian Theory.' July: Mimeo: University of Massachusetts, Amherst.

Davidson, P. 1978. *Money and the Real World.* Second edition. London: Macmillan.

Davidson, P. 1986. 'Finance, Funding, Saving, and Investment.' *Journal of Post Keynesian Economics* 9(1), Fall: 101-10.

Diamond, D. and Dybvig P. 1983. 'Bank Runs, Deposit Insurance, and Liquidity.' *Journal of Political Economy* 91: 401-19.

Dymski, G. 1990. 'Money and Credit in Radical Political Economy: Survey of Contemporary Perspectives.' *Review of Radical Political Economics* 22(2/3), Summer/Fall: 38-65.

Dymski, G. 1994. 'Fundamental Uncertainty, Asymmetric Information, and Financial Structure: "Post" Versus "New" Keynesian Microfoundations,' in *New Directions in Monetary Macroeconomics: Essays in the Tradition of Hyman P. Minsky.* Ed. G. Dymski and R. Pollin. Ann Arbor: University of Michigan Press: 77-103.

Dymski, G. and Pollin R. 1992. 'Hyman Minsky as Hedgehog: the Power of the Wall Street Paradigm.' In *Financial Conditions and Macroeconomic Performance.* Ed. S. Fazzari and D. Papadimitriou. Armonk, NY: Sharpe: 27-62.

Epstein, G. 1994. 'A Political Economy Model of Central Banking.' In *New Directions in Monetary Macroeconomics: Essays in the Tradition of Hyman P. Minsky,* Ed. G. Dymski and R. Pollin. Ann Arbor: University of Michigan Press: 231-77.

Fazzari, S. 1992. 'Theories of Investment: Neo-, Post- and New,' in *Financial Conditions and Macroeconomic Performance.* Ed. S. Fazzari and D. Papadimitriou. Armonk, NY: Sharpe, 1992: 121-32.

Fazzari, S., and Variato A. M. 1994. 'Asymmetric Information and Keynesian Theories of Investment.' *Journal of Post Keynesian Economics* 16(3), Spring: 325-50.

FitzGerald, E. V. K. 1993. *The Macroeconomics of Development Finance: a Kaleckian Analysis of the Semi-Industrialized Economy.* New York: St. Martin's Press.

Greenwald, B. and Stiglitz, J. 1990. 'Macroeconomic Models with Equity and Credit Rationing.' In *Asymmetric Information, Corporate Finance, and Investment,* Ed. G. Hubbard. Chicago: University of Chicago Press: 15-42.

Harcourt, G. C. 1987. 'Preface' to P. Kriesler, *Kalecki's Microanalysis: the Development of Kalecki's Analysis of Pricing and Distribution.* Cambridge: Cambridge University Press.

Harcourt, G. C. and Hamouda O. F. 1992. 'Post-Keynesianism: from Criticism to Coherence?' In *On Political Economists and Modern Political Economy: Selected Essays of G. C. Harcourt.* Ed. C. Sardoni. London: Routledge: 209-32.

Kalecki, M. 1954. *Theory of Economic Dynamics*. London: Allen and Unwin.

Kalecki, M. 1991a. *Collected Works, I: Capitalism, Business Cycles and Full Employment*. Ed. J. Osiatynski. Oxford: Clarendon Press.

Kalecki, M. 1991b. *Collected Works, II: Capitalism, Economic Dynamics*. Ed. J. Osiatynski. Oxford: Clarendon Press.

Kalecki, M. 1993. *Collected Works, V: Developing Economies*. Ed. J. Osiatynski. Oxford: Clarendon Press.

Keynes, J. M. 1936. *The General Theory of Employment, Interest and Money*. London: Macmillan.

Keynes, J.M. 1937. 'The "ex-ante" theory of the rate of interest.' *Economic Journal* 47(188), December: 663-669. Reprinted in J. M. Keynes, *The General Theory and After: Part II Defence and Development*, Ed. D. Moggridge. London: Macmillan.

Keynes, J. M. 1973. *The General Theory and After: Part I. Preparation*. Ed. D. Moggridge, Vol. 13 of the *Collected Writings*. London: Macmillan.

Kohn, M. 1981. 'In Defense of the Finance Constraint.' *Economic Inquiry* 19(2), April:. 177-95.

Kregel, J. 1976. 'Economic Methodology in the Face of Uncertainty: the Modelling Methods of Keynes and the Post-Keynesians.' *Economic Journal* 86(342), June: 209-25.

Kregel, J. 1986. 'A Note on Finance, Liquidity, Saving, and Investment.' *Journal of Post Keynesian Economics* 9(1), Fall,: 91-100.

Kregel, J. 1989. 'Savings, Investment, and Finance in Kalecki's Theory.' In *Kalecki's Relevance Today*. Ed. M. Sebastiani. London: Macmillan: 193-205.

Kregel, J. 1994. 'Causality and Real Time in Asimakopulos's Approach to Saving and Investment in the Theory of Distribution.' In *Income and Employment in Theory and Practice*.

Kriesler, P. 1989. 'Methodological Implications of Kalecki's Microfoundations.' In *Kalecki's Relevance Today*. Ed. M. Sebastiani. London: Macmillan: 121-35.

Kriesler, P. and McFarlane B.1993. 'Michal Kalecki on Capitalism.' *Cambridge Journal of Economics* 17(2), June: 215-34.

Messori, M.1991. 'Financing in Kalecki's Theory.' *Cambridge Journal of Economics* 15(3), September: 301-13.

Minsky, H. 1986. *Stabilizing an Unstable Economy*. New Haven: Yale University Press.

Mott, T. 1990. 'Kaleckianism vs. "New" Keynesianism.' Mimeo. Boulder: University of Colorado.

Mullineux, A. W. 1990. *Business Cycles and Financial Crises*. Ann Arbor: University of Michigan Press.

Osiatynski, J. 1986. 'Kalecki's Theory of Economic Dynamics after Thirty Years.' *IDS Discussion Paper*, University of Sussex.

Pollin, R. and Justice C. 1994. 'Savings, Finance and Interest Rates: an Empirical
    Consideration of Some Basic Keynesian Propositions.' In *New Directions in
    Monetary Macroeconomics*. Ed. G. Dymski and R. Pollin. Ann Arbor:
    University of Michigan Press: 279-309.
Robinson, J. 1962. *Essays in the Theory of Economic Growth*. London: Macmillan.
Robinson, J. 1966. 'Kalecki and Keynes.' In *Problems of Economic Dynamics and
    Planning: Essays in Honour of Michal Kalecki*. Oxford: Pergamon Press:
    335-42.
Rogers, C. 1989. *Money, Interest and Capital: a Study in the Foundations of Monetary
    Theory*. Cambridge: Cambridge University Press.
Sawyer, M. 1985a. *The Economics of Michal Kalecki*. London. Macmillan..
Sawyer, M. 1985b. 'Toward a Post-Kaleckian Macroeconomics.' In *Post Keynesian
    Economic Theory*. Ed. P. Arestis and T. Skouras: 146-79.
Schumpeter, J. 1954. *History of Economic Analysis*. Oxford: Oxford University Press
Steindl, J. 1966. 'On Maturity in Capitalist Economies.' In *Problems of Economic
    Dynamics and Planning: Essays in Honour of Michal Kalecki*. Oxford:
    Pergamon Press: 423-32.
Steindl, J. 1991. 'Some Comments on the Three Versions of Kalecki's Theory of the
    Trade Cycle.' Annex 3 in Kalecki, *Collected works, II*. 1991b: 597-605.
Stiglitz, J. 1992. 'Banks vs. Markets as Mechanisms for Allocating and Co-ordinating
    Investment.' In *The Economics of Co-operation*. Ed. J. Roumasset and S. Barr.
    Boulder: Westview Press: 15-38.
Targetti, F. and Kinda-Hass B. 1982. 'Kalecki's Review of Keynes' *General Theory*.'
    Australian Economic Papers 21(39), December: 244-60. Reprinted in Kalecki
    Collected Works,I. 1991a.

7 KALECKI AND THE AMERICANS

J.E. King

I do not think that it is necessary, if one would advance Keynes's claims to greatness, to argue that we might not have reached the same destination by other routes or at a later date; to name only one other, Michal Kalecki was independently approaching the same goal (A. Robinson 1946, 42).

Mr. Kalecki's discovery of the General Theory independently of Keynes was a classic example of the coincidences of science. His version of the analysis led directly (which Keynes' did not) to a model of the trade cycle. Based upon the same conception of short-period equilibrium, his theory fitted naturally into Keynes' scheme, and became absorbed into it in the subsequent development of the General Theory. By now it is impossible to distinguish what one has learned from which (J. Robinson 1952, 159).

I am grateful for comments from Philip Arestis, Simon Chapple, Gary Dymski, Geoff Harcourt, John Henry, Mike Howard, Peter Kriesler, Marc Lavoie, Bruce McFarlane, Malcolm Sawyer and participants in the Eighth Political Economy Conference, Great Malvern, August 1994, and at a seminar at the University of Newcastle, N.S.W. The usual disclaimer applies.

Introduction

My title is, of course, borrowed from Marjorie Turner's valuable book on Joan Robinson, who made several visits to North America towards the end of her life and had a significant impact on the evolution of Post Keynesian thought in the United States (Turner 1989). Unlike Robinson, however, Michal Kalecki actually lived in America for almost ten years. Yet, she wrote in a review of Axel Leijonhufvud's *On Keynesian Economics and the Economics of Keynes*, he 'had very little influence on American doctrines' (J. Robinson 1969, 582). As will be seen below, this is something of an exaggeration. But it does contain an important element of truth.

This chapter is in three parts. The first outlines Kalecki's work in his North American period (1945-55) and attempts to uncover what effect, if any, America had on him. The second and third sections ask how Kalecki affected the development of economics in America, beginning with the early US Keynesians. For reasons of space I have been forced to omit any discussion of the transatlantic Post Keynesians Victoria Chick and Jan Kregel, or the important Canadian theorists, Lorie Tarshis and Athanasios (Tom) Asimakopulos. Further belying my title, I have ignored Kalecki's influence on Latin American economists, although this is a topic which would certainly repay detailed research. Instead I focus upon four prominent Post Keynesian theorists: Sidney Weintraub, Hyman Minsky, Paul Davidson and Alfred Eichner. In brief conclusion I return to the apparent paradox, already noted, of Kalecki's physical presence and intellectual absence.

Kalecki in America

Except for the second half of 1946, which he spent in Poland, Kalecki lived in North America continuously from March 1945 until the beginning of 1955; this represents almost one-quarter of his active professional life.1 For the first fifteen months he was in Montreal at the International Labour Office, where he conducted research into the problems of postwar reconstruction. Then, at the end of 1946, he began an eight-year spell in New York as head of the Economic Stability Section of the Division of Economic Stability and Development of the Economic Department of the United Nations (which was, evidently, already a fully-fledged bureaucracy). Kalecki was a frequent participant in seminars at McGill and the University of Montreal, and while at the ILO he also lectured (in May 1946) at the University of Chicago, presumably on the initiative of Oskar Lange (Kalecki 1947, 393n). His US experiences were mixed, the pleasures of life in New York failing to compensate fully for repeated clashes with the UN authorities and for the McCarthyite witchhunts which eventually led him to resign - not for the last time - on a point of principle (Feiwel 1975, 293-4).

This part of Kalecki's career has been somewhat neglected by scholars. Feiwel's massive intellectual biography, for example, devotes only a few pages to his writings during this period (*ibid.*, 207-12, 303, 381-2, 387-91), while the tribute by his former colleague, Sidney Dell, although it includes a very useful summary of Kalecki's work at the UN, is very short indeed on personal detail. Dell does provide a list of his more important collaborators at the UN (Dell 1977, 32); Feiwel refers briefly to 'the visits of foreign economists who stopped off at the UN, often for the sole purpose of meeting and debating with him' (Feiwel 1975, 294), without mentioning names. And Paul Sweezy confirms that Kalecki was a regular visitor to the informal editorial meetings of the independent Marxist journal, *Monthly Review* (Sweezy, interview). Apart from this, very little has been recorded of Kalecki's life in America.

Much of Kalecki's writing for the United Nations was descriptive in character, involving assessments of the economic situation in member countries and discussion of their implications for domestic and international economic policy (Dell 1977). In his background papers and briefing documents, however, Kalecki did raise some broader theoretical issues. The most important of these papers, a 1949 report *on Inflationary and Deflationary Tendencies, 1946-1948*, reveals a very significant change in his thinking on the question of income distribution. In his published work, Kalecki had argued that the *share* of profits depended exclusively on the degree of monopoly and the price of raw materials relative to the money wage rate, while the *level* of profits was determined (in a closed economy with no government) by the sum of investment and capitalists' consumption expenditure (Kalecki 1942, 260; cf Kalecki 1941). This allowed Nicholas Kaldor to assert, in his celebrated *Review of Economic Studies* article, that his own model of distribution was original because, unlike Kalecki's, it was explicitly macroeconomic in nature (Kaldor 1956, 94n3).

In the 1949 report, however, Kalecki had set out precisely such an analysis. He began by stating the fundamental condition for macroeconomic equilibrium, that the flow of savings be equal to the sum of investment, net exports and the budget deficit (United Nations 1949a, 5). Abstracting from the government and overseas sectors, Kalecki then considered the effect of an increase in private investment:

> If there is a rise in the net non-consumption payments, e.g., through a rise in investment in a situation of full employment, there will be a shift in resources from personal consumption to non-consumption purposes. The supply of goods for personal consumption will therefore fall without a decline in money

incomes. This will lead to a rise in prices of consumption goods. Such a rise in prices generates new incomes and thus increases the demand for consumption goods. This increase in prices, however, leads to a relative shift to profits in the distribution of private income. Since less is consumed out of profits than out of labour income, a point is reached in the increase in prices where the relative shift to profits is sufficiently great to balance the demand for consumption goods with the reduced supply available. Alternatively the equilibrium may be described as the point where profits have increased sufficiently in relation to private income so as to raise the ratio of current private saving to private income, up to the increased level of the ratio of the net non-consumption payments to private income (*ibid.*, 7).

This is the Kaldor model of distribution without the algebra2. Kalecki extended it to allow for the inflationary effects of fiscal policy: 'In normal inflation when a budget deficit arises, prices increase up to the point where the resulting shift towards profits in the distribution of income increases savings by the amount of the budget deficit'. No further increase in prices will result unless, as in hyper-inflationary conditions, the capitalists' savings propensity falls to zero and 'the additional profits are immediately spent on the hoarding of goods' (*ibid.*, 13).

Although all this was a matter of public record, it appeared in a document which was both anonymous and (presumably) sufficiently obscure to escape the notice of the Cambridge Post Keynesians, as was its subsequent restatement (United Nations 1953, 4). The Kalecki bibliography reveals that he also continued to publish in his own name, albeit (understandably) much less prolifically than in the previous decade. His article, 'The Maintenance of Full Employment After the Transition Period', which came out in the *International Labour Review* in November 1945, was probably written in Montreal, though it drew heavily on Kalecki's earlier work at the Institute of Economics and Statistics in Oxford. In it he argued that savings in the postwar United States could be expected to outrun private investment by some $15 billion, a sum far exceeding any conceivable export surplus and requiring a large budget deficit if full employment were to be preserved. The United Kingdom faced a far less serious problem, owing to its much lower propensity to save (Kalecki 1945). This article provoked a heated response from the statistician, W.S. Woytinsky, then employed by the US Social Security Administration, who disputed Kalecki's projections and predicted an inflationary rather than a deflationary gap for the year 1950 (Woytinsky 1946). Kalecki's reply, in which he reasserted the plausibility of his original estimates, represents his one and only appearance in the *American Economic Review* (Kalecki 1947).

In 1946 he published two short papers on topics related to this question. One discussed the difficulties posed by the principle of multilateral trade for those countries attempting to maintain full employment, and suggested that the burden of adjustment be placed on surplus (not deficit) nations, requiring from them either increased domestic expenditure or long-term international lending (Kalecki 1946b). This added little to the Oxford writings of Kalecki himself, Thomas Balogh and E.F. Schumacher (see Kalecki and Schumacher 1943; Balogh and Schumacher 1944). The other paper was a contribution to a *Review of Economics and Statistics* symposium on domestic fiscal and monetary policy. Here Kalecki expanded on earlier work (Kalecki 1944) to deny that full employment could be assured by stimulating private investment. Contemporary estimates had revealed that

> the 'deflationary gap' is likely to be considerable in the U.S.A. even when the rate of investment is *not* at the depression level but at a level which corresponds roughly to the long-run trend line. It follows that filling the 'deflationary gap', so defined, by stimulation of private investment would in the long run create 'over-investment', i.e., reduce the rate of profit and thus prove a self-defeating measure. It also would create overcapacity, which is a sheer waste of resources (Kalecki 1946a, 82).

This passage anticipates Kalecki's later analysis of the 'tragedy of investment', and hints at an underconsumptionist (or 'overinvestmentist') theory of crisis. He expressed very similar concerns in several of his UN briefing papers (United Nations 1947, 1-3; 1949b, 1-5).

Kalecki called for any necessary budget deficit to be financed by issuing short-term securities, not, as L.W. Mints (1946) had suggested, through the issue of currency. Interest rates must be kept low enough, Kalecki argued, for interest payments on the public debt not to rise faster than national income. Finally he urged, against Mints, that frictional unemployment be reduced by retraining workers instead of reducing wages through increased labour market competition, and expressed what reads in hindsight as a very complacent attitude towards the possibility of wage inflation under full employment:

> ... if the annual increase in wage rates does not exceed the increase in the productivity of labor the price level will not tend to rise. It is very difficult to say whether in fact wage increases would be at a higher rate than this, and, if so, what means would be found to keep prices stable. This would depend on the institutional setup of the regime of full employment. It is no good to conjecture too much about all aspects of the future functioning of such a regime. Let us have it and try it out (Kalecki 1946a, 84).

Joan Robinson, for one, was very much less sanguine on this question (Robinson 1937, 23-8).

Two further notes by Kalecki appeared in the *Review of Economics and Statistics* in 1948, one a short discussion of the impact of price decontrol on the rate of inflation, the other a technical analysis of US national accounting data (Kalecki 1948a, 1948b). In the previous year Kalecki had attended the September meeting of the Econometric Society in Washington, acting as discussant of Oskar Lange's paper on planning and the optimal allocation of resources (Lange 1949; Kalecki 1949a). Unfortunately neither Kalecki's own contribution, a paper on 'Inflation and Unemployment', nor the related discussion is reprinted in the special supplement of *Econometrica*; so far as I know, Kalecki's paper has not survived. His views on inflation at this time may perhaps be inferred from an article which, although published as late as 1962, was apparently written while he was in the US. Here Kalecki takes a quasi-monetarist position on the analysis of hyper-inflation (Kalecki 1962; cf. Sawyer 1985, 124 n4).

In an important theoretical article in the *Review of Economic Studies*, Kalecki modified his earlier model of the trade cycle by respecifying investment as a function either of the level and the rate of change of income or, equivalently, of current savings and the rate of change of income. Both variables reflected the influence of expected profitability, Kalecki claimed, the rate of change of income via something similar to the acceleration principle, while 'the stream of new savings stimulates investment because it makes [it] possible to undertake investment without increasing indebtedness' (Kalecki 1949b, 61).3 Kalecki concluded that this formulation was 'fairly close' to that of his earlier model (*ibid.*, 62, citing Kalecki 1943, 61), though this is perhaps debatable.

Except for a rather slight note (again in the *Review of Economic Studies*) on cyclical and secular aspects of demand deficiency (Kalecki 1950), this was Kalecki's last theoretical work to be published in English until the appearance of his *Theory of Economic Dynamics* in February 1954. This book, as he explains in the foreword,4 was a substantially rewritten version of his two previous books (Kalecki 1939, 1943), and was intended as a substitute for a second edition of those volumes. 'Although', as he put it, 'the basic ideas are not much changed, the presentation and even the arguments have been substantially altered', and new material on the business cycle and shocks (chapter 13) and the process of economic development (chapter 14) was introduced (Kalecki 1954, 5; cf Steindl 1981).

In August-September 1950 Kalecki visited Israel at the invitation of the Finance Minister to investigate the country's balance of payments, unemployment and inflation problems. There were no significant innovations in his report (Kalecki 1951), which drew heavily on his war-time experiences in Britain, and the Israeli government adopted policies which were the exact opposite of what he had recommended (Feiwel 1975, 381). He did, however, break new ground in 1953 in a series of lectures given in Mexico on the economic difficulties facing developing countries; a summary was published in Spanish in 1954 and in English, in the *Indian Economic Review*, in the following year (Kalecki 1955). The article is important because in it he uses an overtly Marxian framework of analysis for the first time in his professional career (though it is implicit in much of his earlier work in English, and explicit in at least one Polish article).5 The standard disclaimer was thus more forceful than usual.6

Kalecki's model of economic development distinguishes three classes (workers, capitalists, and small proprietors) and two departments (producing investment goods and consumer goods respectively). It uses these Marxian categories in a very flexible and undogmatic way, demonstrating first that the sectoral balance condition of Marx's reproduction schemes corresponds to the modern requirement that savings be equal to investment: 'This equation shows that in a sense investment finances itself' (Kalecki 1955, 3). Kalecki then argues that the elasticity of supply of consumer goods - especially food - in response to demand is crucial in determining whether or not a given level of private investment will generate inflationary pressures. He introduces successively into the model productivity growth, monopolistic tendencies in industry, foreign trade, capital imports, public investment and taxation, ending with a critique of credit restrictions as an anti-inflation policy. This article, a genuine *tour de force*, formed the basis for all Kalecki's subsequent writing on the economics of development (see, for example, Kalecki 1976; McFarlane, this volume).

Early Keynesian Responses

Keynes's ideas had of course arrived in America long before Kalecki. Lorie Tarshis was one important propagator (Harcourt 1982). But, as J.K. Galbraith puts it, 'The trumpet ... that was sounded in Cambridge, England, was heard most clearly in Cambridge, Massachusetts. Harvard was the principal avenue by which Keynes's ideas passed to the United States' (Galbraith 1975, 135). Among the old guard, by far the most important proponent of Keynesian ideas was Alvin Hansen, whose conversion to the new way of thinking owed nothing to Kalecki (Barber 1987). The same was true of Paul Samuelson of MIT, the most prominent of the younger Keynesians and co-inventor, with John Hicks, of the neoclassical synthesis. Hicks seems to have developed the IS-LM model independently, prior to the publication of the *General Theory*, under the influence of Pareto and Walras, and to have made little effort in the 1930s to understand Keynes although he did, of course, subsequently disavow IS-LM (Hamouda 1986; cf. Hicks 1980-1). Samuelson was, much more directly, a Keynesian, but he never showed any great interest in Kalecki, who rates only two passing references in the *Foundations*7 and is not mentioned at all in Samuelson's 'brief survey of post-Keynesian developments' (Samuelson 1963)8 nor in his more recent autobiographical sketch. Here Samuelson pays tribute to 'the wonder generation of Frisch, Hotelling, Harrod, Myrdal, Tinbergen, Ohlin,

Haberler, Hicks, Joan Robinson, Lerner, Leontief, Kaldor and others too numerous to mention' - among them Kalecki (Samuelson 1981, 6).

Samuelson was by no means alone in his neglect. Robert Solow always preferred Keynes to Kalecki, although he remembered finding the latter's work exciting as a student, using a well-thumbed copy of *Essays in the Theory of Economic Fluctuations* (Kalecki 1939), held together by tape, and buying his own copy of the 1943 *Studies in Economic Dynamics* (Solow 1975, p 1333-4). The former book was courteously reviewed, Simon Kuznets describing it as a set of 'interesting and imaginative first approaches to the problems involved'. Kuznets did however object to Kalecki's 'often .... cavalier disregard of available evidence' and his 'use of statistical analysis of a crude but suggestive character' (Kuznets 1939, p 805-6). Oskar Lange registered similar criticisms, but also made two significant positive suggestions which Kalecki was later to follow up. He should reformulate his theory of income distribution on non-marginalist lines, Lange argued, and incorporate a growth trend into his analysis of the trade cycle (Lange 1941, 281-2). Kalecki's two later books attracted less attention. *Studies* was received with rather muted enthusiasm by Richard Goodwin (1945), and the 1954 *Theory of Economic Dynamics* appeared somewhat to mystify R. W. Pfouts (1955) in the *Southern Economic Journal*; it was ignored by the *Journal of Political Economy* and the *American Economic Review*.

There were a handful of references to Kalecki in Seymour Harris's 661-page compilation, *The New Economics* (Harris 1946), demonstrating that Harris himself, Benjamin Higgins, Richard Goodwin, James Tobin and Abba Lerner were aware of his work; but none of them is at all substantial.9 Some of the contributors to the American Economic Association's two-volume set of surveys of contemporary economics revealed their acquaintance with Kalecki's writings[10] while the *Festschrift* for Alvin Hansen contained sixteen essays and precisely one reference to Kalecki, this time by Evsey Domar (Hansen 1948, 45n20). Even this was one more than can be found in Joseph Schumpeter's magisterial *History of Economic Analysis*, although this arch-opponent of Keynesian theory had devoted two pages to Kalecki in his treatise on business cycles (Schumpeter 1939, p185-8).[11] If Galbraith regarded Kalecki as 'the most innovative figure in economics I have known, not excluding Keynes' (Galbraith 1981, 75), he failed signally to persuade his Cambridge (Mass.) colleagues. Indeed, Galbraith admitted as much in a 1969 letter to Kalecki written to commemorate his seventieth birthday: 'I am struck to this day by the number of people at Harvard who mention your ideas without associating themselves with your name. Or even, on occasion, use the name Kalecki as an abstraction' (Feiwel 1975, 17).

Generous recognition came from only one young Keynesian. Lawrence Klein was at this time a socialist, who rated Marx as Keynes's equal in economic analysis (Klein 1947a). Not surprisingly, he found Kalecki's ideas congenial. In his *Keynesian Revolution*, a book dedicated in the most fulsome terms to his teacher, Paul Samuelson (Klein 1947b, viii-ix), Klein advocated a greatly expanded role for the state to ensure full employment. To rebut conservative objections he cited 'an informal talk' by Kalecki, who had remarked that the regimentation of unemployment and poverty was infinitely worse than the regimentation imposed by economic planning (*ibid.*, 179). In 1947 Klein appears not to have realised the full extent of Kalecki's theoretical achievements. Reviewing Harrod's *Life of Keynes* four years later, he made comprehensive amends: 'Recently, after having re-examined Kalecki's theory of the business cycle, I have decided that he actually created a system that contains everything of importance in the Keynesian system, in addition to other contributions' (Klein 1951, 447). Kalecki had no theory of liquidity preference or the rate of interest, Klein claimed[12], and could be criticised for his unrealistic assumption that the workers' savings propensity was zero. In some respects, however, Kalecki's model was clearly superior to that of Keynes, since it was explicitly dynamic, explained the distribution as well as the level of income, and distinguished investment orders from investment expenditures (*ibid.*, 448). But Keynes's reputation and ability to command attention had ensured that his genius was fully recognised, while Kalecki's talents had gone largely unnoticed.

Weintraub, Davidson, Minsky

Despite its generosity, this assessment had no effect whatever on the course of American economics. Mainstream macroeconomics in the postwar United States came to mean what Sidney Weintraub would later scornfully describe as 'classical Keynesianism': the Hicks-Samuelson neoclassical synthesis, with IS-LM at its core, Keynes (not Kalecki) as its inspiration, and the *General Theory* as the single authoritative source. When first Weintraub, then others, rebelled against the orthodox Keynesian analysis, it was this interpretation of Keynes which became their target.

Weintraub was to become the founding father of Post Keynesian economics in the US. He had spent a year in Britain in 1938-9, striking up a personal friendship with Nicholas Kaldor while he was there. Weintraub was unusually well-read, took a strong interest in the history of economic thought (including Marxism), and even devoted an early article to a critique of Kalecki's proposals for comprehensive consumer rationing, which he regarded as administratively cumbersome and excessively egalitarian (Weintraub 1942). Weintraub's attempt to model the macroeconomic consequences of an increase in the degree of monopoly was Kaleckian in spirit, without mentioning his name (Weintraub 1946), and in his text on *Price Theory* he cited the principle of increasing risk as one important factor limiting the size of the firm under conditions of uncertainty (Weintraub 1949, 370). But Kalecki seems to have played no real part in the development of

Weintraub's thinking. In his most important work, *An Approach to the Theory of Income Distribution*, Weintraub acknowledged Kalecki (along with Kenneth Boulding) as one of the pioneers of macro-distribution theory, and also alluded briefly to his analysis of changes in the degree of monopoly over time (Weintraub 1958, 21,68). However, Kalecki's role in the book was a very minor one, Weintraub's trenchant criticisms of macroeconomic models of relative shares being reserved for Kaldor (*ibid.*, 104-7). In his own *General Theory*, published in the following year, Weintraub dismissed as 'doubtful in the extreme' Kalecki's 'ingenious *a priori* analysis ... that the constancy in income shares was due to a fortuitous growth in monopoly power which, somehow, just by happenstance counterbalanced productivity influences' (Weintraub 1959, 41).

As I have shown elsewhere (King 1995b), Weintraub's ideas were evolving rapidly in the late 1950s and early 1960s as he broke with orthodox US Keynesianism. In the *Approach* he attributed the 'classical' savings assumption - workers save nothing, capitalists consume nothing - to Kalecki, Robinson and Kaldor, and tentatively accepted it as an 'ingenious simplification' of rather minor significance (Weintraub 1959, 88). Soon he was taking much more seriously the views of the 'Cambridge Keynesians', by whom he meant Robinson, Kaldor and Kahn (but not Kalecki) (Weintraub 1961, 176). Weintraub's first reference to what he would thereafter repeatedly describe as the 'Kalecki-Robinson-Kaldor thesis' on relative shares came five years later (Weintraub 1966, 90), and he subsequently expressed a more sympathetic view of Kaleckian pricing theory (Weintraub 1969, 150-1). For Weintraub the Post Keynesian, Kalecki was a respected forerunner (Weintraub 1970, 209n5).

But Weintraub could never be described as a Kaleckian. Keynes was his inspiration, a Keynes liberated from the shackles of the neoclassical synthesis; in effect, Weintraub was the first of the 'fundamentalist Keynesians' (Coddington 1976). His principal theoretical contribution was his revival of the aggregate supply and demand analysis which Keynes had set out in chapter 3 of the *General Theory* and then neglected, and which Kalecki totally ignored. Weintraub became famous for his emphasis on the wage-push component in postwar inflation and for his advocacy of a tax-based income policy to combat it (Wallich and Weintraub 1971). For Kalecki these were minor issues, while the formal models of the trade cycle and of cyclical growth, which were fundamental to the Kaleckian vision, left Weintraub cold. Kalecki's mark-up was grounded in a model of the firm's pricing behaviour; Weintraub's mark-up was simply an empirically observed macroeconomic constant (Weintraub 1982, 449-50).[13] Even where the two men shared common ground, above all in their concern with income distribution, Weintraub's irrepressibly eclectic approach (which always included a marginal productivity element) was quite alien to the austerity of Kalecki's thought. A comparison of their last papers on distribution theory is very revealing in this regard (Kalecki 1971; Weintraub 1981). There is no reason to doubt Weintraub's own assessment: 'In origin I owed nothing to Kalecki;

it was only after I found the wage *share* (or price mark-up) "constant" that I recalled, and referred to, his work. I resist differentiating my product too much from Kalecki, but its analytical and empirical coverage are [*sic*] *not* "identical"' (Weintraub 1983, 229; original stress).[14]

Weintraub's best-known pupil, Paul Davidson, was well acquainted with Kalecki's work from the very beginning of his own academic career. Davidson's doctoral dissertation on theories of relative income shares was completed in 1958 and bears the very clear imprint of Weintraub's supervision. The chapter on 'Monopoly as a determinant of class shares' is devoted largely to a discussion of the various models of income distribution devised by Kalecki between 1937 and 1954, with a brief assessment of the Kaleckian analysis of Ashok Mitra (1954). Davidson objects to Kalecki's microeconomics, in particular to the assumption of constant marginal cost and to the cavalier assertion that it is possible satisfactorily to define an 'industry' in conditions of monopolistic competition (Davidson 1960, 52-4). His principal criticisms, however, are macroeconomic and methodological. Even in the short run, Davidson argues, there is no reason to suppose that the degree of monopoly will be constant at all levels of output (*ibid.*, 59). Nor are there any grounds to support Kalecki's claim that his analysis can be applied to the long run, since technical change will leave the degree of monopoly unaltered only in the event of 'synchronous fortuitous changes in the demand and marginal revenue curves' (*ibid.*, 53).

Davidson had already rejected the marginal productivity theory of distribution on the grounds of its inability to deal with the macroeconomic dimension to relative shares (*ibid.*, 42-3). He concluded that the same fatal weakness undermined Kalecki's analysis:

> Kalecki and Mitra attempted to construct hypotheses based on individual market structures, without paying sufficient attention to changes in the macroeconomic variables. Although it can be demonstrated that higher prices, given the money wage rate and the level of output, imply a lower relative wage share in the proceeds of the firm, neither Kalecki nor Mitra were able to aggregate this microphenomena [*sic*] without involving their systems in the neoclassical fallacy of an assumed independence of product demand and factor prices' (*ibid.*, 102-3).

Keynes had been on the right track with his 'widow's cruse' or 'Danaid jar' model in the *Treatise on Money* (*ibid.*, 62), and Weintraub had made considerable progress in the *Approach*. Davidson recognised that Kalecki had indeed advanced a macroeconomic theory of the *level* of profits, and that this had exerted a significant influence on the later work of Joan Robinson and Nicholas Kaldor (*ibid.*, 71, 81-2), but he dismissed Kalecki's theory of the profit *share* as wholly unsuccessful.

In his dissertation, Davidson displayed a broadly favourable attitude towards Joan Robinson, and thus, by implication, towards Kalecki as one of her principal sources. By 1972, with the publication of his *magnum opus*, *Money and the Real World*, this had changed. His rather stormy relation with Robinson during his visit to Cambridge in 1970-1 is well documented (Davidson 1992a, 111-12). As he told Weintraub at the time, 'My meetings with Joan Robinson varies [*sic*] from lukewarm to sizzling hot. She is obviously interested in brainwashing me ... She is obviously less open-minded than most and has just about abandoned Keynes for Kalecki'.[15] This verdict is reflected in the book, in which Davidson now distinguished five schools of contemporary macroeconomic thought. Two - the 'monetarist-neoclassical' and 'socialist-radical' streams - made no claim to legitimate descent from Keynes. A third, the 'neoclassical-Bastard Keynesian school' of Samuelson, Solow, Patinkin, Tobin and Hicks, had distorted Keynes's ideas. So too, though rather less seriously, had the 'neo-keynesian school ... who have attempted to graft aspects of Keynes's real sector analysis onto the growth and distribution theories of Ricardo, Marx, and Kalecki', under the leadership of Robinson, Kaldor and Pasinetti. The truth lay with what Davidson termed 'Keynes's School', which he described as 'an exceedingly small group who have attempted to develop Keynes's original views on employment, growth, and money, e.g., Harrod, Lerner, and Weintraub' (Davidson 1972, 2-3) - and, by implication, Davidson himself.

The few subsequent references to Kalecki in *Money and the Real World* are to his - apparently rather slight - role in the 'neo-Keynesian' school and his impact on Robinson's thought. In effect Kalecki had been relegated to the status of a minor pre-Robinsonian. There is just one reference to Kalecki in the index to Davidson's 1200-page *Collected Writings*,[16] and this sums up his mature judgement as to Kalecki's significance.[17]

The contrast with Hyman Minsky is a substantial one. Kalecki's principle of increasing risk is crucial to Minsky's analysis of 'borrower's risk' (Fazzari 1992, 127-8; cf Dymski, this volume). And the Kaleckian theory of profits is central to Minsky's broader vision of capitalist reality, in which economic crisis results from financial instability, itself the consequence of business borrowers' inability to meet their financial obligations. This 'financial instability hypothesis' may briefly be summarised. In each upswing, lending standards are relaxed as the memory fades of previous financial disasters. A growing proportion of loans is made on 'speculative' rather than 'hedge' terms; that is to say, money is lent to borrowers whose cash flows are inadequate to finance the repayment of principal (in addition to interest payments) without further borrowing. The period immediately before the crisis is characterised by what Minsky terms 'Ponzi finance', where loans are extended on projects so dubious that even interest payments can be made only from the proceeds of yet further loans. Eventually the weakest borrowers default, and a chain of bankruptcies initiates a debt-deflation crisis in which asset prices fall, real investment is discouraged, and output and employment levels decline sharply (Minsky 1978, 14-17). The world recession of the early 1990s began in precisely this way.

Minsky is quite explicit about the macroeconomic foundations of his microeconomic theory of financial relations. In aggregate, repayments by borrowers cannot exceed total profits. This means that, in a closed economy with no government, 'current investment determines whether or not the financial commitments on business debts can be fulfilled' (Minsky 1978, 14). More generally, aggregate profits depend (as Kalecki insisted) on the sum of investment, the trade surplus, and the budget deficit. Thus Minsky cites Kalecki in support of a vitally important policy prescription: big government, with a large and perhaps a growing deficit, is an essential condition for avoiding debt-deflation crises (*ibid.*, 13, 21; Fazzari 1992, 6).

All this is very clear, and has been frequently reiterated in Minsky's writings. It is much less obvious, however, whether Kalecki exerted any significant influence on him in his formative years or whether Minsky (like Weintraub) realised their affinities only after his own ideas had crystallised. Like Weintraub, Minsky was initially fairly close to orthodox US Keynesianism, albeit with an unusually strong interest in monetary theory (Wray 1992). On his own account it was a real-world development,[18] the 'near-miss' of 1966 in which a major financial crisis was only narrowly avoided, that was the decisive factor in his intellectual development (Minsky 1976, 27; cf Minsky 1972, 97-8). The first full statement of the financial instability hypothesis came in 1972,[19] followed by numerous reiterations and by a systematic analytical treatment in his book, *John Maynard Keynes*, published in 1975 but completed three years earlier (Minsky 1975; see Papadimitriou 1992, 22). Intriguingly there is no reference to Kalecki in this book, and no attempt to establish a theory of aggregate profits. Not until the late 1970s, in fact, does the Kaleckian profit equation appear in Minsky's published work, the first statement I have been able to discover being that in Minsky (1977, 10-11). His 1978 restatement of the financial instability hypothesis is explicitly Kaleckian (Minsky 1978, 13-14), and Kalecki's analysis has been a consistent theme in Minsky's writing ever since. In the formation of his ideas, however, Irving Fisher, Henry Simons, Oskar Lange, Joseph Schumpeter and, above all, Keynes, were much more important to him than Kalecki (Papadimitriou 1992, 24-5).

Eichner meets Robinson

If the development of Minsky's ideas leaves scope for conjecture, there is no mystery about the course of Alfred Eichner's thinking. The voluminous correspondence between Eichner and Joan Robinson[20] allows us to document the way in which a young, independent-minded but mentally very flexible critic of orthodox economics shifted his ground under continuous and insistent prompting from a much older and more dogmatic mentor. In 1969, when he first met Robinson at Columbia University in New York, Eichner had just completed the first draft of a book on the giant corporation. He had written his PhD dissertation on the emergence of oligopoly in the US sugar refining industry (Eichner 1969), and combined theoretical curiosity with an unusual knowledge of economic history and a taste for comparative economics and institutionalism. All were brought to bear on an analytical problem which Robinson had posed, but not solved, in her own work: the determinants of the mark-up in oligopoly.

Eichner's solution was to establish him as one of the most original of the US Post Keynesians. He argued, in short, that the 'megacorp' was guided in its pricing decisions by the need to raise sufficient finance to implement its investment decisions, subject to the constraints imposed by consumer substitution, the threat of potential entry, and the fear of government intervention if the mark-up seemed too high (Eichner 1973, 1976).[21] His concept of the 'corporate levy' was derived by analogy from the turnover tax imposed by Soviet planners, which Eichner had studied under Alexander Erlich at Columbia. Thus, as he told Robinson, Eichner's original interests were in microeconomics:

> While I have always been interested in static macro models - even though they are badly neglected here at Columbia - the macro dynamic models had seemed hardly worth bothering with. This was because to me, an economic historian, their influence in explaining the secular factors affecting economic growth was close to zero. The reliance on the assumption of perfect competition, together with a marginal productivity theory of income distribution, further repulsed me. However, now that I have thought a great deal about what you said, I realise that my own work on oligopoly contains an implicitly macrodynamic model. ...
>
> This is not readily apparent from the article you saw, but it can be gleaned from the chapters of the projected book you did not see. Moreover, now that I have read your *Essays in the Theory of Economic Growth*, I see that the real value of macrodynamic models is not in understanding the factors influencing long run economic growth but rather in understanding why the possible growth rate is not likely to be achieved. Since it is this latter question which prompted my own work on oligopoly, I am now very much interested in making explicit the macrodynamic model implicit in my previous work (Eichner to Robinson, [?] March 1969).

Robinson replied at some length, favourably but with a series of painstaking criticisms, two of which are especially relevant here. Like so many others, she wrote, Eichner had confused the erroneous Walrasian system of supply and demand with the more easily defensible Marshallian variant:

> Imperfect competition is implicit in the General Theory, otherwise there could be no part-time working of plant. Marshall himself introduced imperfect competition to defend profit margins in a slump. Kalecki cleaned up this element in the General Theory. There is no difficulty in stepping from Marshall to Keynes-Kalecki but there is an absolute impossibility of stepping from Walras' (Robinson to Eichner, 19 June 1969).

And Eichner had neglected the macroeconomics of corporate profitability: I very much agree with your concept of the Corporation [sic] levy but you still need a theory of what governs the rate of profit that is obtainable in the system as a whole' *(ibid.)*.

Eichner accepted Robinson's defence of Marshall but was at first unconvinced by her (implicitly Kaleckian) theory of aggregate profits:

> Your system seems to imply that profits are simply something that happens, largely as a result of aggregate factors over which the individual firm has no control. While I would not deny that this is an important part of the picture, I would nonetheless insist that profits or the realised corporate levy, and thus savings in the oligopolistic sector, are also something that are deliberately planned (Eichner to Robinson, 13 August 1969).

As he put it in a later letter,

> .... realised profits in the sense that you use the word depend both on the amount of investment being undertaken in the aggregate and on the profit margin set by business firms. ...
>
> Basically, what I am suggesting is that firms in the oligopolistic sector because of the pricing power they possess, are able to alter the value of s_p and while this cannot alter the overall value of S, it can affect the level of employment and the rate of capacity utilisation ...
>
> (Are we still apart on the issue?) (Eichner to Robinson, late April 1970).

In her reply Robinson seemed to indicate that they were not:

> I was very pleased to know that you have seen the point of my *Accumulation*. As for the relation between investment and profit I start from Kalecki's epigram 'the workers spend what they get and the capitalists get what they spend', ie, overall gross profit ex post is equal to gross investment plus consumption out of profits. (Of course this is a simplification but you know of the assumptions ...) [the rest of the letter is not readable] (Robinson to Eichner, 4 May 1970).

But, when Eichner suggested that he was simply supplying microfoundations for Cambridge macroeconomics, Robinson demurred:

> (You don't seem to ask, how is it possible to make profits. You give only one half of the two-sided action.) (If there was no investment there would be no profits.)
>
> I think I made this point when I first wrote to you, so perhaps you have a blind spot about it; anyway when you are reading me, remember that I think of investment already going on and profits already being earned (Robinson to Eichner, 1 April 1971).

She proceeded to write the Kaleckian profit equation

$$P = I + (1 - s_p)P - s_w W,$$

where aggregate profits equal investment plus capitalist consumption less workers' saving, so that

$$P = \frac{1}{s_p} I$$

if $s_w = 0$. 'This', she reminded Eichner, 'is true whether firms are competitive or oligopolistic and whether they finance [their investment expenditure] from retained profits or go to the market' (*ibid*.). Eichner's acceptance was immediate (Eichner to Robinson, 6 April 1971), and was repeated in a subsequent letter after Robinson (16 April 1971) had expressed a lingering suspicion that he did not entirely understand the relation between his ideas and her own:

> I accept the argument that profits depend on investment. That is, that $P = 1/s_p \times I$. In the revision of my work, I intend to incorporate your equations into the discussion. ...
>
> It is because my chapter 3 deals with the desired level of corporate levy, or savings, and not the realised level, that it did not focus more directly on the actual level of investment. I hope that by now you have had a chance to read chapter 6, and what I have said is apparent to you (Eichner to Robinson, [?] April 1971).

Robinson was still not satisfied. She found his chapter 6 (on the relations between micro and macro) 'terribly confusing':

You seem to boil investment decisions and current investment together. You should say when income is high in the present period (whether because I is high within or without the megacorp sector or because thriftiness is low) then output is high relatively to capacity in the megacorp sector, profits are high and savings are high. Therefore there are good prospects for investment and finance is becoming available, so that investment decisions, affecting investment in the *next* period, are high (Robinson to Eichner, 17 June 1971).

The general point', she concluded, 'is that you should be using Kalecki's version of the *General Theory*, not Keynes' (*ibid.*). Eichner now claimed to have identified 'a basic disagreement between us about the determinants of the investment demand function'. Robinson appeared to believe that current investment was a function of past profits, as Kalecki had suggested. Eichner himself thought that past sales, acting as a proxy for anticipated future demand, were the critical variable (Eichner to Robinson, 13 July 1971).

This, Robinson replied, had appalled her:

I was quite stunned by your letter. Certainly there is a deep misunderstanding. How could you possibly think that I hold that past saving out of profits determined present investment? Did you think I have joined the pre-Keynesian camp? It is present investment that determines present profits. $P = I + (I-s_p)P$ (Robinson to Eichner, 20 July 1971).

The same principle could even be applied at the micro level: 'I think the corps always have a good cushion of liquidity, and can vary their investment plans when they like. It is rather their investment that generates savings outside' (*ibid.*).

Eichner was not, of course, a defender of Say's Law[22], nor had he consciously made Robinson out to be one. Subsequent correspondence, together with personal discussions during her visit to the US in November-December 1971, appeared once again to have resolved their differences, which Robinson now dismissed as purely 'a matter of exposition' (Robinson to Eichner, 15 February 1972). As she told him in the following November, his theory is perfectly straightforward and convincing. It is a thousand pities that you insist on muddling it up But I know from sad experience that it is hopeless to try to help you (Robinson to Eichner, 1 November 1972).

Their correspondence continued, rather fitfully. By the summer of 1974 Robinson had narrowed the issue to a confusion between the ratio of investment to income and the rate of accumulation. But

the important part of your argument, which I fully support, is that the investment policy, the price policy and the financial policy of a firm, ex ante,

> have to be co-ordinated. What happens ex post will vary, and policy have to be
> reconsidered accordingly (Robinson to Eichner, 31 July 1974).

With this Eichner readily agreed.

The final stage of the Eichner-Robinson correspondence relates to the survey article on Post Keynesian theory that Eichner was writing for the *Journal of Economic Literature* with Robinson's former student, Jan Kregel. 'The general introduction is excellent', she wrote of an early draft, 'but I think both Kalecki and von Neumann should be mentioned along with Keynes'. So should Eichner himself:

> Now you have published your bit (E.J.) [Eichner 1973] surely it ought to be
> treated as one of the contributions and integrated into the general movement.
> E.g. what (if any) are the differences between A.S.E.'s substitution effect and
> Kalecki's degree of monopoly as a limit on the possible level of margins?
> (Robinson to Eichner, 11 September 1974).

Eichner agreed, and the published version included the significant statement that 'Certainly the work of Michal Kalecki has been no less important than that of Keynes' (Eichner and Kregel 1975, 1293n1). Kaleckian influences are apparent in much of Eichner's subsequent work (see, for example, Eichner 1987).

Conclusion

It is evident from the correspondence that Eichner's conversion to a Kaleckian view of economics was the result of a continuous intellectual bombardment by Joan Robinson over several, vitally important, years. He was, perhaps, unusually susceptible to her onslaught. Unlike Weintraub, Davidson and Minsky, Eichner's devotion to Keynes was never unqualified. As an industrial economist, he knew more than most about the defects of orthodox microeconomics. He had never been impressed by marginalism, static maximising models, or the neoclassical synthesis, and at the very start of his contact with Robinson had informed her of his commitment to a 'neo Marxian theory of income distribution purged of all elements of marginal productivity theory' (Eichner to Robinson, March 1969). Eichner shared Kalecki's faith in formal modelling and determinate solutions to precisely-defined problems (see Sawyer 1985, 193, 204-7). Almost uniquely among US Post Keynesians, he worked on the construction of large-scale macroeconometric models[23]. And his emphasis on the megacorp led him, even more than Kalecki, to play down the role of monetary factors in the theory of investment and growth.[24]

These idiosyncrasies of Eichner's help to explain why Davidson was never a Kaleckian, Weintraub only a very partial Kaleckian, and Minsky's conversion was incomplete and long-delayed. As far as Weintraub, at least, was concerned, physical distance was an important factor: had he been able to meet Robinson and the other Cambridge theorists in the 1950s, his ideas might have developed rather differently (Weintraub 1983, 234); by the time transatlantic travel had become easier, it was too late. A second clue is provided by the significant neoclassical vestiges in the thinking of Weintraub, Davidson, and (to a lesser extent) Minsky. Third, there is the rather paradoxical fact that filial loyalty to Keynes increased with the distance from Cambridge. Coddington's 'fundamentalist Keynesians' were always more prominent in the US than they were in Cambridge; Eichner is again an exception. This points to a fourth factor, particularly relevant to Davidson and Minsky, which is the essential role of money in US Post Keynesian theory. Kalecki's relative neglect of monetary questions, exaggerated though it clearly was by his critics, undoubtedly served to distance them from him.

There is one final clue to our puzzle: politics. There seems no doubt that Kalecki's spell in North America was blighted by McCarthyism, which also limited his influence among academic economists outside the United Nations. His views on economic policy - a greatly increased role for the state, substantial redistribution of income, permanent budget deficits - were also exceptionally radical by contemporary US standards. At a time when even the very mild Keynesianism of Lorie Tarshis was getting him into serious political trouble at Stanford (Harcourt 1982, 617), it would have been very difficult (not to say dangerous) for American economists to associate themselves with an avowed socialist like Kalecki.[25] Later on, continuing hostility to the Marxian foundations of Kalecki's ideas is evident in Davidson's tabulation of unorthodox schools (1972, 4), in which the 'Keynes school', with which Davidson associates himself, occupies the 'centre' of the political spectrum, with the 'neo-Keynesian' (Cambridge) school located 'left of centre' and the 'Socialist-Radical' school found on the 'extreme left'. Weintraub, like Davidson a lifelong liberal Democrat, was also a self-proclaimed non-radical (Weintraub 1983, 233). It is almost certainly no accident that the two theorists most sympathetic to Kalecki's method of thinking - Lawrence Klein and Hyman Minsky - had themselves been socialists in their youth (Minsky 1992), while Alfred Eichner was one of the most radical of the US Post Keynesians.

Politics certainly had some effect on Kalecki's reception in North America, and perhaps also in Cambridge, where the political centre of gravity was considerably to the left of that in the US.[26] In the United States his reputation was highest on the socialist fringes of academia, above all in the heterodox *Monthly Review* school of Marxism, where Paul Baran and Paul Sweezy paid handsome tributes to Kalecki (both directly, and indirectly via their appreciation of his disciple Josef Steindl) in their writings on the political economy of growth and the theory of monopoly capital (Baran 1957; Baran and

Sweezy 1964).[27] The full story of Kalecki's influence on the development of radical - as opposed to post Keynesian - economics in North America has yet to be told. His analysis of the political business cycle (Kalecki 1943b) was certainly often quoted. I suspect, however, that Kalecki's impact is easily over-stated. When radicalism found a mass audience on the campuses, in the 1970s, it all too frequently repudiated Kalecki (and Robinson, and Sraffa) in favour of a dogmatic fundamentalist Marxism that none of them would have endorsed.

Notes

1. This lasted just over forty years: Kalecki first published (in Polish) in 1927; he died in 1970.

2. Simon Chapple reminds me that an informal Kaldorian model of distribution can be found in several of Kalecki's early papers (for example, Kalecki 1932), and suggests that the dichotomy between determinants of the profit share and the profit level emerged only after his 1938 Econometrica paper on the distribution of national income (Kalecki 1938).

3. This is extremely similar to the subsequent analysis of Eichner (1976), discussed below.

4. Kalecki's foreword is dated February 1952. This is probably a typographical error; there is nothing to account for a two-year delay in publication.

5. This is Kalecki's important article, 'Three systems', published in Polish in 1934 but in English only in the first volume of his *Collected Works* (Kalecki 1990, p201-19).

6. 'The author was [in 1953] an official of the Department of Economic Affairs of the United Nations; the points of view expressed in the article should, however, be considered as his own, without committing the above organisation in any way' (Kalecki 1955, 1). A milder disclaimer is made in some papers (Kalecki 1947, 1948a, 1951), and no disclaimer in others (1948b, 1949a, 1950). Kalecki (1954) contains neither a disclaimer nor any reference to the author's employment by the United Nations.

7. A footnote mention of his views on general rationing (Kalecki 1941) and a one-paragraph discussion of the mathematical properties of the (1935) trade cycle model (Samuelson 1947, 167n31, 337).

8. His use of the term 'post-Keynesian' (lower-case 'p'; hyphen) is purely chronological.

9. The substantive references are by Higgins, who cites Kalecki (1943) on political resistance to subsidising mass consumption (Harris 1948, 480n30); and Tobin, who refers to the 1939 *Essays* on the constancy of marginal cost and the efficacy of raising wages to combat depression (*ibid.*, 577n13, 579n16). The citations by Harris, Goodwin and Lerner are more cursory (*ibid.*, 60, 488n6, 632n10, 653n15).

10. Significant references were made by Bernard F. Haley on the principle of increasing risk and the limits to the growth of the firm (Ellis 1949, 15-16, 27-8); Henry H. Villard, on the relationship between Kalecki's proposals for general consumer rationing and Milton Friedman's suggested expenditure tax (*ibid*, 338, 342-3); Moses Abramowitz, on income distribution theory and on Kalecki's contribution to the stagnation debate (Haley 1952, 140, 171); and Paul Baran, on Kalecki's 'masterful analysis' of the problems of maintaining full employment (*ibid.*, 362-364). (I am grateful to Simon Chapple for these references).

11. There is a bare mention of Kalecki in the notes to the unpublished portion of the *History* (Feiwel 1975, 458n5); it is certainly not the case, as Feiwel suggests, that Schumpeter was unaware of Kalecki's work.

12. Wrongly: see Sawyer (1985, 96-101) and Dymski, this volume.

13. 'It was only after I made the calculations ... that I recalled Kalecki on the constancy, but not in his pricing formula which I always found both limited and complex ... Mine, I thought - and still do - had the virtue of simplicity and generality, without assigning k to "monopoly"' (Weintraub to Jan Kregel, 20 January 1976, Sidney Weintraub Papers, Special Collections Department, Duke University Library, Durham, North Carolina, Box 10, Folder 16). See also Weintraub to Sheila Dow, 20 June 1980 (Box 8, Folder 5).

14. Or even very similar.

15. Davidson to Weintraub, Cambridge, 21 October 1970, Weintraub Papers, Box 2, Folder 1.

16. This is to a favourable comment on the theory of the political business cycle (Davidson 1991, volume 1, 100).

17. Kalecki's name again appears only once in the index to Davidson (1994).

18. There is another close parallel here with Weintraub, for whom a different historical episode - the first signs of stagflationary tendencies in the US economy in 1957-8, was crucial in his break with orthodox Keynesianism (Weintraub 1981, 10).

19. Though this paper was written in 1966 and revised for publication in January 1970 (Minsky 1972, 96).

20. I am grateful to Fred Lee for providing me with a copy of this correspondence.

21. Similar models were developed, independently of Eichner, by Ball (1964), Harcourt and Kenyon (1976) and Wood (1975).

22. Though, as Malcolm Sawyer has suggested to me, he is perilously close to it in his insistence that corporations actually can generate the profits they require through adjustments to their own profit margins.

23. Though, as Philip Arestis has suggested to me, it was not without serious misgivings. Eichner's 'flirtation' with large-scale econometric modelling, Arestis believes, was motivated by his desire to challenge the neoclassicals rather than by a firm belief in them *per se*.

24. See Kregel (1990), Milberg (1992) and - much more critical - Davidson (1992b); cf Dymski, this volume. Marc Lavoie objects to this characterisation of Eichner, pointing to his significant published work on the role of money (Forman, Groves and Eichner 1985; Arestis and Eichner 1988). On Kalecki, see Dymski, this volume.

25. I am grateful to Malcolm Sawyer and Bruce McFarlane for emphasising this point.

26. Paul Davidson is convinced that Joan Robinson's enthusiasm for Kalecki was largely political (King 1995a, 28), though this is surely an exaggeration.

27. Note, however, that the core ideas of both books can be found in Sweezy's (1942) *Theory of Capitalist Development*, which was written under the influence of classical Marxism and without any reference to Kalecki.

References

Arestis, P. and Eichner, A.S. 1988 'The Post Keynesian and Institutionalist Theory of Money and Credit'. *Journal of Economic Issues* 22(4), December: 1003-21.
Arestis, P. and Sawyer, M.C. (eds) 1992. *A Biographical Dictionary of Dissenting Economists*. Aldershot: Elgar.
Ball, R.J. 1964. *Inflation and the Theory of Money*. London : Allen and Unwin.
Balogh, T. and Schumacher, E.F. 1944 'An International Monetary Fund'. *Oxford University Institute of Statistics Bulletin* 6, 29 April: 81-93.
Baran, P. A. 1957 *The Political Economy of Growth*. New York: Monthly Review Press.
Baran, P. A. and Sweezy, P. M. 1964 *Monopoly Capital* New York: Monthly Review Press.
Barber, W .J. 1987 'The Career of Alvin H. Hansen in the 1920s and 1930s: a Study in Intellectual Transformation'. *History of Political Economy* 19(2), Summer: 191-205.
Coddington, A. 1976 'Keynesian Economics: the Search for First Principles'. *Journal of Economic Literature* 14(4), December: 1258-73.
Davidson, P. 1960. *Theories of Aggregate Income Distribution*. New Brunswick, N.J.: Rutgers University Press.
Davidson, P. 1972. *Money and the Real World*. London: Macmillan.
Davidson, P. 1991. *Money and Employment: the Collected Writings of Paul Davidson, Volume 1*, ed. L. Davidson. London: Macmillan.
Davidson, P.1991. *Inflation, Open Economies and Resources: the Collected Writings of Paul Davidson, Volume 2*, ed. L. Davidson. London: Macmillan.
Davidson, P.1992a. Paul Davidson (Born 1930). In Arestis and Sawyer 1992: 109-15.
Davidson, P. 1992b. 'Eichner's Approach to Money and Macrodynamics'. In Milberg 1992: 185-90.
Davidson, P.1994. *Post Keynesian Macroeconomic Theory*. Aldershot: Elgar.
Dell, S.   1977.   'Kalecki at the United Nations, 1946-54', *Oxford - Bulletin of Economics and Statistics* 39(1), February: 31-45.
Dymski, G.A. 1995. 'Kalecki's Monetary Economics'. This volume.
Eichner, A. S. 1969. *The Emergence of Oligopoly: Sugar Refining as a Case Study*. Baltimore: Johns Hopkins University Press.
Eichner, A. S. 1973. 'A Theory of the Determination of the Mark-Up under Oligopoly'. *Economic Journal* 83(332), December: 1184-1200.
Eichner, A. S.1976. *The Megacorp and Oligopoly: Micro Foundations of Macro Dynamics*. Cambridge: Cambridge University Press.

Eichner, A. S. 1987. *The Macrodynamics of Advanced Market Economies*. Armonk, N.Y.: Sharpe.

Eichner, A. S. and Kregel, J.A. (1975) 'An Essay on Post-Keynesian Theory: a New Paradigm in Economics'. *Journal of Economic Literature* 13(4), December: 1293-1314.

Ellis, H.S. (ed.) 1949. *A Survey of Contemporary Economics, Volume I*. Homewood, Ill: Irwin for the American Economic Association.

Fazzari, S. 1992 'Introduction: Conversations with Hyman Minsky. In Fazzari and Papadimitriou 1992: 3-12.

Fazzari, S. and Papadimitriou, D.B. (eds) 1992 *Financial Conditions and Macroeconomic Performance: Essays in Honor of Hyman Minsky*. Armonk, N.Y.: Sharpe.

Feiwel, G.R. 1975 *The Intellectual Capital of Michal Kalecki: a Study in Economic Theory and Policy*. Knoxville: University of Tennessee Press.

Forman, L., Groves, M. and Eichner, A.S. 1985. 'The Demand Curve for Money Further Considered'. In M. Jarsulic ed., *Money and Macro Policy*. Boston: Kluwer-Nijhoff: 29-45.

Galbraith, J.K. 1975. 'How Keynes Came to America'. In M. Keynes (ed.), *Essays on John Maynard Keynes*. Cambridge: Cambridge University Press: 132-41.

Galbraith, J.K. 1981. *A Life in Our Times*. Boston: Houghton Mifflin.

Goodwin, R.M. 1945. Review of Kalecki (1943). *American Economic Review* 35(4), September: 709-10.

Haley, B.F. ed. 1952 *A Survey of Contemporary Economics, Volume II*. Homewood, Ill: Irwin for the American Economic Association.

Hamouda, O.F. 1986 'Beyond the IS/LM Device: Was Keynes a Hicksian?'. *Eastern Economic Journal* 12(4), October-December: 370-84.

Hansen, A.H. 1948. *Income, Employment and Public Policy: Essays in Honor of Alvin H. Hansen*. New York: Norton.

Harcourt, G.C. 1982. 'An Early Post Keynesian : Lorie Tarshis (or : Tarshis on Tarshis by Harcourt)'. *Journal of Post Keynesian Economics* 4(4), Summer: 609-19.

Harcourt, G.C. and Kenyon, 1976. 'Pricing and the Investment Decision'. *Kyklos* 29(3): 449-77.

Harris, S.E. (ed.) 1947. *The New Economics: Keynes 'influence on Theory and Public Policy* New York: Knopf.

Hicks, J.R. 1980-1. 'IS-LM : an Explanation'. *Journal of Post Keynesian economics* 3(2), Winter: 139-54.

Kaldor, N. 1956 'Alternative Theories of Distribution'. *Review of Economic Studies* 23(2): 83-100.

Kalecki, M. 1932. 'The Business Cycle and Inflation' [first published in Polish]. In J. Osiatynski ed., *Collected Works of Michal Kalecki, Volume I*. Oxford: Clarendon Press, 1990: 147-55.

Kalecki, M. 1935. 'A Macrodynamic Theory of Business Cycles'. *Econometrica* 3(3), July: 327-44.

Kalecki, M. 1938. The Determinants of Distribution of the National Income, *Econometrica* 6(2), April: 97-112.

Kalecki, M. 1939. *Essays in the Theory of Economic Fluctuations*. London: Allen and Unwin.

Kalecki, M. 1941. 'The Theory of Long-Run Distribution of the Product of Industry'. *Oxford Economic Papers* 5, June: 31-41.

Kalecki, M. 1942. 'A Theory of Profits', *Economic Journal* 52, June-September: 258-67.

Kalecki, M. 1943a. *Studies in Economic Dynamics*. London: Allen and Unwin.

Kalecki, M. 1943b. 'Political Aspects of Full Employment'. *Political Quarterly* 14(4): 322-31.

Kalecki, M. 1944a. 'Employment in the United Kingdom During and After the Transition Period'. *Oxford University Institute of Statistics Bulletin* 6, 4 December: 265-87.

Kalecki, M. 1944b. 'Three Ways to Full Employment', in *The Economics of Full Employment : Six Studies in Applied Economics Prepared at the Oxford University Institute of Statistics*. Oxford: Blackwell: 39-58.

Kalecki, M. 1945a. 'The Maintenance of Full Employment After the Transition Period: a Comparison of the Problem in the United States and the United Kingdom'. *International Labour Review* 52(5), November: 449-64.

Kalecki, M. 1945b. 'Full employment by stimulating private investment?'. *Oxford Economic Papers n.s.*, 7, March: 83-92.

Kalecki, M. 1946a. 'A Comment on "Monetary Policy". *Review of Economics and Statistics* 28(2), May: pp 81-4.

Kalecki, M. 1946b. 'Multilateralism and Full Employment'. *Canadian Journal of Economics and Political Science* 12(3), August: 322-7.

Kalecki, M. 1947. 'The Maintenance of Full Employment After the Transition Period. A Rejoinder to Mr Woytinsky's Note'. *American Economic Review* 37(3), June: 391-7.

Kalecki, M. 1948a. 'Determinants of the Increase in the Cost of Living in the United States'. *Review of Economics and Statistics* 30(1), February: 22-4.

Kalecki, M. 1948b 'Further Comments on the Department of Commerce Series'. *Review of Economics and Statistics* 30(3), August: 195-7.

Kalecki, M. 1949a. Contribution to Discussion, *Econometrica* 17, Supplement, July: 176-7.

Kalecki, M. 1949b. 'A New Approach to the Problem of Business Cycles'. *Review of Economic Studies* 16(2): 57-64.
Kalecki, M. 1950. 'A Note on Long-Run Unemployment'. *Review of Economic Studies* 18(1): 62-4.
Kalecki, M. 1951. *Report on Main Current Economic Problems of Israel.* Tel Aviv: Government Printer.
Kalecki, M. 1954. *Theory of Economic Dynamics. An Essay on Cyclical and Long-run Changes in Capitalist Economy.* London: Allen and Unwin.
Kalecki, M. 1955. 'The Problems of Financing of Economic Development'. *Indian Economic Review* 2(3), February: 1-22.
Kalecki, M. 1962. 'A Model of Hyperinflation'. *Manchester School* 30(3), September: 275-81.
Kalecki, M. 1971. 'Class Struggle and the Distribution of National Income'. *Kyklos* 24(1): 1-9.
Kalecki, M. 1976. *Essays on Developing Economies.* Hassocks: Harvester.
Kalecki, M. and Schumacher, E.F. 1943. 'International Clearing and Long-Term Lending'. *Oxford University Institute of Statistics Bulletin* 5(Supp: 5), 7 August: 29-33.
King, J.E. 1995a. *Conversations With Post Keynesians.* London: Macmillan.
King, J.E. 1995b 'Sidney Weintraub: the Genesis of an Economic Heretic'. *Journal of Post Keynesian Economics,* forthcoming.
Klein, L.R. 1947a. *The Keynesian Revolution.* New York: Macmillan.
Klein, L.R. 1947b. 'Theories of Effective Demand and Employment'. *Journal of Political Economy* 55(2), April: 108-32.
Klein, L.R. 1951. 'The Life of John Maynard Keynes'. *Journal of Political Economy* 59(5), October: 443-51.
Kregel, J.A. 1990. 'The Integration of Micro and Macroeconomics through Macrodynamic Megacorps: Eichner and the "Post Keynesians"'. *Journal of Economic Issues* 24(2), June: 523-34.
Kuznets, S. 1939. Review of Kalecki (1939). *American Economic Review* 29(1), March: 805-6.
Lange, O. 1941. Review of Kalecki (1939). *Journal of Political Economy* 49(2), April: 279-85.
Lange, O. 1949. 'The Practice of Economic Planning and the Optimum Allocation of resources'. *Econometrica* 17, Supplement, July: 166-71.
McFarlane, B. 1995. 'Michal Kalecki and the Political Economy of the Third World', this volume.
Milberg, W. (ed.) 1992. *The Megacorp and Macrodynamics: Essays in Memory of Alfred Eichner.* Armonk, N.Y.: Sharpe.

Minsky, H. 1972. 'Financial Instability Revisited : the Economics of Disaster'. In *Reappraisal of the Federal Reserve Discount Mechanism, Volume 3*. Washington, D.C.: Board of Governors of the Federal Reserve System: 96-136.

Minsky, H. 1975. *John Maynard Keynes*. New York: Columbia University Press.

Minsky, H. 1976. 'How "Standard" is Standard Economics?' *Society* 14(3), March-April: 24-9.

Minsky, H. 1977. 'The Financial Instability Hypothesis: an Interpretation of Keynes and an Alternative to "Standard" Theory'. *Nebraska Journal of Economics and Business* 16(1), Winter: 5-16.

Minsky, H. 1978. 'The Financial Instability Hypothesis: a Restatement'. *Thames Papers in Political Economy*, Autumn.

Minsky, H. 1992. 'Hyman Minsky (Born 1919)'. In Arestis and Sawyer 1992: 352-8.

Mitra, A. 1954. *The Share of Wages in National Income*. The Hague: Central Planbureau.

Papadimitriou, D.B. 1992. 'Minsky on Himself'. In Fazzari and Papadimitriou 1992: 13-26.

Pfouts, R.W. 1955. Review of Kalecki (1954). *Southern Economic Journal* 22(1), July:117-18.

Robinson, A. 1947. 'John Maynard Keynes', *Economic Journal* 57, March: 1-68.

Robinson, J. 1952. *The Rate of Interest and Other Essays*. London: Macmillan.

Robinson, J. 1969. Review of A. Leijonhufvud, *On Keynesian Economics and the Economics of Keynes* (1968). *Economic Journal* 79(275), September: 581-3.

Samuelson, A. 1947. *Foundations of Economic Analysis*. Cambridge, Mass.: Harvard University Press.

Samuelson, A. 1964 'A Brief Survey of Post-Keynesian Developments'. In R. Lekachman (ed.), *Keynes' General Theory, Reports of Three Decades*. New York: St Martin's Press: 341-56.

Samuelson, A. 1981. 'Economics in a Golden Age: a Personal Memoir'. In E.C. Brown and R.M. Solow (eds), *Paul Samuelson and Modern Economic Theory*. New York: McGraw-Hill, pp 1-13.

Sawyer, M.C. 1985. *The Economics of Michal Kalecki.*, London: Macmillan.

Schumpeter, J.A. 1939. *Business Cycles* (two volumes). New York: McGraw-Hill.

Schumpeter, J.A. 1954. *History of Economic Analysis*. London: Allen and Unwin.

Solow, R.M. 1975. Review of Feiwel (1975). *Journal of Economic Literature* 13(4), December: 1331-5.

Sweezy, M. 1992. Interview with J.E. King, 6 December.

Turner, M.S. 1989. *Joan Robinson and the Americans*. Armonk, N.Y.: Sharpe.

United Nations 1947. *Background Paper on National Measures Concerning Full Employment*, Economic and Employment Commission, Sub-Commission on Employment and Economic Stability, document E/CN.1/Sub.2/2, 10 November.

United Nations 1949a. *Inflationary and Deflationary Tendencies, 1946-1948*. Department of Economic Affairs, Lake Success, N.Y.

United Nations 1949b. *The Structure of Full Employment*, Economic and Employment Commission, Sub-Commission on Employment and Economic Stability, document E/CN.1/Sub.2/10, 9 March.

United Nations 1953. *Consideration of the Provisional Agenda for the Sixteenth Session of the Council. Note by the Secretary-General* [on measures designed to reconcile the attainment and maintenance of full employment with the avoidance of the harmful effects of inflation], Economic and Social Council, document E/2404, 16 April.

Wallich, H.C. and Weintraub, S. 1971. 'A Tax-Based incomes Policy'. *Journal of Economic Issues* 5(2), June: 1-19.

Weintraub, S. 1942. 'Rationing Consumer Expenditure'. *Harvard Business Review* 21(1): 109-14.

Weintraub, S. 1946. 'Monopoly Pricing and Unemployment'. *Quarterly Journal of Economics* 61, November: 108-24.

Weintraub, S. 1949. *Price Theory.* New York: Pitman.

Weintraub, S. 1958. *An Approach to the Theory of Income Distribution.* Philadelphia: Chilton.

Weintraub, S. 1959. *A General Theory of the Price Level, Output, Income Distribution and Economic Growth.* Philadelphia: Chilton.

Weintraub, S. 1961. *Classical Keynesianism, Monetary Theory, and the Price Level.* Philadelphia: Chilton.

Weintraub, S. 1966. *A Keynesian Theory of Employment, Growth and Income Distribution.* Philadelphia: Chilton.

Weintraub, S. 1969. 'A Macro-Theory of Pricing, Income Distribution, and Employment'. *Weltwirtschaftliches Archiv* 102(1), March: 11-28.

Weintraub, S. 1970. 'Solow and Stiglitz on Employment and Distribution: a New Romance with an Old Model?' *Quarterly Journal of Economics* 84(1), February: 144-52.

Weintraub, S. 1981. 'An Eclectic Theory of Income Shares'. *Journal of Post Keynesian Economics* 4(1), Fall: 10-24.

Weintraub, S. 1983. 'A Jevonian Seditionist: a Mutiny to Enhance the Economic Bounty'. *Banca Nazionale del Lavoro Quarterly Review* 146, September: 215-34.

Wood, A. 1975. *A Theory of Profits.* Cambridge, Cambridge University Press.

Wray, L.R. 1992. 'Minsky's Financial Instability Hypothesis and the Endogeneity of Money'. In Fazzari and Papadimitriou 1992:161-80.

8 KALECKI, MARX AND THE ECONOMICS OF SOCIALISM

Jan Toporowski

Introduction

In this paper Kalecki's economics of socialism is put forward as rooted in a marxian critique of capitalism and his understanding of the limits of Keynesian stabilisation policies. At the heart of his analysis was central economic planning and control over investment in a socialist economy, which were needed for rational management of the economy. Kalecki's analysis suggests that errors of economic strategy and, in particular, weak planning of investment, rather than an absence of markets, disturbed the balance of the Eastern European socialist economies, leading to the 'Collapse of Communism' at the end of the 1980s.

Socialism and the Rational Economy

As is well known, the founders of the systematic radical critique of capitalism, Marx and Engels, did not speculate on the economics of socialism. As a result, this branch of economics had to be 'invented' as new with the establishment of the first socialist regimes in Central and Eastern Europe in 1917.

I would like to thank John King, Haroon Akram-Lodhi, Philip Arestis, Simon Chapple, Victoria Chick, Geoffrey Harcourt, Jan Kregel, Bruce McFarlane, and Malcolm Sawyer for the helpful comments on an earlier draft of this paper.

Among those who sympathised with the socialist project, the economics of socialism that emerged started with the political fact of the takeover of power by a socialist party, and then proceeded to examine more systematically the economic problems that forced themselves onto the political agenda of the new socialist governments. Debates over War Communism, Lenin's New Economic Policy, and Socialism in One Country, gave rise to economic analyses of the problems of industrialization, rural infrastructure such as electrification, and the establishment of basic social welfare facilities (Lenin 1921; Preobrazhensky 1965; Domar 1957; Bukharin and Preobrazhensky 1969).

These concerns were a far cry from the state of material prosperity envisaged by Marx and Engels when they thought of the transition to socialism. For them, the problems of socialism were simply the political one of the conquest of power, and the economic one of co-ordinating the enthusiastic labour of the enfranchised proletariat (Marx 1875, 318-319; Engels 1975 326-327). Contrary to their prediction, the socialist revolutions of this century took hold not in the most advanced capitalist countries, but in the two continental powers (Russia and China) which were too backward to become capitalist, but too powerful to be colonised, and subsequently in countries that were dependent on those powers.

Between Marx and the Russian Revolution there emerged neoclassical economics, which narrowed the scope and focus of political economy from production, distribution and accumulation, to prices and markets. Neoclassical economics engaged Marxism on the issue of value sending Marx's most faithful followers, from Engels onwards, into a largely sterile defence of the labour theory of value as a price-determining mechanism (the Transformation Problem). The neoclassical theory of socialism identified co-ordination of economic activities as the main economic problem facing a socialist regime (Mises 1935). When Lange pointed out that markets do exist under socialism, and central planners can vary prices to eliminate shortages and surpluses, Hayek's riposte was that the co-ordination problem was really one of incentives to efficient entrepreneurial behaviour (Lange 1937; Hayek 1945). In various guises, the core of the neoclassical approach continues to be that a socialist economy is doomed to shortages and inefficiency because it abolishes the free price system and entrepreneurship that are supposed to characterise dynamic capitalism. In Eastern Europe, Kornai emerged as an exponent of this view, seeing socialism as a particular form of disequilibrium economy (Kornai 1959, 1992).

Whereas socialist economists began their economics of socialism with the immediate practical problems of 'building socialism' in backward, impoverished countries, and neoclassical economists begin their economics of socialism with the state of rational efficiency which they believe laisser-faire capitalism to embody, Kalecki began his socialist economics implicitly with the problems of capitalism and, in the course of his exposition, refers repeatedly to the capitalist economy to show how differently adjustments to particular problems occur in the two types of economies. The chief problem of capitalism according to Kalecki is market instability. The fundamentalist Marxist reaction to the neo-classical revolution had been to defend the labour theory of value and argue around the principal policy issues raised by it, namely exploitation and the falling rate of profit as the main factors in capitalist crisis (Engels 1894; Mandel 1975). However, most Marxists including Engels recognised chronic instability as the central problem of capitalism[1].

The most damaging form of instability in the capitalist economy is the business cycle in which, at best, full employment is only achieved temporarily at the peak of an economic boom, so that unemployment persists most of the time under capitalism, except where a Tugan-Baranovsky strategy (see below) is implemented. Business cycles were the focus of Kalecki's studies of capitalism (Kalecki 1969, 1971). Central issues in this analysis were whether cycles were characterized by increasing or diminishing amplitude, and whether the trend was rising, falling or static (Steindl 1981). Behind these ostensibly obscure mathematical arguments lies a question concerning the rationality of capitalism that is fundamental to neo-classical economic theory and the political argument for capitalism: does the economy converge onto an efficient equilibrium? If it does, then general equilibrium theorists, the Real Business Cycle School, believers in Rational Expectations, and New Keynesians are correct in believing that capitalism is basically 'rational'; so that 'rational' decisions by individual agents create an efficient equilibrium or at least, in the view of Hayek and his followers, the least disequilibrium that is compatible with human freedom.

For Keynes, with whom Kalecki's work on capitalism is usually associated, the problem with capitalism is that the capitalists' rationality is limited by uncertainty and this makes their decisions subject to volatile shifts in their expectations (Keynes 1936, chapter 12; Keynes 1937). This theory of the 'bounded rationality' of capitalists is most developed in the work of George Shackle who, among Post-Keynesian economists was the least influenced by Kalecki (despite having been introduced to Keynesianism by Kalecki at the London School of Economics in 1936). While those Post-Keynesian economists who have been most influenced by Kalecki (e.g., Joan Robinson, G.C. Harcourt, Jan Kregel) have tended to be the least committed to 'bounded rationality', many have tried to combine Keynes's insights into uncertainty with Kaleckian analysis (e.g., Arestis 1992, chapter 4).

Kalecki himself was distinct from Keynes and his followers in believing, like Rosa Luxemburg and Marx, that the irrational characteristics of capitalism could not be attributed to defects in the faculties of capitalists. They too are at the mercy of an irrational system, that distorts the outcome of their rational decisions. That outcome depends on the response of capitalists as a class to situations which impose decisions on them that may be individually rational, but collectively disastrous. In a laissez-faire capitalist economy, economic aggregates which are critical for employment, trade and financial and economic stability, are merely the incidental outcomes of narrowly focused individual decisions, however rational they may be.

Examples of this individual rationality/collective irrationality in capitalism are numerous in Kalecki's writings on capitalism and socialism. Perhaps the best example is in his treatment of the relationship between wages and profits. While it is clearly rational for an individual capitalist to reduce the wages of his workforce, it is to their disadvantage when entrepreneurs as a whole act rationally like this. The effect is to deflate the wage goods market and redistribute profits from entrepreneurs to rentiers[2].

In his writings on socialism, Kalecki repeatedly points out that, contrary to the view widespread among economists and economic commentators, a market economy responds less flexibly and more haphazardly than a socialist economy to changes in supply. This does not just reflect the Hicksian 'fix-price' market imperfections that are widely believed to characterize the Keynesian economics in which Kalecki's work is usually located. For example, suppose that steel supply is reduced. Prices may rise, but the response of steel-using industries is likely to be a further increase in prices of their output, which may have little effect on demand in steel-using industries. Reaching equilibrium between supply and demand may take a long time, with the effects of the steel shortage being spread across industries in a haphazard manner that may be unrelated to social or consumer priorities. It is rational then for a central planning agency to identify a major steel-using industry and reduce its output modestly (Kalecki 1986, 30). Elsewhere Kalecki argued that the introduction of 'free market' forces in the socialist economy would give rise to macro-economic instability (Kalecki 1986, 52).

Kalecki's proposed solution to irrationality in the capitalist economy may be contrasted with Keynes's proposed solution. In Keynes's theory, the 'bounded rationality' of capitalists needs to be supplemented by government fiscal policy. In particular, the volatility of expectations of rentiers needs to be eliminated in order to remove the 'liquidity premium' on long-term interest rates, and bring them down to rates that will allow investment to rise to the level that will secure full employment (Keynes 1936, 374-375). Because the main problem of capitalism arises from a psychological defect of rentiers and entrepreneurs, it can be remedied, according to Keynes, by the 'socialization of investment' and the 'euthanasia of the rentier' (Keynes 1936, 375-376).

However, even if it were possible, through the kind of social control that is associated with Swedish social democracy or French indicative planning, to regulate investment in a Keynesian way to maintain near-full employment as well as foreign trade balance, a 'political business cycle' may emerge, as capitalists use their economic power to impose deflationary policies on governments in between elections (Kalecki 1943). A more serious and longer-term problem arises in the balance between investment and the level of aggregate demand needed to maintain the high rates of capacity-utilization that are necessary to sustain the rate of investment. We may call this the Tugan-Baranovsky problem, after the economist who first identified this 'disproportion' in Marx's extended scheme of capitalist reproduction, and suggested how it may be resolved. The stabilization of economic growth by regulating investment is only possible by having consumption rise more slowly than investment, and over time moving to more and more capital-intensive techniques (cf Kalecki 1967 and 1944). In the second half of this century, this Tugan-Baranovsky solution has appeared in the form of growing trade surpluses in countries that have achieved full employment through investment and export-led growth, in effect raising the capital stock relative to domestic consumption. Needless to say, the cost of this stability for export surplus countries has been chronic trade deficits in other countries, and consequent financial, monetary and economic instability.

For Kalecki, the problem is inherent in the way in which market forces operate, so that even the most rational decisions by agents are constrained by the flow of funds and the circular flow of income. Even if rentiers were eliminated and investment were guided by central planners, the economy would still experience instability because of the operation of market forces. Hence Kalecki's opposition to 'market socialism' (Kalecki 1986, 29-31). For Kalecki, the essential feature of the socialist economy was that investment and aggregate balances were planned, so that 'irrational' demand and financial constraints on production were removed.

Underlying this, implicitly if not explicitly in Kalecki's work, is the idea that reliable information which would not normally influence the decisions of agents in a free market economy or might influence them too weakly, can be used by central planners to guide economic decision-making. Such information might be on the state of foreign trade and opportunities in it, economic aggregates in the economy, or future productive capacity requirements. The Hayek critique of socialism, recently echoed by Kornai, assumes that all such information is either irrelevant, misleading, or fully reflected in price and cost alternatives (Toporowski 1982, 7; Hayek 1945; Kornai 1992)[3].

Planning under Socialism

Economic planning was therefore central to Kalecki's thinking about socialism, not because it allowed the working class to take back the fruits of their exploitation by capitalists, but because it liberated them from the misery of unemployment, and from insecurity when in employment. It also determined the issues which Kalecki examined in his studies of the socialist economy. Although attempts have been made to reconstruct from Kalecki's work 'a consistent system of socialist reproduction' (Osiatynski 1988, 171; see also Nuti 1986), his analysis is not comprehensive in this respect. There are two obvious and major gaps in his analysis of the socialist economy: consumption and the labour market (Toporowski 1986). In respect of consumption, Kalecki developed a methodology of estimating, by chain indices, sets of consumption bundles for use in calculating the efficiency of investment. These are similar to the equivalent consumption bundles of neo-classical indifference curve analysis, with the important difference that equivalence in Kalecki's approach is determined by central planners and not by consumers (Kalecki 1963; Osiatynski 1988, 144-147). However, this is far from constituting a systematic conceptual framework for the study of consumption under socialism.

In the case of the labour market under socialism, Kalecki provides only fragmentary analysis and original insights, beyond applied studies of the incomes of different strata of workers (Kalecki 1964), his advocacy of workers' councils as a democratising element in economic planning (Kalecki 1956), and repeated admonitions about the effects of reducing consumption on socialist sentiment among the working class. This lacuna in his analysis became the pretext for the accusations of revisionism that were made against him in 1968, when it was argued that his theory of growth in the socialist economy was 'an investment model of growth...mechanistic reasoning...[lacking] appreciation of the fundamental growth factor - human labour' (J. Gorski, quoted in Osiatynski 1988, 112). In fact, it is quite easy to re-arrange Kalecki's growth equations to give more general, labour-based equations for economic growth (*ibid.*).

Kalecki did not do so because he was not concerned to provide a 'general theory' of the socialist economy. He really wanted to elucidate certain arguments that had been put forward about the socialist economy, in effect using his formidable capacity for systematic thinking to identify the logic and pre-suppositions behind them, and to demonstrate the consequences of looking more realistically at the economic problems under discussion. Epistemologically, general economic theories are prone to mis-attributing reality to heuristic or pedagogic devices (cf Whitehead 1938, 74). Applied studies of problems in the real world are less likely to do this. Whereas a general theory needs merely to put forward an explanation that logically satisfies a general curiosity, applied work is about operational solutions, whose success or failure may be regarded as supporting or disproving the theory advanced in a particular solution. Applied analysis of the type that Kalecki undertook has rather more stringent criteria of verification (see Sohn-Rethel 1978). In the course of it he was able to identify much more crucial factors than those indicated by more academic general theorizing.

Kalecki's work on the socialist economy therefore has to be seen as it was actually advanced: not as a general theory, but as a set of studies of problems in economic planning under socialism. Criticisms of a lack of generality and Eastern European particularism (e.g. Nuti 1986) are beside the point. Kalecki was not concerned with merely making serious generalizations, but with clarifying the 'central problems of our time' (Kalecki 1970; Toporowski 1991). In the laissez-faire capitalist economy, there are no economic problems for the state to resolve, because all problems are eventually remedied, where at all possible, by individuals and the 'hidden hand' of market forces (see Hayek 1945; Kornai 1992). But in the socialist economy, economic problems are, or should be, the responsibility of economic planners. Hence Kalecki emphasized that a socialist economy had to be centralized. In particular, central planners should set the prices and production targets for the main commodities produced, and control the main investment projects and foreign trade. He was especially insistent that each enterprise's wage bill should be centrally determined. This was to avoid cost-minimizing by enterprises of the kind that would lead to unemployment and falling real wages. In this way, as was argued in the first section of this paper, socialism would avoid the chief problem of capitalism.

Kalecki was nevertheless aware of the limitations of central planners, and he became more aware of them as he experienced during the 1960s their various policy errors, in particular their propensity for 'heroic' plan construction, with extravagant targets set to win acclaim among the masses and offer them opportunities for material sacrifice for the sake of future prosperity. In the 1950s, Kalecki had advanced the view that over-centralization in economic organisation and shortages were the result of such heroism (Kalecki 1957), rather than being caused by over-centralization itself, as most economists have argued (e.g. Kornai 1959; Brus 1972; Brus and Laski 1989). In his view, workers' councils were necessary to avoid excessive bureaucratization, but not as part of a market system of control over production ('Workers' Councils and Central Planning' in Kalecki 1986). While he saw workers' councils as an effective check on the consistency of economic planning in individual enterprises, Kalecki made no mention of how democratic organs of government, the legislature perhaps, could act as a check on the macro-economic consistency of economic plans (Toporowski 1986). Perhaps he realized that there were going to be few votes for the modest, realistic aspirations that he advocated. If so, then this is a political inconsistency in his view of socialism, since it is so dependent on the articulation of social priorities by central authorities. Behind the over-ambitious economic plans that caused the Polish economy to decelerate in the 1960s was a sanguine optimism about the future of socialism that rapidly became demagogic and caused Kalecki to fall out with his employers, the Polish government.

However, Kalecki did introduce two major changes to Polish economic planning. The first was in articulating the longer-term aims of economic planning in a fifteen-year perspective plan. The idea behind this was not to give a forecast, or even the main economic data on the economy in a decade-and-a- half's time, but to act as a focus of research, as the plan was periodically up-dated, and to guide shorter-term, annual and five year, economic plans. A combination of demographic projections and forecasts from agriculture and industry were used to calculate overall economic growth rates and targets. An important advantage of the perspective plan over the medium-term, five or six year plans, was that it covered a period during which the benefits for consumption of particular investments should be capable of being demonstrated. In preparing a shorter, medium term, plan, it was much easier to justify excessive investment by inflating consequent increases in consumption which did not need to be specified because they fell beyond the period of the plan.

The aims of the perspective plan were perhaps the nearest that Kalecki ever came to drawing up his 'social welfare function'. They were the maximisation of consumption and a modest but good standard of housing for all households. These were subject to the constraints of maintaining full employment, realism in setting sectoral and industrial growth rates, and no medium or long-term foreign debts. These targets were then used to determine the investments that were needed to achieve them.

In any real economy, such a plan requires adequate supply information in order to check its consistency and realism. Foreign trade is a major unknown in most of the equations making up the plan. For Kalecki this underlined the importance of long-term trade agreements within the socialist bloc, the Council for Mutual Economic Assistance, and with politically sympathetic developing countries. He devoted much of his time during the early 1960s to discussions in the CMEA aimed at coordinating its members' perspective plans.

Investment and Economic Growth

In Kalecki's system of socialist economic planning, the chief instrument which the central planners have for achieving the plans which they draw up is their control of investment. Its total and distribution were supposed to be laid down by the perspective plan. Kalecki's work on investment efficiency was intended to minimize the investment outlays needed to obtain the consumption targets in that plan, and its five year and annual editions. In that respect, Kalecki's planning theory and practice differed radically from more traditional Stalinist economic planning, which emphasized the scarcity of capital equipment as a factor in economic backwardness and low standards of consumption. In traditional Stalinist planning, raising the share of investment in national income is a sufficient condition for higher consumption, and this was supported by economists who were not necessarily Stalinist in their politics (Domar 1957; Dobb 1959; Sen 1957). Kalecki's views on economic planning were informed by a systematic critique of this approach in his *Introduction to the Theory of Growth in a Socialist Economy*.

The starting point for this critique is a Harrod-type growth equation in which the increase in national income, dY, in a given year, is a function, $1/m$, of gross fixed investment, I, less depreciation, which Kalecki makes a function of national income, aY; plus the effect of disembodied technical progress, uY:

$$dY = (1/m)I - aY + uY \qquad\qquad (8.1)$$

Parameter m is the incremental capital-output ratio, while depreciation and disembodied technical progress are functions of national income on the implicit simplifying assumption of a fairly constant average capital-output ratio, and full capacity utilization, which Kalecki believed was made feasible by central planning (Kalecki 1972, 12; see also the previous section). Although, as we shall see, Kalecki developed the theory to consider increasing the capital-output ratio, the simplifying assumption of a constant ratio reflected the use of this equation in economic planning where parameters are relatively fixed in the short run, and are variable only in the longer term.

Dividing equation (8.1) by national income, Y, gives a linear growth equation:

$$dY/Y = r = (1/m)(I/Y) - a + u \qquad\qquad (8.2)$$

Kalecki then extends this equation to allow for changes in inventories and shows that, where there are labour reserves (i.e., effective unemployment), and where the capital-output ratio is allowed to vary, planners are faced with a choice of techniques which may be used to accelerate the rate of growth. However, once labour reserves have been taken up, then the rate of growth of national income settles down at the rate of growth of the labour force and its productivity due to disembodied technical progress (Kalecki 1972, chapter 5). The growth rate may still be accelerated by introducing more capital-intensive techniques, or rejuvenating the capital stock by a more rapid depreciation and replacement of it. While these may temporarily increase the rate of growth, it will still return eventually to the rate which is determined by the growth of the labour force and its productivity, albeit at a higher eventual level of national income. Kalecki's growth theory is therefore far from being an 'investment' model of growth in which labour is not accorded a key role, since labour is the key factor whose productivity is enhanced, or diminished by investment.

Kalecki then proceeds to the heart of his analysis, his critique of the strategy of adopting more capital-intensive techniques even when unused labour reserves are available. He shows that this strategy is limited in initial periods by the productivity of labour in the consumption goods sector. If this is insufficient to accommodate the increase in employment in the investment goods sector, then real wages will fall. In fact all net investment that is not financed from abroad involves some sacrifice of current consumption for future consumption. Even if a constant real wage constraint is imposed upon the switch to capital-intensive production, so that consumption rises with employment, Kalecki shows that the eventual increment in national income, due to the adoption of more capital-intensive techniques, is likely to be small once technical progress is taken into consideration (Kalecki 1972, 88). However, Kalecki was introducing a form of technical progress which Dobb and Sen had not taken into account, or rather had assumed away by positing that technical progress enhances only capital productivity. In that case, switching to capital-intensive techniques becomes marginally more attractive than when technical progress is neutral, irrespective of the capital-output ratio (Nuti 1986).

Kalecki points out that economic growth is limited by foreign trade as well as by current consumption. Beyond a certain growth rate, the balance of trade goes into deficit, raising the prospect of higher foreign indebtedness if growth is not reduced. The effect of these 'barriers' to growth is to reduce labour productivity and increase investment costs, beyond a certain threshold share of investment in national income, effectively raising the incremental capital-output ratio. Thus ambitiously capital-intensive growth strategies eventually become absolutely less efficient than less capital-intensive variants.

Kalecki derived from this analysis a 'government decision curve' summarizing his arguments about the correct way in which an economic growth strategy should be selected. Having established that capital-intensive growth strategies are unlikely to be significantly more productive, and that the share of investment in national income is subject eventually to diminishing returns, the incremental capital-output ratio is shown as a function of the share of investment that is constant and then rises ($1/m$ - $1/m'$ in the diagram).

Superimposed on this is a government decision curve which 'serves only to illustrate the attitude of the government towards "sacrificing the present for the future"'. Kalecki thereby indicates that this is not an optimisation calculation. The decision curve (G - G') shows the rising amount of economic growth that would induce the economic planners to reduce the share of consumption in national income. Hence at low rates of investment, they are likely to be more willing to sacrifice consumption for higher growth than at higher rates of investment (I/Y), and the curve is therefore upward-sloping. The position of the curve is determined by their policy on real wages during the period of

The Government Decision Curve

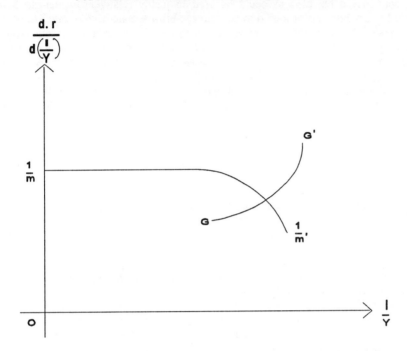

m is the incremental capital/output ratio; r is the growth rate of national income; I is gross investment; Y is national income.

growth acceleration and by balance of trade considerations. The existence of labour reserves, or an improvement in terms of trade would shift the decision curve up, allowing the economy to secure a given growth rate at a lower rate of investment[4].

The preferred share of investment, multiplied by the current level of national income gives a volume of investment resources which is then distributed to the various branches of industry in accordance with the perspective plan. The branches are also given parameters by the central planners to assist in drawing up the enterprises' own investment plans. Kalecki's second contribution to economic planning was to modify the calculations used in this industrial investment planning in Poland. From the mid-1950s these were based on Soviet practice, essentially applying to investment projects a standard recoupment period set by the central planners.

In principle, given a sufficiently accommodating attitude on the part of the central planners to the share of investment in industry (i.e., a flatter government decision curve), recoupment period calculations could be used to justify relatively capital-intensive projects[5]. The amendments proposed by Kalecki and his associate Mieczyslaw Rakowski were intended to economise on investment resources by discouraging new capital undertakings, and encouraging capital spending on improvements to existing capacity. Kalecki and Rakowski incorporated labour-saving modernization schemes in the calculation, the costs of output losses due to the tying up of investment resources in uncompleted projects, and an allowance for differences in the expected life-time of projects. The formula that they eventually produced was one in which effective expenditure on capacity is minimized:

$$E = \frac{I(1/T)(1 + q.z) + C.y_n}{X.z_n} = \text{min.} \qquad (8.3)$$

where I is the investment cost of the project; T is the standard recoupment period; q is the net yearly product of one unit of investment unfrozen by adopting a more rapidly-yielding variant; z is the average period during which investment resources are frozen; C is the total of the project's operating costs; y_n is the ratio of the total costs of the project to the total costs of a project operating to the standard project life-time laid down for the industry; X is the target capacity of the project; and z_n is the project's capital-output ratio divided by the capital-output ratio of plants of standard durability[6]. The formula was published by the Polish Planning Commission as an instruction to Polish enterprises, with tables of standard project parameters for different branches of industry. Kalecki developed another formula, similar in some respects to the investment efficiency equation, to calculate the efficiency of foreign trade (Osiatynski 1988, 91).

The equation is an ingenious compromise between the old pay-back period of assessment, and rates of return, implicit in the $1/T$, z_m, and y_n parameters. Nuti has argued that this approach was 'untidy and messy' by comparison with discount rate methods of selection (Nuti 1986). But the editor of Kalecki's *Collected Works* has pointed out that discounting future returns would require 'correct' price information which simply would not exist in a centrally planned economy (Osiatynski 1988, 143). (Nor, we may add, is such price information available in any market economy). Kalecki himself was aware of the limits of any calculation precisely because he regarded investment as an instrument, rather than an aim, of central economic planning. The calculation was only to be decisive for relatively minor projects. Larger projects were supposed to be decided upon in perspective and five year plans, in accordance with the requirements of target standards of consumption and the availability of labour. For these larger projects, investment calculations would inform, but not determine, the choice of techniques where such a choice was available (Kalecki 1972, chapter 12).

Moreover, for the whole system (that is, the selection of growth and investment rates, the choice of the main projects, and investment and foreign trade calculations) to work it is necessary to have strong and disciplined planners. Otherwise there arises a socialist version of the Tugan-Baranovsky problem that is inherent in Stalinist planning and the weak central planning that superseded it. In principle, higher rates of investment are supposed to facilitate higher levels of consumption at the end of the plan period. In practice, the utilities of particular outputs are not interchangeable, and higher outputs of investment goods are not automatically transformed into higher outputs of consumption goods. Machine tools, for example, have no direct household or agricultural uses, and need the intervention of a central planner to allocate them to the production of consumer goods or agricultural equipment. It is worth recalling here (as Kalecki was prone to do when discussing appropriate methods of adjustment in a socialist economy) what happens in a free market capitalist economy following an investment boom: an excess of investment goods capacity results in a fall in investment. This, in turn, causes economic activity to decline until excess capacity is eliminated. According to Kalecki, only central planning can simultaneously redirect the excess investment goods capacity towards the production of, say, consumer durables and agricultural implements *and* raise wages and advance agricultural credits to increase demand for such production.

Under Stalinist and weak central planning, the central planners allowed excessive investment and did not re-direct it towards the production of consumer goods. The excessive production of investment goods drained material resources away from the consumption sector of industry and agriculture, reducing efficiency in those sectors and giving rise to the shortages that Kornai regards as inherent features of socialism (Kornai 1992, chapter 11). In Poland, the revulsion against Stalinist excesses gave way to a somewhat tighter control over investment, but the benefits of this were vitiated by faulty strategic choices which reduced the effectiveness of the investment programmes as a whole, and resulted in a slow-down in economic activity in the later 1960s (Kalecki 1958, 1959, 1964b). During the 1970s, investment planning was liberalized, with the central planners merely setting the parameters for investment managers to decide on individual projects. This resulted in a huge investment boom that was accommodated by rising foreign indebtedness. At the same time, the 'modernising' post-1970 government pursued a policy of widening income differentials in the state sector, in order to create stronger economic 'incentives'. The scope of free market activity was extended, and the resulting inflation of higher incomes created a large demand for luxury goods that further enhanced the excess demand in the consumer goods market (cf Toporowski 1993). The realization that the boom had got out of hand led to a re-centralization of investment decision-making after 1976. However, the foreign indebtedness that was incurred placed new constraints on the economy. Efforts to secure a convertible currency trade surplus in order to service the growing foreign debt undermined the central planners' attempts to direct the new industrial capacity towards domestic consumption and agricultural production. This time, shortages of imported materials, spare parts and equipment reduced capacity utilization and hence industrial efficiency. In this way weak central planning and strategic blunders gave rise to the crisis of socialism (Toporowski 1981) and the eventual collapse of Communism in Poland.

In addition to his work on economic planning, Kalecki also undertook a study of economic delinquency (i.e., black market activities) which suggested that, with the development of industry, planning and methods of control, petty pilfering was giving way to large-scale networks of criminal activity (Kalecki 1962), from which are descended the criminal business mafias that have emerged in laissez-faire post-communism. He also headed an investigation of the distribution of income which up-dated his 1937 study of income distribution in Poland. In a comparison of changes in manual and white-collar workers' incomes between 1937 and 1954, Kalecki was able to show that the establishment of socialism had equalized incomes across the two strata. Perhaps surprisingly, the real wages of manual workers had not risen, but the real earnings of white collar workers had fallen by around a third. Kalecki suggested that this was why workers tended to compare their post-War earnings unfavourably with their pre-War earnings. Despite this, living standards had risen for all households, principally because of full employment: households had more members in employment, and hence higher real household incomes (Kalecki 1964a).

Conclusion

Kalecki's work on the socialist economy adds up to a strong economic rationale for socialism and a consistent view of how it should operate. The starting point of his analysis was a clear appraisal, in the marxist tradition, of the fundamental problems of capitalism, and the limits of Keynesianism, which could only be overcome by central planning in a socialist economy. At the core of his analysis was the planning of investment, not only because it is the vehicle for economic progress in backward economies, but also because the efficiency of the socialist economy at full employment was determined by the strict control of investment. This clear understanding of the fundamental economic problems of socialism makes Kalecki's analysis more relevant than theories of socialism that claim greater generality and comprehensiveness but either idealize capitalism (Hayek 1945; Kornai 1992), and hence can only explain post-Communist difficulties by past Communism, or those theories which overlook the all-too-obvious difficulties of socialism (Stalin 1952; Bettelheim 1975).

Notes

1 Engels even hinted that the chronic instability may be a new stage of capitalism. In a letter to August Bebel dated 20-23 January 1886, he wrote :

This is now already the eighth year of the pressure of over-production on the markets and, instead of getting better, it is always getting worse. There is no longer any doubt that the situation has essentially changed from what it was formerly, since England has got rivals on the world market the period of crises, in the sense known hitherto, is closed. If the crises change from acute into chronic ones but at the same time lose nothing in intensity, what will be the end? A period of prosperity, even if a short one, must after all return sometime, when the accumulation of commodities has been exhausted; but how all this will occur I am eager to see. But two things are certain: we have entered a period incomparably more dangerous to the existence of the old society than the period of ten-yearly crises; and secondly, when prosperity returns, England will be much less affected by it than formerly, when she alone skimmed the cream off the world market (Marx and Engels 1936, 444-5).

2 'One of the main features of the capitalist system is the fact that what is to the advantage of a single entrepreneur does not necessarily benefit all entrepreneurs as a class. If one entrepreneur reduces wages he is able *ceteris paribus* to expand production; but once all entrepreneurs do the same thing, the result will be entirely different' ('The Mechanism of the Business Upswing' in Kalecki 1969, 26; see also 'Class Struggle and the Distribution of National Income' in Kalecki 1971, 156-164).

3 The editor of Kalecki's *Collected Works*, Jerzy Osiatynski, argues that, for at least three reasons, central planners themselves suffer from 'bounded' rationality. These reasons are the absence of an agreed and consistent social welfare function, inadequate information transmission, and the absence of a 'hard' budget constraint under socialism (Osiatynski 1988, 182-187). 'Hard' budget constraints were precisely what Kalecki was trying to avoid because of their deflationary consequences when excess capacity appears.

4 Nuti calls this planners' decision curve 'a supply function of savings on the part of the planners'. This may give a misleading impression that the curve is determined by the thrift of planners, whereas in fact it represents the productivity of labour and the terms of trade, *given* a certain *attitude* on the part of the planners towards household consumption in the near future (Nuti 1986; see also Laski 1960). The possibility of misinterpretation is perhaps enhanced by Nuti's comparison of Kalecki's growth function to the golden rule of accumulation in neoclassical growth theory (see also Harcourt and McFarlane 1990).

5 In his unique laconic style, Kalecki summed up virtually all the problems of investment planning with the remark 'Just as economists have a weakness for calculation, technicians want to have the latest technical toys, and we should not hold this against them, but we do not need to offer them these toys immediately' (Kalecki 1965, 322).

6 This version of Kalecki's investment efficiency calculation is given in Nuti 1986.

References

Arestis, P. 1992. *The Post-Keynesian Approach to Economics: An Alternative Analysis of Economic Theory and Policy.* Aldershot, Elgar.

Bettelheim, C. 1975. *The Transition to Socialist Economy.* Hassocks: Harvester Press.

Brus, W. 1972. *The Market in a Socialist Economy.* London: Routledge and Kegan Paul.

Brus, W. and Laski K. 1989. *From Marx to the Market: Socialism in Search of an Economic System.* Oxford: Clarendon Press.

Bukharin, N.I. 1979. *The Politics and Economics of the Transition Period.* London: Routledge and Kegan Paul.

Bukharin, N.I. and Preobrazhensky E.A. 1969. *The ABC of Communism.* Harmondsworth: Penguin.

Dobb, M. 1960. *An Essay on Economic Growth and Planning.* London: Routledge and Kegan Paul.

Domar, E. 1957. 'A Soviet Model of Growth' in Domar, *Essays in the Theory of Economic Growth.* Oxford: Oxford University Press : 223-61.

Engels, F. 1894. 'Preface' to Marx, K. *Capital Volume III: The Process of Capitalist Production as a Whole.* London: Lawrence and Wishart 1974.

Engels, F. 1975. *Anti-Dühring: Herr Eugen Dühring's Revolution in Science.* Moscow: Progress Publishers.

Harcourt, G.C. and McFarlane B., 1990. 'Economic Planning and Democracy'. *Australian Journal of Political Science* 25(2), November: 326-32.

Hayek, F.A. von 1945. 'The Uses of Knowledge in Society'. *American Economic Review* 35(4), September: 519-30.

Kalecki, M. 1943. 'Political Aspects of Full Employment'. *Political Quarterly* vol. 14(4): 322-31.

Kalecki, M. 1944. 'Three Ways to Full Employment'. In *The Economics of Full Employment. Six Studies in Applied Economics Prepared at the Oxford Institute of Statistics.* Oxford: Basil Blackwell: 39-58.

Kalecki, M. 1956. 'Workers' Councils and Central Planning'. In Kalecki 1986: 25-37.

Kalecki, M. 1957. 'Do not Over-estimate the Role of the Model'. In Kalecki 1992: 69-73.

Kalecki, M. 1958. 'Perspective Plan for 1961-1975'. In Kalecki 1992: 221-31.

Kalecki, M. 1959. 'The Basic Problems of the 1961-1965 Five Year Plan'. In Kalecki 1992: 209-16.

Kalecki, M. 1962. 'On the Causes of Economic Delinquency'. In Kalecki 1993: 220-5.

Kalecki, M. 1963. 'The Problem of the Optimum Structure of Consumption'. In Kalecki 1993: 147-58.

Kalecki, M. 1964a. 'A Comparison of Manual and White-Collar Worker Incomes with the Pre-War Period'. In Kalecki 1993: 226-33.

Kalecki, M. 1964b. 'Observations on the 1961-1965 Five Year Plan'. In Kalecki 1993: 243-54.

Kalecki, M. 1965. 'Theses on Technical Progress and Its Types'. In Kalecki 1993: 314-16.

Kalecki, M. 1967. 'The Problem of Effective Demand in Tugan-Baranovsky and Rosa Luxemburg'. In Kalecki 1971: 146-51.

Kalecki, M. 1969. *Studies in the Theory of Business Cycles 1933 - 1939*. Oxford: Blackwell.

Kalecki, M. 1970. 'Theories of Growth in Different Social Systems'. *Scientia* 105, May-June: 311-16.

Kalecki, M. 1971. *Selected Essays on the Dynamics of the Capitalist Economy 1933 - 1970*. Cambridge: Cambridge University Press.

Kalecki, M. 1972. *Selected Essays on the Economic Growth of the Socialist and the Mixed Economy*. Cambridge: Cambridge University Press.

Kalecki, M. 1986. *Selected Essays on Economic Planning*. Cambridge Cambridge University Press.

Kalecki, M 1992. *Collected Works of Michal Kalecki. Volume III Socialism. Functioning and Long-Run Planning*. Ed. J. Osiatynski. Oxford: Clarendon Press.

Kalecki, M. 1993. *Collected Works of Michal Kalecki. Volume IV. Socialism Economic Growth and Efficiency of Investment*. Ed. J. Osiatynski. Oxford: Clarendon Press/

Keynes, J.M. 1936. *The General Theory of Employment, Interest and Money*. London. Macmillan.

Keynes, J.M. 1937. 'The General Theory of Employment'. *Quarterly Journal of Economics* 51(2), February: 209-23.

Kornai, J. 1959. *Overcentralization in Economic Administration*. Oxford. Oxford University Press.

Kornai, J. 1992. *The Socialist System: The Political Economy of Socialism*. Princeton : Princeton University Press.

Lange, O. 1936-7. 'On the Economic Theory of Socialism'. In B.E. Lippincott ed. *On the Economic Theory of Socialism*. Minneapolis: University of Minnesota Press, 1938: 55-143.

Laski, K. (1960). 'Warunki rownowagi ogolnej mindzy produkcjn a sponyciem w gospodarce socjalistycznej' in Lange, O., (ed.) *Zagadnienia ekonomii politycznej socjalizmu*. Warszawa, Ksinka i Wiedza, 1960: 176-237.

Lenin, V.I. 1921. 'Theses for a Report on the Tactics of the R.C.P.' In Lenin, V.I. *Selected Works*. Moscow : Progress Publishers 1968: 631-8.

Mandel, E. 1975. *Late Capitalism*. London: New Left Books.

Marx, K. 1875. 'Critique of the Gotha Programme'. In Marx, K., and Engels, F., *Selected Works*. London: Lawrence and Wishart 1970: 311-31.

Marx, K. and Engels F. 1936. *Selected Correspondence 1846 - 1895*. London: Lawrence and Wishart.

Mises, L. von 1935. 'Economic Calculation in the Socialist Commonwealth'. In Hayek, F.A. von (ed.) *Collectivist Economic Planning*. London: Routledge and Kegan Paul: 87-130.

Nuti, D.M. 1986. 'Michal Kalecki's Contribution to the Theory and Practice of Socialist Planning'. *Cambridge Journal of Economics 10(4), December: 333-53.*

Osiatynski, J. 1988. *Michal Kalecki on a Socialist Economy*. London: Macmillan.

Preobrazhensky, E. 1965. *The New Economics*. Oxford: Clarendon Press.

Sen, A.K. 1957. 'Some Notes on the Choice of Capital Intensity in Development Planning'. *Quarterly Journal of Economics* 71, November: 561-84.

Sohn-Rethel, A. 1978. *Intellectual and Manual Labour: A Critique of Epistemology*. London: Macmillan

Stalin, J.V. 1952. *The Economic Problems of Socialism in the USSR*. Moscow: Foreign Languages Press.

Steindl, J. 1981. 'Some Comments on the Three Versions of Kalecki's Theory of the Trade Cycle'. In Steindl, *Economic Papers 1941 - 1988*. London : Macmillan: 1990: 139-48.

Toporowski, J. 1981. 'Polish Realities'. *The Tablet* 235, 12 December: 1220-1222.

Toporowski, J. 1982. *Sources of Disequilibrium in a Centrally Planned Economy*. Unpublished Ph.D. thesis, University of Birmingham.

Toporowski, J. 1986. 'Introduction'. In Kalecki 1986: 1-18.

Toporowski, J. 1991. 'Two Enigmas in the Methodology of Michal Kalecki'. *History of Economics Review* 16, Summer: 90-6.

Toporowski, J. 1993. 'Housing as a Wage Good and a Luxury Good: Absolute Poverty and the Distribution of Income in Supply-side Economics'. *International Review of Applied Economics 7(3).*

Whitehead, A.N. 1938. *Science and the Modern World*. Harmondsworth, Penguin.

9 MICHAL KALECKI AND THE POLITICAL ECONOMY OF THE THIRD WORLD

Bruce McFarlane

The difference between highly developed and underdeveloped (non-socialist) economies can be formulated in a very simple way. In one case, existing resources have to be utilised and modern capitalism has learned the trick of doing it. In the other case, resources have to be built up and this requires far-reaching reforms amounting to revolutionary changes. This simple fact explains the difference in the economic and political situations in those two groups of countries and, in a sense, determines the present phase of history.

(Kalecki 1976, 27)

Introduction

Michal Kalecki's work on countries of the Third World (formerly the 'underdeveloped' world, now the 'developing world') covered two main dimensions of his career as a practical economist. This observation first spans his work at the United Nations in New York (late 1946 to late 1954) in which Third World problems came up in a number of contexts. The second phase encompasses his work as a visiting adviser to Mexico (1953), India (1960) and Cuba (1960) and his establishment of a Centre for Research on Underdeveloped Countries in Warsaw in 1963 which trained young economists from Asia, Africa and Latin America.

A main feature of Kalecki's writings in this area is that they are policy-oriented. Although informed by an incisive theoretical scaffolding, the aim is to give advice that can be acted upon to improve the rate and structure of growth with full incorporation of the limiting effects of bottlenecks and the generation, within the process of development itself, of new fetters on accelerated development.

Kalecki at the United Nations: His Writings and Talks

Kalecki's involvement with international and national issues impinging on Third World countries began in 1946. In March that year, Kalecki took up a senior post at the International Labour Office in Montreal. He interrupted the job with a rather long visit to Poland later in the year. Returning after three months to the ILO, he represented that body on a number of official and non-official committees that had been set up in 1946 under the new Bretton Woods and UN frameworks, committees looking into post-war international stability, payments and trading arrangements. However, feeling that he was unable really to influence ILO policy, Kalecki joined the staff of the UN on 16 December 1946.

With official Polish support, he became a Deputy-director of a Division (Stability and Prices) under the UN Department of Economic and Social Affairs in New York, where he remained until his resignation at the end of 1954. During his stint at the UN, he directed the compilation and publication of UN reports on various national and international aspects of full employment, and the *World Economic Report* series. His work at the UN also brought to his attention the economic problems of developing countries, (Interview with S. Braun in Kriesler 1991c).

In this section some of his inputs to UN reports will be reviewed. However, it is also important to recall the conditions under which he wrote at that time. Internationally, the victors of World War II were concentrating their attention on post-war stability - of the developed and the underdeveloped areas. Destabilising forces in international trade and payments were seen as major threats to political settlements after the war and to the full employment objective that the UN was adopting. At the UN itself there was a great deal of early tension exacerbated by the onset of the Cold War, the atomic bomb and the Rightist surge within the USA that reached its apogee in McCarthyism.

Kalecki, then, had to do his work against this breakdown of normal study - there could be no writing for the sake of research as such. With his well known strong stands on principles and a willingness to resign to support them, Kalecki was inevitably drawn into a number of incidents to which some attention needs to be paid. A number of these have been brought to light in Peter Kriesler's intensive interviews with the former UN economists, Sidney Dell and Stanislaw Braun, as well as with Ada Kalecki (Kriesler 1991a, 1991b, 1991c). Among the problems faced by the Polish economist were: American FBI interference with Kalecki's staff; his rift with a close colleague, J. J.Mosak, who had felt outside 'pressure'; and the refusal of UN Secretary-General Dag Hammerschold to meet a Mexican government request that Kalecki be sent as an adviser. (He had previously lectured to young planners there, but this time there came an official application from the Mexican government to send Kalecki as an adviser). Finally, in 1954, came the setting up of an external committee to review Kalecki's reports.

The circumstances under which Kalecki worked at the United Nations were, then, very difficult for him[1], as interviews with those in the know reveal (Kriesler 1991a, 1991b, 1991c). However, from 1948 till his retirement in 1954 he wrote the main part of the UN *World Economic Report*, and some special reports on price stabilisation in the post-war era. In informal discussions he criticised the excessive interference with Third World countries being contemplated by the IBRD or the IMF. He did, however, debate with some economists on these issues, which had already been flagged in his article on multilateralism (Kalecki 1946). For example, two issues which touched on that interest were (a) the international conditions needed for full employment and (b) the international arrangements needed for its maintenance. Some of Kalecki's positions are set out in an early post-war paper (Kalecki 1946) where he suggests that, in an international economy with freer trade, a domestic Keynesian-style full employment policy would have to be modified severely to take into account large changes in the capital account of the international balance of payments of a country. He rejected elimination of current account deficits by means of exchange rate manipulation. What had to be done, he thought, was to look at various *parts* of the international economy: some countries' growth involves current account deficits, while others run up balance of payments surpluses. Hence the latter should expand domestic output to draw in more imports. This action would go a long way towards eliminating their surpluses and the deficits of their trading partners. (The resemblance of Kalecki's scenario, written in 1946, with recent Japanese actions, is obvious). As to maintaining the full employment objective, which was so important a part of Kalecki's (1945) piece 'Three Ways to Full Employment', he did not write much at the UN, but he did work with T. C. Chang on the devaluation of sterling.

One incident in 1947 concerning Kalecki and the Third World is recorded in Kriesler's interview with Braun (Kriesler 1991c). A Mr McCloy, from an international bank, asked for UN participation at a conference on future development strategies for Third World countries. Kalecki attended, but did not respond in the way hoped for when McCloy's plan to limit the industrialisation of Third World countries was outlined. India should, in the planned scenario, avoid constructing metals industries and stick to textiles. Some Third World economies should specialise on agriculture and not industry; otherwise the harmony of the world economy would be disturbed. Kalecki criticised some of the American and English economists present, quoting past and present Western advocates of protectionism: 'You are using double standards. You are doing certain things or you did them in the past and this allowed you to develop, and now you are trying to forbid the less developed countries to do just that'. After this speech the majority present voted down the McCloy-inspired resolution. It appears that this incident irked quite a few UN officials when they heard about it, hastening the inevitable departure of Kalecki from the organisation.

This process seems to have been reinforced by Kalecki's arguments within the UN Divisions in favour of an intra-American Development Bank (Dell, interview with Kriesler; see Kriesler 1991b). Dell has noted: 'The Americans were absolutely dead set against this because for them it was equivalent to treason to propose intra-American banking for development purposes - it would upset the whole US applecart in Latin America'. On this occasion, Hammerschold appears to have given Kalecki some support, but backed off 'after all hell broke loose' when a Kaleckian draft proposal was circulated.

With attempts to organise 'checks' on his reports, Kalecki left the UN, but his interest in development issues was to be resumed in 1960 and subsequently (Kalecki 1976). In retrospect quite a few of the issued Reports of the UN Economic and Social Commission reveal an influence of Kalecki, either direct, or indirect through close colleagues and subordinates.

His background at Oxford was important here; certain well-honed skills were brought to his UN section dealing with post-war stability. First, he brought an unrivalled knowledge of the operation of the British war economy, including methods of financing priority sectors and raising resources; rationing of scarce foods and raw materials; and ways of ensuring that price controls achieve their objectives. Oskar Lange was fond of saying that the early days of economic planning for a country embarking on rapid economic development were analogous to 'planning a war economy'. If there is any truth in this, Kalecki would have been a most useful contributor to UN discussions on the link between stability and the planning of accelerated growth, for he had already worked on ways of achieving full employment in developed countries as price controls and rationing were taken off.

Certainly the topics discussed around him daily at the UN, such as post-war stability and financing economic development, would have been 'grist to the mill'. Kalecki set to work on these important post-war issues for the 'new' countries emerging from a colonial past, or about to emerge. An example is a report by UN development economists, specifically one sub-commission dominated by Kalecki, the Division of Economic Stability and Development. It was published as *Methods of Financing Economic Development* by the UN Department of Economic Affairs in 1949. There are many wise remarks about controls, forced saving, methods of increasing public and private savings and the usefulness of foreign investment in promoting development in the underdeveloped world (and some of the dangers of this). While it is impossible to pin down what parts, if any, were written by Kalecki, one can feel his influence. Whether the paper was written by one of his close associates has not yet been established by me or other biographers. However, Part I anticipates many ideas that re-appeared in Kalecki's remarks on the Third Indian Five Year Plan, written in January 1960 when he was a visiting adviser to the Planning Commission.

Methods has two halves. The second is a reprint of various reports from a number of bodies and persons. (IMF, International Bank for Reconstruction and Development, FAO, R.K.R.V. Rao, the ILO). The first half is a summary and running commentary on these submissions, which also remarks that 'it may be said that the subject of direct controls in underdeveloped countries is somewhat neglected in the documents of Part II' (UN 1949, 10).

The Kaleckian themes in Part I are: the need to raise national savings by means additional to 'interest rate inducement' (the role of interest rates is criticised and said to be uncertain) and the undue dependence of underdeveloped countries on one or two commodities for their export trade, leading to instability (a topic which was a main focus of Kalecki's UN sub-division at that time). One also notices an emphasis in this report on raising resources by taxation *(ibid.,* 9-10) and a clear endorsement of the view that the role of fiscal policy is four-fold: to eliminate inequalities, increase the total volume of savings, moderate the rate of inflation and provide incentives. This is a list that was reiterated several times during Kalecki's stay in India in early 1960.

Instability of foreign exchange earnings and its effect on development planning were featured in a 1952 publication of the UN Economic Development section: *Instability in Export Markets of Developing Countries in Relation to Their Ability to Obtain Foreign Exchange.* Again, one senses Kalecki's presence in the compilation of this report, whether or not he actually authored the final version (which cannot be known). The Report's main arguments were:

(a)   *price* fluctuations were not the major factor in the instability of export proceeds for underdeveloped countries; rather, volume changes were more significant;

(b)   the above phenomenon was more evident in the sales of specific varieties and of grades of primary products on the part of the underdeveloped countries;

(c)   instability of export volumes was present in three respects: year-to-year movements; cyclical; and longer-term, notably in the cases of rubber, linseed, sodium nitrate and wheat. Rubber was also found to have been unstable in terms of *price* fluctuation in all three time periods. The six most stable primary commodities were found to be: copper, coffee, hemp, silk, tea and wool;

(d)   the only two commodities for which the instability of *proceeds* would have been significantly reduced by the elimination of price fluctuations were wool and silk, but significant reductions in instability of proceeds for seventeen commodities would have occurred if *long-term* price trends were eliminated with retention of long-term trends in volume terms.

The remainder of the report reviews points raised in Kalecki's 1946 analysis as to whether capital movements tended to stabilise or aggravate fluctuations in the international balance of payments resulting from changes in proceeds. The text also evaluates export proceeds as a source of foreign exchange, compared to currency receipts obtained from capital movements. In fact, chapter 6 of *Instability in Export Markets of Underdeveloped Countries* has a distinctively Kaleckian flavour, because back in 1946 Kalecki had posed the question of whether full employment could be maintained if no controls remained on capital movements, pointing out that this would only happen if those capital movements offset the current accounts deficits of countries which have chronic balance of trade deficits. The world economy in the 1980s moved towards the kind of arrangements which, in 1946, Kalecki had postulated in his model of international trade and finance.

The purely theoretical and literary work pursued by Kalecki in his UN years may be summed up as an emphasis on the key role of the wages-goods sector in developing countries in the framework of the rigidity of supply and the degree of monopoly in the economic system.

In August 1953 he gave a series of lectures and seminars during a three week stint in Mexico, with these issues emphasised, and sketching what H. W. Arndt has termed (following Little) the 'structuralist approach'. The Mexican lectures were later published in *El Trimestre Economico* (October 1955) and the English edition is in Kalecki (1976). Another of Kalecki's Mexican lectures appeared in English in the *Indian Economic Review*, dealing with the problem of financing economic development. However the first lecture was clearly of greater importance. Its chief point was to stress that in LDCs the supply of food may be fairly rigid, and that the inelastic supply of food, will cause a fall in real wages if aggregate demand increases, raising food prices.

These, then, were the lectures which caused the Mexican government to ask the UN (Hammerschold in particular) to send Kalecki to the Mexican government agencies as an adviser on planning. The UN refused, on the grounds that member countries could ask for an adviser or team of advisers, but not for a particular individual to assist them.

Some echoes of Kalecki's line of thinking and his influence can still be seen with the UN *World Economic Survey for 1956* (even though it was prepared shortly after Kalecki had ceased to be in charge of the surveys):

> An additional key element in inflationary pressure in underdeveloped countries is the high degree of immobility of resources .... which prevents the structure of production from adapting itself sufficiently rapidly to the pattern of demand .... Thus, in underdeveloped countries with limited supplies of food and other essential consumer goods, severe inflationary pressures may be generated even in the absence of budget deficits and with relatively low rates of investment.

One also needs to look at the UN World Economic Report for the early 1950s to see Kalecki's general views on inflation in Third World countries. If productivity rises in the non-agricultural sectors, but not in agriculture, then (assuming that the demand for food depends purely on the level of real wages and is inelastic with respect to the relative prices of food and non-food items), an expansion of the money supply in step with rising GDP would raise money wages. It might even happen that a rise in money supply could cause (by a series of steps) a sufficient rise in food prices (relative to both wages and non-food prices) as to offset totally the increase in real earnings in terms of non-food items.

According to Stanislaw Braun (Kriesler 1991c), Kalecki also did some mathematical economics in this period which may have emerged in his later writings on both Third World and socialist economies. Braun recalled:

> In the UN period he had already started work on a theory of growth in socialist economies. As far as his later algebraic formulas were concerned, they started to emerge at the time he worked on *World Economic Survey*. I was myself writing something about the relationship between [the] change in productivity, investment and consumption. When Kalecki read it, he said, 'why don't you put this in mathematical form, it is much easier'. So he added some and several things emerged which I hadn't dreamt of. It was so much changed, I really had no contribution to it all.

What Braun reveals here is that Kalecki's period at the UN, despite all the problems and disappointments he encountered as an economic official, was also a period in which new ideas were generated - ideas that were to be fully developed into concepts and mathematical models by Kalecki in the 1960s, work which was to have a strong bearing on the study of the socialist planned economies and the Third World.

After leaving North America in early 1955 for his native Poland, Kalecki worked on the dynamics of national income growth (Kalecki 1969) and problems of Polish economic planning. In early 1960 he spent three months in India at the Perspective Planning Division of the Indian Planning Commission and lectured at the Indian Statistical Institute, as well as the Universities of Delhi and Lucknow. The main focus of attention in 1960 was the discussion around Pitambar Pant's *Certain Dimensial Hypotheses Concerning the Third Five-Year Plan* published by the Indian Planning Commission as a discussion document in 1959. After this he discussed problems of raising agricultural output in India, the issue of land reform, and methods of raising government savings and tax revenue (see below).

Later in 1960 the Kaleckis made a rather disastrous visit to Cuba (Kriesler 1991a). Though initially well received, they discovered that the government was in a 'Great Leap Forward' mood, and many top economic officials were actually away in China. Michal never actually met Castro on his trip, though he had been invited as an official adviser. Bizarre things followed. Kalecki was forced to rely on historical economic statistics kept in the American Embassy and smuggled out. He could get few indicators from Cuban officialdom itself. Despite these difficulties he presented a brilliant economic blueprint in the form of a draft plan (Kalecki 1976, chapter 19). At that time, it was rejected by the Cubans and some of their other handpicked foreign advisers as 'too pessimistic', but later suffered the curious fate of being set as textbook reading on 'how to plan' for up-and-coming young economists.

Kalecki's comments on India and Cuba were based on some acute economic analysis of concrete problems facing Third World coun tries. The analysis, in turn, was backed by a scaffolding of ideas about the inter-relationship between economic variables, and between growth and income distribution, to which we now turn.

Issues of Economic Theory

Growth Theory for Guidance of Underdeveloped Economies

The prevailing economic theory that Kalecki had to confront in the 1950s and 1960s was the older neo-classical contributions of Meade and Bauer. Arthur Lewis had written on the implications of unlimited supplies of labo ur. Some innovative thinking about 'labour accumulation projects' had been presented by Ragnar Nurkse (Nurkse 1957). The dominant textbooks dealt with problems of underdevelopment from an orthodox point of view (McFarlane 1989, 98-102) of which the main elements were:

(a)   growth is largely constrained by the size of a country's pre-existing savings fund;

(b)   to promote the savings fund, it is necessary to establish a network of savings banks and financial institutions;

(c)   the rate of interest and individual time preference are the best guides to the rate of capital accumulation in underdeveloped countries;

(d)   choice of technique should be according to the state of factor proportions;

(e)   all foreign aid and investment is good, almost by definition, since it augments domestic capital formation and raises the feasible rate of national investment, ensuring higher economic growth if efficiency of capital utilisation is maintained;

(f)   if the underdeveloped country opens up to trade and specialises on its traditional commodities, growth will flow from the application of comparative advantage principles.

All of this created a problem for Kalecki. In 1938 he had joined Manoilesco in his devastating critique of 'comparative cost' (Kalecki 1938). Because of his well known views on excess capacity, he did not see the 'pre-existing savings fund' as an immutable signpost for how much growth could be attempted. He knew there was a world iron and steel shortage, so that a number of countries, notably India, had decided on the construction of such industries simply because they could not get supplies - their attitude on factor proportions, comparative cost or import-substitution as an ideal strategy had little to do with it.

So, with a few exceptions, he could have found little to guide planning for growth in the orthodox neoclassical approach (perhaps a bit about the behaviour of economic agents if one believes in the idea of a *homo economicus* in the largely rural environment of the Third World).[2] Something could, in 1960, no doubt be said about the functioning of various markets, although the neoclassical investigators would scarcely be able (as Kalecki was able) to classify the systems that had semi-feudal elements in a country like India (Kalecki 1976, 148-50). Yet such a recognition of the nature of underdeveloped country markets would seem essential: it surely won't do, in the rural context of India, to be talking about 'decision-making under uncertainty', 'simultaneous transactions over all markets', and the like. Perhaps J.S. Mill's laws of production might be relevant to the production function for wheat, but his laws of distribution, so well described in this case by Kalecki (*ibid.*, 148-50) would seem to be more relevant, and crop yields for those who are tenants and those who are owners vary widely.

Kalecki, by contrast with neo-classical economists, focussed on practical issues: tenancy and sharecropping; profit-gouging and rack-renting[3]; usury in rural interest rates; lack of countervailing power against the power of private grain merchants. This was in part due to the circumstances of his being an economic adviser to governments (eg India, Mexico, Israel, Cuba). Yet it was also, much more, a matter of his temperament, which favoured practical measures to improve conditions for the poor within a political-social context that could not be changed in the short-run. It is a matter for the reader to judge which approach is more useful in the Third World development context: Kalecki or neo-classical theory? M. Kalecki or C. J. Bliss?

Comparative Cost, Factor Proportions and the Role of Trade

Kalecki attacked static comparative cost theory (Kalecki 1938) although he accepted a commonsense approach that trade can be beneficial. Yet comparative advantage theory contained essential weaknesses (Kalecki 1938, 708-11). Kalecki criticised the theory for its assumption of a given supply of capital, arguing that it is more realistic to assume reserves of unused capital and that the supply of capital will rise as new investment opportunities open up as new industries are protected. In the context of his remarkable and early venture into the economics of underdevelopment, Kalecki mentions there is likely to be some unemployment in any agricultural country, 'manifest or disguised' (Kalecki's terminology). He also has a discussion in the review of Manoilesco about what later came to be called 'Nurkse savings' - the direct creation of capital stock by employing those without much work on social overhead capital formation using primitive techniques of production.

Kalecki's review of Manoilesco's book, which he describes as 'a daring attack on the theory of comparative costs', is itself a gem: 'To represent free trade as the *only* obstacle for the economic progress of backward countries is to divert attention from such internal social problems as land reform and others' (Kalecki 1938, 711). Kalecki attacks the notion that trade is the only factor in economic development but he does not agree with the viewpoint later associated with 'dependency theory', a school which argues that free trade is the main reason for underdevelopment (see, for example, the work of A. Emannuel or S. Amin). The latter day critics of dependency theory, like Kalecki, have argued that internal agrarian and industrial class relations ought to be more the focus of discussion about the causes of underdevelopment (Limqueco and McFarlane, 1983; Limqueco, Odhnoff and McFarlane 1989).

The Role of the Wage-good Sector

To someone familiar with Marx's famous 'schemas of expanded reproduction' there would be nothing surprising about Kalecki taking the output of the wage-good sector as a key lever of development. In his 1953 Mexico lecture and his subsequent development of it (Kalecki 1976, chapter 7) an intriguing relationship is sketched, linking the level of investment and the possibility of expanding the supply of wage-goods. Kalecki then considers the case where, in Department 2, the supply of consumer goods is elastic in some sectors and not in others. He also warns against Ragnar Nurkse's too-easy assumption that migration of labour from the countryside to work on urban construction projects means that such migration will leave behind an extra supply of food which will find its way to urban markets. In Kalecki's view it is more likely the peasants will use the food to eat more.

An interesting extension of Kalecki's analysis (noted also below) here has been carried out by Filipino economist Joseph Lim (1991). In his analysis the wage-good sector, the luxury goods sector and the capital goods sector are all examined.

The Financing of Economic Development

A constant theme in Kalecki's work on Third World political economy was the issue of financing of development (Kalecki 1976, Chapters 5 and 7). The first major piece, delivered in 1953 as a lecture in Mexico, was outlined within a Marxian 2-sector model. Later, in 1970, the scaffolding set out in the Mexican lecture was greatly modified[4] (*ibid,* chapter 7), although the policy conclusions he drew were similar. The new framework (originally developed after extensive discussion with colleagues within the Warsaw-based Centre for Research in Developing Countries in the 1960s) combined the emphasis on bottlenecks in the wage-goods sector with the position first established in his observations on the Third Indian 5-year plan, that no taxes be levied on the poor or on necessities.

Kalecki began with a model in which the rate of increase of demand for necessities is a linear function of the rate of growth of national income. He shows that this relationship is quite different from a linear relationship between the rate of growth of *total* consumption and that of the national income. With *total* consumption, part is deducted annually to be diverted to investment. This should not be the case with necessities (*ibid.*, chapter 7). If investment plans overshoot, additional taxes must be levied on higher income groups or on non-essential goods and services. In general, Third World countries should exercise fiscal discipline in this way, by staying carefully within any target for the annual investment to national income ratio (the *rate* of investment) in each year of an economic program. Otherwise, the fiscal problems of the state will tempt government into allowing inflationary deficits which, Kalecki showed (*ibid.*, chapters 5, 7 and 9), are more to the advantage of the upper classes than to the broad masses. However, capital imports can be used to raise the rate of non-inflationary growth by supplementing the home supplies of necessities (and this event could also reduce the pressure for more taxes). Care should, of course, be taken to ensure that increased demand flowing from growth is not directed towards foreign non-essentials (*ibid.*, chapters 6 and 7).

At the policy level, Kalecki's funding ideas point to the need for finding an efficient mechanism of mobilising saving as a way to fund investment. This is the vital supplement to raising government savings from higher taxes in the face of the narrow fiscal base available to governments in Third World countries. Toporowski (1991) and others have queried the efficiency of capital markets in fulfilling this function, preferring a mature banking system to finance both fixed and circulating capital. The struggles and difficulties within the People's Republic of China since 1986 in developing a stockmarket to supplement the banking network, lend credence to this scepticism. Capital markets in 'developing' countries outside China (notably India and the Philippines) are also notoriously unstable, due to high volatility of expectations, the key to the demand for securities. Uncertainty about returns and the problem of investors being 'locked into' shares once the full market phase ebbs, have been the major causes of instability in both industrialised and developing countries. Moreover, companies in Third World societies are likely to have lower internal reserves and higher gearing ratios which, by exposing them to increasing risk, mean a high rate of bankruptcy in depressions. With low reserves, the microeconomic functioning of such companies will be such as to encourage low capital-intensity in their technology, trading and services, reinforcing a low-productivity economy.

Ultimately, at the macroeconomic level, the topic of the financing of investment involved Kalecki in the whole theory of the relationship between rates of growth of investment and consumption. This may be seen in his advocacy that planners should always consult a 'government decision function' showing the trade-offs between accelerated investment and levels of consumption. The need to 'be careful' in economic policy to ensure regular increases in material consumption standards of the masses was a feature of Kalecki's work in relation to a socialist economy.[5] However, it is equally relevant to the Third World.

Growth, Savings and Fiscal Reforms

Kalecki set to work on fiscal implications of raising the growth rate of the Indian economy (Kalecki 1976, chapter 4). While considering that investment created savings through higher income levels, Kalecki also favoured an increment in the savings pool to assist the process of accelerated growth. A higher growth target implied (a) higher government savings or (b) higher private savings or (c) more government revenue from existing tax sources.

The idea of levying an indirect tax on non-necessities was a truly innovative suggestion by Kalecki here. He had his team draw up two lists of individual products. One consisted of products that the masses did not buy: finished cloth, consumer durables; processed foods. The other comprised the daily necessities of a poor family: kerosene, ghee, coarse cloth, unprocessed foods. This list, said Kalecki, was to bear zero tax. This whole exercise was done to get around the almost intractable problem of income tax avoidance. Kalecki thought that in the very special conditions of a country like India a tax on goods was *not* regressive (as it would be in the West), since the masses would rarely buy a product subject to taxation.

This simple, brilliant plan cut through all the mystifications of orthodox tax theory. If implemented, it would have raised Indian government revenues by 20% per annum over the first five years and reduced dependence on other items like the land tax, customs duties and income tax. Above all, it would have contributed to *growth with equity*, something Kalecki advocated a decade before Chenery and some rebellious economists in the IMF/World Bank complex made it fashionable, or at least put it on the agenda of development economics.

Investment Effectiveness

While most of Kalecki's work on this topic consisted of an elaboration of formulae worked out in Warsaw and designed for use by Polish managers (Kalecki and Rakowski 1959), quite a lot can be learned by officials of Third World countries willing to study his ideas. By avoiding waste caused by bad investment decisions, large financial resources can be saved. Examples which Kalecki was fond of citing during his India stint include (a) avoiding expensive 'shells' for buildings and factory sites (bamboo is better than concrete); (b) choosing appropriate levels of technology (his advice was that it is not always necessary to adopt 'state of the art' techniques; (c) subjecting any capital-intensive technology to tough evaluation criteria, including fiscal implications. Kalecki did not agree with Maurice Dobb's (Dobb 1960) view that a case can be made out for highly capital-intensive techniques due to re-investment of the profits from such projects.

The 'effectiveness of investment' in Kalecki's theories was also connected to issues touching on the appropriate sectoral allocation of investment, as well as to the opportunity cost of capital and the rate of scrapping of machines. The 'efficiency' issue also relates to the elaboration of coefficients guiding the choice of techniques of production. The increment of production from new investment may be 'realised' by investment variants representing different techniques; in effect we are talking about various combinations of investment outlays (valued at constant prices) and labour cost (valued at constant wages). Kalecki also recognised (1969, 17) that two complications arise: (a) investment choices are subject to change as a result of technical progress, and (b) different volumes of investment may result from the choice of techniques. Kalecki worked out a most ingenious way (using a 'scrapping' coefficient) for handling these two problems in order to ensure a proper evaluation of investment efficiency (*ibid.*, 260-3). He therefore, greatly developed his earlier 'generalised formula' (Kalecki and Rakowski 1959) which had incorporated different durabilities and different opportunity-costs of 'locking up' or 'freezing' capital in projects with longer gestation periods.

Land Reform

Michal Kalecki wrote before the Green Revolution in Asia had raised rice and wheat productivity dramatically. Yet it was this very rise in productivity of agriculture that he advocated, seeing it as the key to the feasibility of Third World development plans, notably in India and Cuba. India, he believed, had to produce 180 million tons of grain in the Third Plan (1961-65) or risk failure. To do this, lacking the Green Revolution seed strains, what methods were available?

Land reform could, Kalecki thought, unlock those farmers' incentives long crushed by heavy debt payments and unfair tenure systems which gave little security. The poor in India, he thought, were 'exploited' in the rural areas, even if exploiters were themselves rather poor. There is not a lot in Kalecki about the role of irrigation dams, or of 'leasing in' arrangements between owners and tenants. Nevertheless, it is clear that he saw the improvement in the general rural atmosphere as crucial; for this reason he wanted an activist role for government wholesale purchasing companies in grain, and government credit banks to loosen the hold of those who bought the crop at cheaper prices when it came in, who were often also those who charged usurious interest rates for rural improvement loans to peasants.

The Balance of Payments Constraint

Kalecki did, of course, introduce this aspect in all his discussions of growth (e.g. the difficulties in expanding Polish bacon exports in the face of Danish and New Zealand competition; the Cuban problem that the Soviets had to take most of the sugar crop for Cuban economy to function). There is some doubt, however, as to whether he gave it the weight we would today. With deregulated banking and financial sectors, increasingly a feature of Third World affairs since 1980, there is now a more direct link between the balance of payments and other variables. For example, the level of overseas borrowing, by increasing total foreign debt, worsens the current account deficit by increasing interest payments. Unless exports boom (often difficult to see in primary producing countries), the debt service ratio also becomes more severe. Kalecki seems to have assumed that if there was a sound fiscal policy (with genuine saving rather than deficit financing) and if productivity in agriculture could be increased by 5% per year, such problems could be kept under control. As well, the objectives he sought - low-cost housing for the poor, clean water - are not import-intensive goods. But after 1970 the urban bourgeoisie in cities like Bangkok, Manila and Calcutta, grew rapidly in absolute numbers and in wealth. Their penchant for imported foods and the like put more strain on the balance of payments than Kalecki, perhaps, allowed. However, he was right in seeing the lack of engineering industries, the absence of a capital-goods sector, as itself the cause of a lot of imports - the typical import bill of the Third World was for final or capital goods (Kalecki and Sachs 1966).

We can recall here Kalecki's 1946 article: in developing countries he argued, foreign direct investment is to a great extent made up of plant and equipment supplied by the foreign company direct to the host nation. This poses the issue of the 'degree of monopoly' exercised by multinational corporations. Kaleckian analysis here would suggest that the increased ability of workers and firms to buy imported wage-goods, luxury goods and capital goods (if available) should reduce somewhat the domestic degree of monopoly. However, this in turn suggests the great need to expand exports, to break the constraint posed by the limits to the import bill and hence to permit more imported investment. The danger on a global scale is a higher degree of monopoly exercised by the multinationals in the host country, which can pose a new challenge for economic policy.

The Environment

Some 30 years ago, development economists paid little attention to 'green' issues (P. Gourou and R. Dumont being notable exceptions). For advisers like Kalecki, job creation, land security and a minimum calorific intake for all were the keys to improving the people's livelihood in Asian and Latin American countries. Today we realise that green economics involves complicated issues - there is a trade-off between growth and pollution in the West, but this is not universally accepted in the Third World. The effort, therefore, is to make a greater push to delineate and assess the relationship between the environment and the world of economics. Taxes, technologies and interest groups are all involved. In other words, it is important to see where particular technologies are compatible with environment protection, where they are neutral, and where they are likely to damage the environment.

It should be pointed out, however that bureaucratic 'blocking' of technology while its 'environmental credentials' are investigated is also a major cause of reduced effectiveness of investment.[6] Kalecki was quite aware that many Third World countries have bureaucracies which take months to process applications for new investment ventures and new technology, or to approve financial arrangements. He was unimpressed with the functioning of import licensing and building licensing in the India of the 1960s. A similar pattern of delay, reducing investment effectiveness, still prevails in Thailand, the Philippines and other developing countries.

Finally, it should be noted that in Kalecki's fundamental growth equation,

$$r = \frac{I}{y} \cdot \frac{1}{m} - a + u \qquad\qquad (9.1)$$

one of the four variables is a defined as depreciation of the capital stock. It would be relatively easy to include in this variable some of the major elements of environmental damage. After all, like the running down of machines, running down of the environment will exercise a negative effect on future attempts to accelerate economic growth.

Kalecki's Political Analysis: The Third World Context

Institutions, the recorded behaviour of social classes under specific conditions of transformation of the state and civil society, and large structural movements in the economy: this was the hub of the Kaleckian focus for a *political economy* approach to the Third World.

As mentioned elsewhere in this chapter, Kalecki disliked many political regimes, but once involved in an official or semi-official capacity with their affairs, he did not seek to be 'left adventurist', to write about the need for revolution or to propose a 'transitional programme' of demands. His guiding principle was, rather, to derive policies and ways to finance them that would best be able to avoid imposts on the poorer members of society.

In relation to the handling of political analysis, Kalecki noted the political barriers to land reform and the political trade-offs within the elite that would be needed for them to be overcome. When it became all too clear that a kaleidoscopic turn to a new coalition of dominant social classes in the exercise of power brought demands for entirely new strategies and policies, Kalecki wrote about these in his celebrated piece on 'Intermediate Regimes' (Kalecki, 1976, 30-41). He began by noting (Kalecki 1976, 30):

> History has shown that the lower-middle class and rich peasantry are rather unlikely to perform the role of the ruling class. Whenever social upheavals did enable representatives of these classes to rise to power, they invariably served the interests of big business (often allied with the remnants of the feudal system). This despite the fact that there is a basic contradiction between the interests of the lower-middle class and big business, to mention only the displacement of small firms by business concerns.

Are there any specific conditions today favouring the emergence of governments representing the interests of the lower-middle class (including in this also the corresponding strata of the peasantry)? It would seem that such conditions do arise at present in many underdeveloped countries.

(a) At the time of achieving independence the lower-middle class is very numerous while big business is predominantly foreign controlled with a rather small participation of native capitalists.

(b) Patterns of government economic activities are now widespread.

Now a social system where the lower middle class operates to support the government in elaborating state capitalism is the 'intermediate' regime. In the system the lower middle class and the rich peasants are favoured. The state capitalist sector concentrates investment on the expansion of the productive potential of the economy:

Thus there is no danger of forcing the small firms out of business, which is a characteristic feature of the early stage of industrialisation under *laissez faire*. Next, the rapid development of state enterprises creates executive and technical openings for ambitious young men of the numerous ruling class. Finally, the land reform, which is not preceded by an agrarian revolution, is conducted in such a way that the middle class which directly exploits the poor peasants - i.e. the money lenders and merchants - maintains its position, while the rich peasantry achieves considerable gains in the process.

The antagonists of the ruling class are, from above, the upper-middle class allied with foreign capital and the feudal landowners and, from below, the small landholders and landless peasants, as well as the poor urban population - workers in small factories and the unemployed or casually employed, mainly migrants from the countryside in search of a source of livelihood. On the other hand, white-collar workers and the not very numerous workers of large establishments - who in underdeveloped countries are in a privileged position as compared with the urban and rural paupers - are frequently, especially when employed in state enterprises, allies of the lower-middle class rather than its antagonists.

However, the stability of the system is not 'unproblematic'. In his observation on the likely working out of the internal contradictions of such 'intermediate regimes', Kalecki looks at some of the more basic class conflicts that could arise:

Potentially at least, the urban and rural paupers are antagonistic towards the ruling class, since they do not benefit from the change of social system such as described above, and profit relatively little from economic development. The land reform is conducted in such a way that a major share of the land available goes to the rich and medium-rich peasants while the small landholders and the rural proletariat receive only very little land. Insufficient effort is made to free the poor peasantry from the clutches of money lenders and merchants and to raise the wages of farm labourers. The resulting agrarian situation is one of the factors limiting agricultural output within the general economic development, as under the prevailing agrarian relations the small farms are unable to expand their production. The same is true of larger farms cultivated by tenants. The lagging of agriculture behind general economic growth leads to an inadequate supply of foodstuffs and an increase in their prices, which is again to the disadvantage of the 'stepsons' of the system. Even if the aggregate real incomes of those strata do not decline as a result of the increase in employment, they do not show any appreciable growth.

Though the poorest strata of the society have thus no reason to be happy, they do not, for the time being at least, constitute a danger for the present system. The poor peasantry and rural proletariat are controlled by some form of a local oligarchy comprised of the petty bourgeoisie (merchants and money lenders), the richer peasants and smaller landlords. The urban population without stable employment, and even home workers and workers in small factories are not too dangerous either, because they are permanently threatened by unemployment and are difficult to organise.

In this context, one can easily understand the repressions against the communists observable in a number of intermediate regimes. This is not a question of competition between parallel ideologies; the communists are simply at least potential spokesmen for the rural and urban paupers, and the lower-middle class is quite rightly afraid of the political activisation of the latter.

Peru, run by modernising military officers was the first example that met political analysis from Kalecki. His aim, in putting forward his views about 'intermediate regimes', was to assess the likely effects of a new political elite based on capitalist farmers rather than 'semi-feudalists', on an expanded civil service rather than a handful of big industrialists. Other writers have taken this up and given a class analysis of India's transition from the older political regimes of Punjab and Bengal to new regimes flowing from the socio-economic effects of the Green Revolution (Webster 1990). Others have written about similar developments in the Philippines (Ofreneo 1983) and Indonesia (Pincus 1990).

What we need to remember about Kalecki's work on Third World problems is the political aspects of that topic. He came to the problems with a Marxist outlook - the questions he posed, the 'vision' he applied, came from this source. What is the mode of production? What is the line-up of social classes? What is the social base of the state? How does the state maintain its legitimacy in the economic field? Among these issues

Kalecki sought to develop his policy recommendations. This was not so much a problem of applying a 'formula' like 'historical materialism' in a mechanical way, but something deeper. As White pointed out, 'Kalecki's analysis does not suffer from a simplistic reductionism - explaining, for example, the political as a mirror reflection of the economic' (White 1977, 318).

Despite his Marxism, Kalecki adopted a moderate approach to the pace of social reform. In India he favoured land reform for the long-run; for the shorter term he proposed a government credit bank and a state-owned wholesale grain purchasing corporation. This outlook reflected what could be called Kalecki's political 'nous'. He sought not to upset his hosts or the circles of academics who came to see him with utopian proposals, but concentrated on *getting the best deal for lower income groups*, given that the social and political system was not going to be fundamentally altered in the short-run.

Stemming from this attitude, Kalecki made a number of simple but effective suggestions in the areas of fiscal policy, manpower policy, price policy and the handling of debt and foreign investment. In *fiscal* policy, his distinction between essential and non-essential goods in a poor country allowed him to advocate indirect taxes as a way of raising the savings rate without harm to lower income groups. This has increasingly been accepted in Third World countries (e.g. the Philippines) as a way of increasing the savings rate in a socially just way. His view of the need for more rather than less labour-using projects is not only a 'Chinese' view, but is now shared within the inner circles of the ILO (e.g. within ARTEP, the Asian Regional Training and Employment Programme) and the Asian Development Bank. In agricultural pricing, a few countries have set up government wholesale grain agencies to compete with rapacious private merchants (India, the Philippines). Similarly, the rural debt question has been at the centre of attention of reforming the social relations in agriculture, including debt cancellation and lowering interest rates through active lending by government-controlled rural banks. All of this speaks for the contemporary relevance of Kalecki's political analysis and his observations on the socio-political nature of semi-industrialized societies.

Kalecki's Influence on Analysts of Third World Economic Problems

Structuralists

In his magisterial summing up of the ongoing debate on 'structuralism' in the environs of United Nations economists, Arndt (1985) traced the origins of structuralist thought among Latin American economists to the visit by Kalecki to Mexico in 1953.[7] Among those influenced were the economists and policy advisors Noyola and Sunkell. These writers seem particularly to have used Kalecki's stress on the importance of the rigidity in supply and on the degree of monopoly within the economic system.

Arndt traces Kalecki's outlook on policy to work done back in the 1940s with a team at the Oxford University Institute of Statistics. Arndt notes that, as a leader of the team of researchers, Kalecki had a 'Marxist' starting point. Equally important was his interest, as early as 1938, in supply constraints and social issues like land reform, already flagged in his review of Manoilesco (Kalecki 1938).

Lim's Extension of Kalecki

While Kalecki considered the impact of exports and foreign capital inflow (Kalecki 1976, chapter 6), and even discussed multilateralism (Toporowski 1991), his strategic thinking was more oriented, in the 1960s, to such huge internal problems as raising the savings ratio, land reform, labour productivity and employment of labour. His well-known supply-side model also emphasised capital productivity (the inverse of the capital/output ratio), depreciation, and a 'betterment factor' (using up excess capacity, saving on waste, etc).

With the movement towards export-oriented growth strategies in the 1970s and 1980s, a systematic link opened up between the export record, structural change caused by accelerated industrialisation and the internal economy. In particular, structural change, in the sense of the changing contribution of capital goods, consumer goods and service industries, became more profound and was happening with some speed.

Absorbing the lessons of the newly industrialising economics of East Asia and South-East Asia, some of the development economists influenced by Kalecki have tried to open up and deepen the Kalecki analysis. The most sympathetic, and earliest, contribution along these lines was by Joseph Lim, an economist from the University of the Philippines, who developed the Kalecki model during a stint of research at Cambridge University. The main thrust of Lim's modification of the original Kalecki approach was his suggestion that the Kaleckian perspective allows study of the distributive implications of export-led promotion in the specific context of a developing country like the Philippines (Lim 1985), since it can handle structural features of a disjointed economy, where government has created an 'extraverted' economic policy (Lim 1991). His method of illustrating the second claim was to extend Kalecki's analysis from a two-sector to a three-sector model in order to incorporate the analysis of a segmented market for industrial luxury goods on the one hand, and mass agricultural goods on the other ('wage-goods').

Lim starts with the specifics of a dependent economy: a large portion of capital-goods and intermediate-goods have to be imported. He continues by setting up a Kaleckian problematic: what sectors of the economy (exports, wage-goods, intermediate goods, capital-goods) need to be developed in a process of successful transformation, and by how much? What will be the impact of differences in technology and capital-intensity as between domestic and export sectors?

His first step is to argue, not for the standard Kaleckian 2-sector model (consumer goods and investment goods), but for the analysis to be extended to three sectors, as Kalecki did in his piece on Marx's equations (Kalecki 1968). Lim's additional assumptions are:

(a)   in the first sector, producer-goods and industrial inputs are entirely imported and paid for completely out of foreign exchange earnings;

(b)   trade is balanced;

(c)   there are no imported consumer-goods;

(d)   no foreign borrowers or investors.

In this scenario, export production becomes Kalecki's Department I; it is the dynamic origin of the growth process.

The new 'departmental schema for expanded reproduction' becomes:

Dept I: export production;

Dept II: luxury goods (produced by import substitution), consumed from rent and income;

Dept III: wage-goods for workers in all departments, consisting of local agriculture and agriculture-related industries.

The next step is that in each sector total value added is divided between workers and profit and rent receivers, so that:

$$E = W_E + R_E \ldots \tag{9.2}$$

$$C = W_C + R_C \ldots \tag{9.3}$$

$$W = W_W + R_W \ldots \tag{9.4}$$

where E = total export of goods and services in value; C = total value of luxury consumption goods; W = total value of wage-goods, W_i = total wage bill for sector i; R_i = total profit and rent in sector i ($i = E, W, C$). X_0 is demand for exports.

Then Lim writes the expenditure flows:

$$E = X_0 \ldots \tag{9.5}$$

$$C = cR = c(R_E + R_c + R_w) \ldots \tag{9.6}$$

$$W = W_E + W_C + W_W \ldots \tag{9.7}$$

This set of three equations indicates that: the demand for exports comes from abroad; demand for luxury goods are a proportion (c) of total profit and rental income; and demand for wage-goods comes from the sum of the wage bills paid out to the work force in the three sectors (exports, luxury goods and wage-goods). Lim now asks: what happens if we adopt the crucial Kaleckian assumption that wage-earners spend all their incomes? He suggests the following results obtain. In the wage-goods sector, equations (9.4) and (9.7) suggest that

$$R_W = W_E + W_C \ldots \tag{9.8}$$

This means that rents and profits in the wage-goods sector will be equal to the wage bills in the export and luxury good sectors. Also, in the luxury goods sector, equations (9.6) and (9.3) suggest that $R_C = [c(R_E + R_W) - W_C] / 1-c$. This indicates that the profits in the luxury goods sector are made up of the value of the consumption of rentiers and profit makers in the export and wage-goods sectors, less wages in the luxury good sector, all multiplied by $1/1-c$.[8]

What Kaleckian conclusions does Lim derive from the above mathematical relationship? First, he shows the likelihood that increased wage bills in the export and luxury sectors will stimulate profits and rents in the wage-goods sector. In terms of the Kaleckian 'intermediate regime' framework[9], the class of landlords and capitalists in the wage goods sector will benefit from the expansion of employment in either the export or luxury goods sector. Second, he suggests that the profits in the luxury goods sector will be augmented by increased profits in the export and wage-goods sector, as well as by any increase in the propensity to consume of the non-wage earners, including capitalists in the luxury goods sector itself. Hence we can say that, under Third World conditions, profit-makers in the luxury-goods sector would get a bigger market and surplus, if non-wage incomes grow in all sectors of the economy.

Now what happens if there is an expansion of demand via the growth of exports, recalling Kalecki on the need to take into account (a) backward social relations in agriculture; (b) excess capacity in luxury goods; (c) oligopoly and a trend to increasing capital-intensity? Lim suggests that, in the extreme case where the wages goods sector has fixed capacity, prices of wage goods will rise, and real wages (as well as the wage share) will fall in the case of a surge of exports or output in the luxury goods sector. Demand is dampened by the restricted wages, and so offsets the original expansion of employment in the export and luxury goods sectors. There will be a rise in the share of rentiers and profit recipients in the wage-goods sector (and, perhaps, in the share of capitalists and workers in the luxury goods sector. Lim argues also that the bigger is the demand injection into the system, the bigger the boost there will be to the output of luxury goods, so long as some non-wage income is spent on luxury goods, although this expenditure will vary with the propensity to consume of the rich.

If the luxury goods sector has no excess capacity, the boost from demand will end when full capacity realisation is reached. Meanwhile, what is happening to a Third World industrial (import-substituting) sector? A number of the bottlenecks about which Kalecki wrote so persuasively will be present, including the foreign exchange balance. It is this sector which depends on imported machinery and industrial materials. But the firms in this sector will not get these inputs if the bottleneck is severe; prices will rise in the luxury sector due to fewer imports there, and there will be a shift in the distribution of profits from the export sector and the wage-good sector (agriculture) to the luxury goods sector, thus confirming the Kalecki-Sachs analysis.

Lim's discussion flows from his making the Kaleckian assumption of an inelastic supply of domestic food production, a perspective Kalecki derived from his close study of Indian agriculture in the 1950s. Given the Lim equations and relationships, this assumption ensures that an expansion of employment in either the luxury goods sector or the export sector will cause food and other wage-good prices to rise and will increase rents to landlords and profits to rural traders and money lenders (Kalecki 1976, 41-62; Lim 1991, 6-7).

What are the implications of Lim's analysis for income distribution? Lim remarks that he agrees with Kalecki that this shift might have some beneficial effects if the peasants were organised in such a way (co-operatives; government rural banks competing with money lenders; a state or co-operative grain marketing body) as to get their hands on part of the economic surplus and then spend it on industrial goods. However, if the social relations are of the 'semi-feudal' type rather than the 'small capitalist farmer' type, then increased prices of food are channelled to higher income for landlords, traders and usurers, not to higher standards of living for the peasantry. Furthermore, even if the peasants do get hold of some of the surplus, the Kaleckian assumption used by Lim, that their incomes will not be high enough for them to afford luxury goods and are spent wholly on wage-goods, will not allow any beneficial effects, since there are bottlenecks to the further production of wage-goods. Even if the peasants could afford some luxury goods, any beneficial effects will depend on whether the foreign exchange balance will allow the luxury goods sector to expand or not.

However, Lim has also studied Kalecki's socio-political analysis of the Third World in his 'Observations on Social and Economic Aspects of Intermediate Regimes' (Kalecki 1976, 30-37). This gives him the possibility of further developing ideas about the consequences of a transformation from 'semi-feudalism' to a more commercial rural capitalism, a change that has clearly occurred in India since Kalecki wrote in 1960, and in the Philippines since Ofreneo wrote *Capitalism in Philippine Agriculture* in 1980 (see also Scott 1976, 20-21). A similar development in South Vietnam was described in Beresford (1989, 53-55,130-135) and was also explicitly tackled by Halevi (1992), as will be described in the next section. For Lim himself, the best way to move from Kalecki's 'semi-feudal' framework to the more modern 'agribusiness' framework was set out in an extension of Kalecki and can be summarized as follows. Assume that a new coalition of social classes (workers, petty-commodity producers and small capitalists in non-wage sectors) exerts its power to go about restructuring the semi-feudal agriculture economy and to assist the peasants to secure higher incomes - as seen in China since 1979. The programme for change can be organised by a coalition of sectoral interests which are anti-feudal and anti-monopoly. Given political control in agriculture, the dynamic would need to come from the non-wage sector, including the 'modern' wing of the export sector. The workers and agriculturalists would have a mutual interest in reforming both the industrial sector (hitherto dominated by a high degree of monopoly) and semi-feudal agriculture. Within the coalition forming the new social base of a 'Kaleckian intermediate regime' (Kalecki 1976, chapter 4), the capitalists of the export sector (and, notably, the exporters of non-traditional exports) will need to be active.

The results of the structural transformation, says Lim, should include: breaking down some of the dichotomous structures; increased real income of workers and peasants; and possible rises in productivity, allowing an end to the 'coolie wage' regime so far as money wages are concerned. In the area of production, the foreign exchange constraint might now be alleviated by rising productivity in the export sector, once backward and forward linkages in exports are pursued; the sectoral dichotomy between exports and luxury goods will also be lessened as the degree of monopoly is broken down and competition heightened between and within the two sectors, and as the lower-income classes slowly become a major market for the output of Department 2.

With some simple mathematical apparatus (Lim 1991, 11), the author shows that successful transformation to a modernising intermediate regime brings the following differences with the category 'semi-feudal economy with limited industrialisation':

(a)   the expansion of the export and the wage-good sectors will increase consumption of the import-substituting goods from workers, capitalists and even rentiers;

(b)   the foreign exchange constraint becomes an even more vital bottleneck, holding the potential to govern the overall rate of economic growth;

(c)   pressure will be intense to raise productivity in both export and import-substituting sectors. A more egalitarian income distribution will assist in encouraging workers to believe that they can benefit from higher productivity.

Looking ahead, Lim indicates that the Kalecki model for developed countries will gradually become relevant, for a new capital-goods sector and intermediate sector will arise; linkages (backwards and forwards) will accelerate structural transformation in which the former type of Department I is replaced by the domestic capital-goods sector, and Department II by the consumption goods sector. Finally, the earlier sectoral differences between export and domestic goods production (as illustrated by differences in technological level, capital-intensity etc) will greatly diminish, and once again a standard Kaleckian two-sector model for a developed economy will serve as a reference point for a structural picture of the economy.

Halevi and Kalecki

Building on his knowledge of the specifics of Asian development Halevi (1992, 1993) canvasses the topic of the role for a Kalecki model in accounting for the acceleration of economic growth in the dynamic section of the world capitalist economy. Halevi finds the missing link that he thinks exists in any attempt to generalise Kalecki for an ASEAN-type economy: vertical integration. Unsatisfied with certain aspects of Kalecki's treatment[10] Halevi opted to integrate 'vertical integration analysis' (Pasinetti 1981) into a model of Asian development. He pointed out that Asian industrialisation processes, experiences and time-scales are so different to those of Western Europe and the USSR that Marxian growth models have been rendered otiose - that of Kalecki included. Due to the export orientation and other special features of the Asian 'course', models based on 'capital-goods sector' and 'consumer goods' division are no longer necessarily useful, because of 'different outcomes as to the output mix and to the reproductive capacity of the social systems which supervised and guided the two different forms of industrialisation' (Halevi 1992, 446). While this criticism is mainly directed at the models of Feldman, Dobb and Mahalanobis, the Kaleckian approach is also involved to the extent that it uses Marxian reproduction models[11] (Kalecki 1965). As Halevi puts it, this family of models is too much geared up to explaining endogenous industrialisation: 'they do not tackle the issue of the relationship between the structure of production and the structure of consumption, nor do they offer a framework for the analysis of sectors which at first sight appear as unproductive, such as services' (ibid., 451). In other parts of his seminal article, Halevi also refers to the need for new models which can explain the problematic of Joseph Lim, the conditions on the basis of which dualism (a backward sector coexisting with a modern one) can be averted.

Much more needs to be said about the foreign exchange constraint, in Halevi's view. It might be observed here that (despite what Halevi suggests about previous Marxian growth models) Kalecki did tackle the 'foreign exchange bottleneck' in two places (Kalecki 1969, 44-54 and Kalecki 1976, 64-73). He referred repeatedly to the fact that, the higher the rate of growth of national income, the more rapidly must exports increase and the more difficult it is to sell them due to limited foreign demand. Here Kalecki can be said to have underestimated the periods of spurts in the volume of world trade. Kalecki also had a rather pessimistic view of the absorptive capacity in relation to foreign aid in Third World countries as a way of plugging trade gaps (Kalecki 1976, 71-73). Moreover he argued that, unless ever-increasing new outlets for exports can be tapped, servicing of the debt will inevitably become a growing burden (Kalecki 1976, 73).

Turning to Pasinetti's (1981) approach, Halevi takes up those problems he believes are not well handled in Marxian models and shows that the Pasinetti approach successfully incorporates them: the spread of consumer-goods; the foreign trade sector; and the role of services in modern economic systems. The main emphasis here (Halevi 1992, 458) is that it is not the departmental approach of the Marxian reproduction models that is the core of a theory of growth, but rather (a) the composition of consumption goods and (b) structural change based on the notion of vertically integrated sectors. Does all of this criticism render Kalecki less useful?

Since there are neither input-output (inter-industry) relations nor vertically integrated sectors in Kalecki, this indicates, indirectly, Halevi's reservations about a Kalecki model for studying Asian industrialisation. Although he does say that while 'at first glance' such an approach might appear to be in opposition to the Marxian 2-sector model, 'it eliminates the reductionism and determinism which tended to characterise Marxian development theory, in which accumulation and consumption were viewed in the short run as conflicting'. One gets the impression that Halevi regards the Marx phase, which was followed by the Kalecki phase, as now superseded: we are now in the Pasinetti phase. This also seems to be the meaning of his comment that 'the intuition put forward by people like Kalecki, Baran and Sweezy corresponds more closely to the historical evolution of the capitalist system' (*ibid.*, 463).

Conclusion

What then, was Michal Kalecki trying to achieve? How successful were his endeavours? In the first place, we must mention justice for low-income groups. Whether looking at the 'blue collar' situation in his native Poland, at Indian or Cuban farm workers, or at the Israeli labour market, this was a priority. The rule he seems to have set for himself was that any policy involving the Third World ought to improve the lot of those at the bottom of the income pyramid.

Second, Kalecki sought the 'opening' of all serious bottlenecks to development. Without this solution, high growth targets could only be disastrous and self-defeating. This foreshadowed to some extent the 'shortage economy' concept used so effectively by Janos Kornai in the 1970s and 1980s.

Third, he was concerned to 'concretize' the mode of production in the country in which he found himself giving advice. This concern is clearest in his comments on the Third Five Year Plan in India. It is the land tenure system, the exploitation of share farmers by big landlords, that comes into play, along with the activities of the money lenders, dealing with peasants whose grandparents may have incurred large debts which were passed down. Similarly, the 'intermediate regime' is an analysis of the social layers controlling the state machine. As we saw, the shift in a number of countries was from a state geared to big landed interests and a small group of powerful industrialists, to one serving more the interests of Green Revolution capitalist farmers and state employees.

Fourthly, there is the all-important 'vision' of how the economy works. While 90% of Kalecki's conclusions came directly from statistical data (notably in the cases of India and Cuba), in the background there was a flexible Marxism or Marxist -influenced paradigm. His article on 'Econometrics and Historical Materialism' (Kalecki 1964) perhaps gives the clue here: there is a feedback mechanism where the superstructure of a society influences the base. Historical materialism can capture this by dividing each social formation into four sectors: natural resources, the economic situation, productive relations and the superstructure. Historical materialism is therefore a generalised econometric model, but Kalecki was really involved with 'dealing with obstacles to development that arose from the class structure of the peripheral formation' (White 1977, 301). To this extent, he sometimes appeared as a left proponent of structuralist theories with a class perspective added. As White reminds us, it is a strength of Kalecki's work that he attempted a theorisation of the State in post-colonial social formations (*ibid.*, 322-3). In his work on the state, lay his Marxism; and the success of his 'vision'. For many of the topical issues in the Third World today have to do with the link between the state and industrialization, as well as the state and the labour movement (Limqueco, McFarlane and Odhnoff 1989).

At the same time, on the theoretical front, the work of Lim and Halevi discussed above indicates how rich was the fruitfulness of the way that economic development theory was brought to a certain stage by Kalecki. However, they also imply the limitations on possible future development of his analysis.

A final point is in order here. Kalecki's influence on some of the younger economists (FitzGerald 1993) arose from his high moral stand on poverty. Kalecki once said he could never return to India, as his humanity was offended by the degree of poverty. This opens a contradiction in his 'perspective', for, as emphasised earlier, it was precisely to defend the poorer elements of society that he took on these jobs advising Third World countries. Yet he personally found it most confusing that the 'exploiters' in India were *themselves* poor! He therefore set about proposing the sort of land reform that would gradually end this situation. This is but one example of the limit he found between diagnosis of the situation of the 'wretched of the earth' and the determination to do something about it.

Notes

1 Apart from office politics and an all-pervading McCarthyism in New York at this time, problems arose because he took seriously data supplied by the governments of the USSR and China, to the great annoyance of the American officials.

2 A most dogmatic example is the application of neoclassical economics to an Indian village in the book *Palanpur: the economy of an Indian village* (Bliss and Stern 1982). A contrary example showing the essential irrelevance of neoclassical theory is provided by Gregory (1983).

3 It is the greatest irony that, in today's neoclassical world, it is those farmers who are in a desperate situation and are seeking government assistance that are called rent-seekers, rather than their landlords.

4 It should be pointed out that working on a 'perspective plan' under Polish conditions probably gave Kalecki an awareness of the points at which financial bottlenecks threaten the growth process.

5 See Toporowski, this volume.

6 A good example here was the 'mothballing' of a nuclear power station at Bataan in the Philippines and failure to fast-track alternative sources of power which inflicted 40 billion pesos of lost production on an ailing Philippines economy.

7 However, as Fitzgerald pointed out, Arndt wrongly treats 'structuralism' as mainly a doctrine of market failure (FitzGerald 1993, 22).

8 This multiplier effect occurs because part of the profits in the luxury goods sector is used to purchase more luxury goods, thus further increasing profits within the luxury goods sector.

9 M. Kalecki, 'Observations on the Social and Economic Aspects of Intermediate Regimes' in Kalecki (1976, chapter 4).

10 While not always stated explicitly, the misgivings appear to amount to a feeling that in adapting Marx's expanded reproduction model, Kalecki left out certain things. He explicitly notes that 'we are not told how the profits in the wage-goods sector are spent in purchasing capital goods from the investment sector' (Halevi 1986, 42).

11 In his comparison of Kalecki and Marx, Sawyer (1985, chapter 8) does not really discuss this 'reproduction models' aspect of Kalecki's work.

References

Beresford, M. 1989. *National Unification and Economic Development in Vietnam.* London: Macmillan.

Bliss, C.J. and Stern, N. 1982. *Palanpur: the Economy of an Indian Village.* Oxford: Oxford University Press.

Dobb, M.H. 1960. *An Essay on Economic Growth and Planning.* London: Routledge.

Domar, E. 1957. 'A Soviet Model of Growth' In Nove and Nuti, 1972: 149-72.

FitzGerald, E.V.K. 1993. *The Macroeconomics of Development Finance: a Kaleckian Analysis of the Semi-industrial Economy.* London: Macmillan.

Gregory, C. 1983. *Gifts and Commodities.* London: Academic Press.

Halevi, J. 1981. 'The Composition of Investment Under Conditions of Non-Uniform Changes'. *Banca Nazionale del Lavoro Quarterly Review* 137, June : 213-32.

Halevi, J. 1992. 'Asian Capitalist Accumulation: From Sectoral to Vertical Integration' *Journal of Contemporary Asia* 21 (4): 444-470.

Halevi, J. 1993. 'Croissance Asiatique et Demand Effective.' *Revue Tiers Monde* XXXIV (135), Juillet-Septembre: 531-34.

Hoffman, W.G. 1958. *The Growth of Industrial Economies*. Manchester: Manchester University Press.

Kalecki, M. 1938. Review of M. Manoilesco, *Die Nationalen Produktivkraefte und der Aussenhandel. Economic Journal* 48(192) December: 708-11.

Kalecki, M. 1946. 'Multilateralism and Full Employment'. *Canadian Journal of Economics and Political Science* 12 (2) : 322-27.

Kalecki, M. 1964a. 'Short papers on economic growth'. *Teaching Materials (1)*. The Higher School of National Economic Planning: Warsaw: 3-89.

Kalecki, M. 1964b. 'Historical Materialism and the Role of the Economic factor.' In *Essays in Honour of Oskar Lange*. Oxford and Warsaw: Pergamon Press.

Kalecki, M. 1968. 'The Marxian equations of Reproduction and Modern Economics'. *Social Science Information* 7, Geneva: UNESCO.

Kalecki, M. 1969. 'On the Choice of Techniques of Production.' *Zastosowiania Matematyki*. The Hugo Steinhaus Jubilee Volume 10: 257-64.

Kalecki, M. 1969. *Introduction to the Theory of Growth in a Socialist Economy*. Oxford: Blackwell.

Kalecki, M. 1976. *Essays on Developing Economies*. Hassocks: Harvester.

Kalecki, M. and Rakowski, M. 1959. 'The Generalised Formula for Investment Efficiency'. *Gospodarcza Planowa* 11, November: 191-201. Reprinted in Kalecki, 1964a: 42-52 and in Nove and Nuti 1972: 252-62.

Kalecki, M. and Sachs, I. 1966. 'Forms of Foreign Aid: an Economic Analysis'. *Social Science Information* 5(1), March: 21-44. Reprinted in Kalecki, 1976.

Kriesler, P. 1988. 'Keynes and Kalecki on methodology'. *School of Economics Discussion Papers* 88 (14), pp 1-33. Sydney: University of New South Wales.

Kriesler, P. 1991a. 'Interview with Ada Kalecki'. Sydney. University of New South Wales. Unpublished manuscript.

Kriesler, P. 1991b. 'Interview with Sidney Dell'. Sydney. University of New South Wales. Unpublished manuscript.

Kriesler, P. 1991c. 'Interview with S. Braun'. Sydney. University of New South Wales. Unpublished manuscript.

Lim, J.Y. 1985. 'The Distributive Implications of Export-led Industrialisation'. *Philippine Economic Journal* 24(4): 223-33.

Lim, J.Y. 1991. 'A Kaleckian Three-Sector Model for Third World Countries'. *Journal of Contemporary Asia* 21 (1) : 3-12.

Limqueco, P. ed. 1989. *Partisan Scholarship*. Manila: Journal of Contemporary Asia Publishing House.

Limqueco, P. and McFarlane, B. 1982. *Neo-Marxian Theories of Development*. London: Croom Helm.

Limqueco, P., McFarlane, B. and Odhnoff, J. 1989. *Labour and Industry in ASEAN*. Manila: Journal of Contemporary Asia Publishing House.

Mahalanobis, P.C. 1953. 'Some Observations on the Process of Growth of National Income.' *Sankhya* 12, September: 307-12.

McFarlane, B. 1971. 'Michal Kalecki's Economics'. *Economic Record* 47 (1), March: 93-105.

McFarlane, B. 1989. 'The Crisis of Development Theory' In Limqueco 1989:98-114.

McFarlane, B. 1992. 'Michal Kalecki: More Biographical Notes'. *History of Economics Review* 18, Summer: 129-49.

Nove, A. and Nuti, D.M. eds. 1972. *Socialist Economics*. Harmondsworth: Penguin.

Nurkse, R. 1953. *Problems of Capital Formation in Underdeveloped Countries*. New York: Oxford University Press.

Nuti, D.M. 1986. 'Michal Kalecki's Contribution to Socialist Economics'. *Cambridge Journal of Economics* 10 (2), December: 333-53.

Ofreneo, R. 1980. *Capitalism in Philippine Agriculture*. Quezon City: Foundation for Nationalist Studies.

Pasinetti, L.L. 1977. *Lectures on the Theory of Production*. New York: Columbia University Press.

Pasinetti, L.L. 1981. *Structural Change and Economic Growth*. Cambridge: Cambridge University Press.

Pincus, J. 1990. 'Approaches to the Political Economy of Agrarian Change in Java'. *Journal of Contemporary Asia* 20 (1): 3-40.

Scott, J.C. 1976. *The Moral Economy of the Peasant*. New Haven: Yale University Press.

Sawyer, M. 1985. *The Economics of Michal Kalecki*. London: Macmillan.

Toporowski, J. 1991a. 'On Multinational Companies in the International Economics of Michal Kalecki.' *Cyprus Journal of Economics* 4 (2), December: 87-95.

Toporowski, J. 1991b. 'A Refinancing Theory of Capital Markets and Their Valuation'. *Research Papers* 17, South Bank Polytechnic, London.

Webster, N. 1990. 'Agrarian Relations in Burdwan District, West Bengal: From the Economics of Green Revolution to the Politics of Panchayati Raj'. *Journal of Contemporary Asia* 20 (2): 177-211.

White, M. 1977. 'Kalecki's Theories of Growth and Development.' *Journal of Contemporary Asia* 7 (3): 298-331.

CONTRIBUTING AUTHORS

Philip Arestis is Professor of Applied Economics at the University of East London, England. He has written many articles on Post Keynesian theory, and has taken a particular interest in monetary economics and econometric modelling. Among his recent books is *The Post-Keynesian Approach to Economics* (Edward Elgar, 1992).

Simon Chapple is Senior Research Economist at the New Zealand Institute of Economic Research in Wellington. He has published several articles on Kalecki (the subject of his doctoral thesis) and on wage and employment problems in the New Zealand economy.

Gary A. Dymski is Associate Professor of Economics at the University of California at Riverside. His principal research interests are in money and banking. Dymski is co-editor (with Gerald Epstein and Robert Pollin) of *Transforming the U.S. Financial System : Equity and Efficiency for the 21st Century* (M. E. Sharpe, 1993).

J. E. King is Reader in Economics at La Trobe University, Melbourne. His principal research interests are in the history of heterodox economic ideas, especially Marxian political economy. He is the author of *Conversations with Post Keynesians* (Macmillan, 1995).

Peter Kriesler is Senior Lecturer in Economics at the University of New South Wales. Together with two other contributors to this volume (Bruce McFarlane and Jan Toporowski) he is currently completing an intellectual biography of Michal Kalecki. Kriesler is editor of *The Australian Economy : the Essential Guide* (Allen and Unwin, 1995).

Bruce McFarlane is Professor of Economics at the University of Newcastle, New South Wales. An authority on the economic development of Asia and on radical economics, McFarlane is the co-author (with Peter Groenewegen) of *A History of Australian Economic Thought* (Routledge 1990).

Peter J. Reynolds is Reader in Economics at Staffordshire University. He has published widely on Post Keynesian pricing and distribution theory. Reynolds is the author of the popular text, *Political Economy : a Synthesis of Kaleckian and Post Keynesian Economics* (Wheatsheaf, 1987).

Malcolm Sawyer is Professor of Economics at the University of Leeds, and is an authority on Kaleckian macroeconomics and the economics of industry. Among his many books are *The Economics of Michal Kalecki* (Macmillan, 1985) and (edited jointly with Philip Arestis) *The Elgar Companion to Radical Political Economy* (Edward Elgar, 1994).

Jan Toporowski is Reader in International Business and Languages, South Bank University, London. In addition to research interests in Kalecki, and in socialist economics, Toporowski has published widely in monetary theory and policy. His latest book is *The Economics of Financial Markets and the 1987 Crash* (Edward Elgar, 1993).

INDEX